THE MAKING OF THE WEST

All roads lead to London – and to the West En
presents a new history of the beginnings of t
London entertainment. Putting female-centrea, g....
managements and styles at the centre, it redraws the map of performance history in the Victorian capital of the world. Bratton
argues for the importance in Victorian culture of venues like the
little Strand Theatre and the Gallery of Illustration in Regent Street
in the experience of mid-century London, and of plays drawn from
the work of Charles Dickens as well as burlesques by the early writers
of *Punch*. Discovering a much more dynamic and often woman-led
entertainment industry at the heart of the British Empire, the book
seeks a new understanding of the work of women including Eliza
Vestris, Mary Ann Keeley and Marie Wilton in creating the template
for a magical new theatre of music, feeling and spectacle.

JACKY BRATTON is Professor of Theatre and Cultural History at
Royal Holloway, University of London. She is the author of *New
Readings in Theatre History* (2003), and, with Ann Featherstone, *The
Victorian Clown* (2006), which published previously unknown
materials by Victorian comedians. She contributes to many radio
and TV programmes about Victorian theatre.

THE MAKING OF THE WEST END STAGE

Marriage, Management and the Mapping of Gender in London, 1830–1870

JACKY BRATTON

Royal Holloway
University of London

CAMBRIDGE
UNIVERSITY PRESS

University Printing House, Cambridge CB2 8BS, United Kingdom

Cambridge University Press is part of the University of Cambridge.

It furthers the University's mission by disseminating knowledge in the pursuit of education, learning and research at the highest international levels of excellence.

www.cambridge.org
Information on this title: www.cambridge.org/9781316620830

© Jacky Bratton 2011

First published 2011
First paperback edition 2016

A catalogue record for this publication is available from the British Library

Library of Congress Cataloguing in Publication data

Bratton, J. S. (Jacqueline S.)
The making of the West End stage : marriage, management and the mapping of gender in London, 1830–1870 / Jacky Bratton.
p.   cm.
Includes bibliographical references.
ISBN 978-0-521-51901-4 (Hardback)
1. Theater–England–London–History–19th century.   2. Women in the theater–England–London–History–19th century.   3. Theater management–England–London–History–19th century.   4. West end (London, England)–History.   I. Title.
PN2596.L6B73 2011
792.09421´09034–dc23

2011018537

ISBN 978-0-521-51901-4 Hardback
ISBN 978-1-316-62083-0 Paperback

Contents

Illustrations

Cover London Street Scene 1835 by John Orlando Parry

John Parry's stage work is discussed in Chapter 3. His watercolour of bills on a wall and adjacent hoardings, with the dome of St Paul's rising from the ruins, as always, in the distance, is partly a private joke – his own imaginary performances figure largely in the advertisements – but also gives a vivid impression of the palimpsest of entertainments that Londoners saw covering, and making sense of, the demolition of Old London and the building of the new capital.

Acknowledgements

This book is the culmination of a long period of work supported by the AHRC, whose assistance is very gratefully acknowledged. I am also grateful to Ann Featherstone, who was my Research Assistant during much of that time, and with whom I explored many of the less frequented places of the nineteenth-century entertainment world; I hope she will be pleased with the place *The Era* now has in this final outcome of our collaboration. I would also like to thank the helpful people I have encountered in many libraries and archives, including those of Royal Holloway (in particular Irene Bittles), the Huntington Library, California, the British Library, the New York Public Library, the Harvard Theatre Collection, the Victoria and Albert Theatre Collection (especially Kate Dorney), the British National Archives, and also to acknowledge the invaluable online resources provided by, amongst others, Gale Cengage's Nineteenth-century Newspaper databases, the Dictionary of National Biography and the genealogical resources of FindMyPast.com. Colleagues who have commented and encouraged are many, but I am particularly beholden to Tracy C. Davis for suggestions, to Christine Webb for careful reading, unflagging interest and support, and to my partner Gilli Bush-Bailey, for her energy, her wisdom and the many hours of discussion that have shaped this project over the years.

Introduction

Introducing a volume of the diaries of a minor dramatist, the Victorian critic Clement Scott speaks of them as a bridge 'over the blank period of unwritten history between Macready and Henry Irving'.[1] It is now generally agreed that the years from 1840 to 1870, roughly the same span, saw the emergence of the West End;[2] but the period remains almost as unmapped as it was when Scott threw his first rope of reminiscences across the chasm. In 2000 Tracy C. Davis provided a massive and challenging incitement to new work on the whole century, in her *Economics of the British Stage 1800–1914*;[3] but there are still very few works exploring the foundation of the West End. This book, taking something of its title and its focus from Maggie Gale's *West End Women: Women and the London Stage 1918–1962*,[4] is therefore setting out upon a new and untold history. Perhaps Scott's image of a bridge, offering to link two high places, suggests a reason for the continued neglect of the early and mid Victorian theatre: it carries the implication that what lies between is a gulf, dark and low and not worth visiting. A few pathways through the undergrowth have been traced, mostly using Shakespeare as a guiding light;[5] and they suggest that this was indeed a space of savagery and darkness. It is the ambition of this book to counter that perception. My intention is not to offer another way of negotiating, getting over, the mid-Victorian theatre, but to make an open-eyed and appreciative foray into its centre; to attempt to suggest a different way of seeing, that does

---

[1] Clement Scott and Cecil Howard, eds., *The Life and Reminiscences of E. L. Blanchard*, 2 vols. (London: Hutchinson, 1891), vol. 1, p. xiv.
[2] See for example James Davis and Victor Emeljanow, *Reflecting the Audience* (University of Iowa Press, 2001), p. 167.
[3] Cambridge University Press, 2000.   [4] London: Routledge, 1996.
[5] See for example Richard W. Schoch, *Shakespeare's Victorian Stage: Performing History in the Theatre of Charles Kean* (Cambridge University Press, 1998) and *Not Shakespeare: Bardolatry and Burlesque in the Nineteenth Century* (Cambridge University Press, 2002).

not picture the formation of the West End as an unfortunate pitfall in the development of theatrical art.

The first question that presents itself is why such a 'blank period' in theatre history should be supposed to have occurred during the most eventful and vigorous years of Victoria's reign: the received understanding that theatre-going was an unimportant and unfashionable pursuit during these decades is not an answer but a restatement of the question. During these years London was rebuilt as the global metropolis, the unchallenged centre of the western world; and this meant huge physical and psychological changes. According to its most recent historian, '[t]he 1860s were the most destructive and the most creative decade in the City's history in the 200 years since the Great Fire', when runaway new building and the urgent necessity for new highways, transport, drainage and lighting to serve it made old London an unceasing chaos, a maze of hoardings, actual bridges – the viaducts of the new railways – deep excavations, broken-off streets, raw demolition and chaotic redevelopment.[6] In the midst of this there were, it would appear, many people eager to be amused and to have their understanding of the world around them shaped by the interpretations of performance: every picture we have of London's ubiquitous hoardings in these years shows them plastered with brilliant and busy posters advertising plays, shows, exhibitions and performances of all kinds (see cover illustration). Already in 1800 this was the largest city in the world; by 1851 it had become a dense mass of more than 2.3 million people, with tens of thousands more within frequent visiting range by train. By 1841 a third of the residents had not been born in the city; and the large majority of them were young.[7] 136,000 houses in 1801 had become 306,000 by 1851. Here was the biggest, most exciting audience in the world.

On the other hand, growth was not a simple matter of addition. The redevelopment undercut not only the old patterns of social assumption and interaction between Londoners, but their very dwelling places, and many communities which were the potential audiences for London theatre were displaced and destroyed, while others were created further from the centre. In the City of London the number of inhabited houses fell by 30 per cent in twenty years, from 14,580 in 1851 to 9,415 in 1871. The middle-class

---

[6] Jerry White, *London in the Nineteenth Century* (London: Jonathan Cape, 2007), p. 47.
[7] Accounts of the Total Population, 1841, *British Parliamentary Papers*, 1841 ii (Sess. 2, 52), p. 277.

workers in the banks and offices of the commercial district chose to move to the suburbs and become commuters on the new trains: and the new train stations meant that, in their turn, the poorer citizens were turned out. Over 56,000 inner-city poor were abruptly made homeless between 1857 and 1874. Since no replacement housing was provided, they crammed into every surviving nook and cranny behind and around the grand new stations and the fine broad roads that were deliberately driven through the worst of the slums; their alienation presented an urgent problem requiring social engineering in an increasingly dangerous city. It was as well that by 1842 all the main thoroughfares were lit by gas – but the dark lanes and back courts were thereby turned even more completely into no-go areas for the well-dressed and vulnerable. The violent underclass were no more of a threat to city life, however, than the chaotic traffic jams in which people and horses were regularly crushed to death, and certainly nothing like as dangerous as the newfangled water closets of the better off, which by 1855 discharged most of the waste of 2.5 million Londoners untreated into the Thames on their doorsteps, and spread successive waves of cholera that thinned the city's population, rich and poor alike. Deaths had reached 43,000 by 1854, when the causes were finally understood and action taken – again in the form of massively disruptive building works, this time to create the Thames Embankments, which still house sewers to intercept and carry away the waste, the work partly financed by having the Embankments also house the tunnel of the first underground railway in the world.[8]

During the second half of the period of this book, from the tipping point of 1851 when the Great Exhibition at the Crystal Palace in Hyde Park inaugurated W. L. Burn's 'age of equipoise',[9] the imperial, industrial wealth that made it possible to undertake these grand designs flowed into leisure and consumption as conspicuously as it did into metropolitan growth. Business responded to demand driven by a new middle-class self-confidence, ever-increasing disposable income and social ambition; the modern West End was developed as the centre of that conspicuous consumption and urgent self-formation.

This development did not only apply to the public lives of men. It is an important part of the project of this book, the reassessment of West End

---

[8] White, *London*, pp. 47, 49–50.
[9] A characterisation of the period that the historian originated well before it became the title of his 1964 book (London: Allen & Unwin), which is interestingly endorsed by the revisionist essays in *An Age of Equipoise? Reassessing Mid-Victorian Britain*, ed. Martin Hewitt (London: Ashgate, 2000).

entertainment, to reinstate women as part of the London public and the professions. The role of women in the making of this new metropolis has already begun to be read anew in the twenty-first century, beginning with Erika Rappaport's significantly titled *Shopping for Pleasure: Women in the Making of London's West End*.[10] The gendering of these developments as feminine and therefore soft and commodified may indeed have something to do with way in which West End theatre, a hugely important part of London's Victorian social history, is still discussed in a largely hostile, dismissive tone. Davis and Emeljanow provocatively offer the analysis that 'the history of the West End in our period . . . shows a deliberate attempt on the part of managers and journalists . . . to construct a "Crystal Palace", which would lure an increasingly assertive middle class to a theatrical theme park to flatter its sensitivity and cultural perspicacity or to satisfy its craving for luxurious spectacle'.[11] To put this less pejoratively, one might say that public spaces for display and shopping, entertainment and instruction, leisure and pleasure were part of the building and development of the new London; and the performance culture there played out is important for our understanding of Victorian times and our own. Jane Rendell in *The Pursuit of Pleasure: Gender, Space and Architecture in Regency London* has shown how the early part of the century set up a matrix of building and buying, looking and owning, on which the Victorian city was built, and suggests that 'the "interdisciplinary" state of knowledge allows new kinds of spaces and alternative modes of interpretation to emerge'[12] through which we might come to understand our culture better. A new and more nuanced understanding of the part played by women in this process is of the essence.

The domestication of leisure in the suburbs, the much discussed swing to the private patriarchy of the fireside, which fed the development of the periodical press and the novel, was not all there was by way of community activity and identity formation in the mid nineteenth century. The Victorians did go out; and many thousands of them went, every night of the week, to the spanking new West End entertainments. Imperious new movements in the arts gathering pace after 1880 have condemned this as simply commercial and commodified activity. The influential critical perspectives of William Archer and Bernard Shaw have enforced a teleological, Modernist view that before the arrival of Ibsen's plays London theatre was in urgent need of reformation and reclamation from vulgar and self-indulgent social rituals. A different view of the building of the

---

[10] Princeton University Press, 2000.   [11] Davis and Emeljanow, *Reflecting the Audience*, p. 173.
[12] London: Athlone, 2002, p. 2.

West End, both literally and in its symbolic dimensions, would read theatre – and also professional and social singing, dancing, music-making, reading and lecturing – differently, alongside the new understandings of public pursuits like shopping, dining out and strolling. This field is, of course, far too large to be remapped in its entirety in one volume; what follows will aim simply to set aside the stubborn rejection of the period's theatre as lacking in interest and excellence, and suggest ways into it as a richer and more flexible field of significance both social/material and symbolic.

PART I: MAPPING

This book is in two parts, each informed by one of the historiographic methods I canvassed in *New Readings in Theatre History*. The first section attempts a denser, more particularised characterisation of the West End entertainment world by several kinds of mapping. Chapter 1 begins by walking in imagination the West End streets that made up the rough parallelogram between the river on the south, Oxford Street to the north, Temple Bar to the east and St James's to the west, and attempts to give a sense of the rich complexity of that unfolding terrain, in its spatial, cultural and temporal dimensions. It culminates in an evocation of the essence of the place, its ideal existence as a portal on to a world of pleasure – an imaginary but insistently desired world that remains discursive. The journey invokes a materialist understanding of the pleasure ground both more detailed and broader than the usual focus on a few theatres and notable moments that led to the next important era. The demise of the patent houses in the 1840s, Charles Kean's management at the Princess's and his competition with Samuel Phelps at Sadler's Wells in the 1850s, the Bancrofts' management at the Prince of Wales's and their sponsorship of Tom Robertson's plays in the 1860s, the rise of Irving's Lyceum in the 1870s are the piers on which previous histories have built their bridge; this section moves about under their shadow, and looks for other marks upon the quite different landscape that lies beneath, seeking there the fairy-lights and half-hidden ways in to other theatres, new entertainments, a different performance.

Chapter 2 reaches for a discursive map to this newly illuminated terrain, turning to the popular press of the day. The explosion of journalism and print culture in general is a conspicuous feature of mid-Victorian Britain, and one often invoked to explain the enduring critical focus upon writing rather than performance in the period. It has been usual to accept the condemnation of the theatre of the day which is found in the prolific commentaries of contemporary writers, the millions of words pumped out by the new steam presses and sold at popular prices to an increasingly literate population. But the very proliferation and endless repetition of these journalistic jeremiads might suggest to us that they were not succeeding in their aim of suppressing or changing the theatre to suit themselves; and amidst the deluge of print there is much that can be read to reveal the shape of the hopes and anxieties that performance provoked. I take a single issue of the trade newspaper *The Era* (that for 6 April 1856) and extrapolate, from its layout, tone and especially its advertisements, a taxonomic, classed view of the entertainment world to which it is a guide, finding there a fuller and more balanced context for the work of the men and women of the theatre.

Having surveyed the West End on the ground and in the press, Chapter 3 makes a final step from a material to a conceptual mapping of the terrain to ask how the creators of Victorian theatre perceived their own world; how they conceived of their work and the social identity it gave them. One of the most intriguing areas for a new history that is revealed by interdisciplinary understanding of the development of the West End is an exploration of an imaginary land that existed within it – the land of 'Bohemia'. Victorian Bohemianism was a notable feature of the mid-century, and it is particularly interesting in a discussion of the gendering of social space; twenty-first-century scholars in gender studies have begun to explore it, taking off from suggestive remarks in Eve Kosofsky Sedgwick's *The Epistemology of the Closet* about a 'semiporous, liminal space' where 'the young, male bourgeois literary subject was required to navigate his way through his "homosexual panic"'.[13] Focussing on the hitherto occluded presence of women in this world of artistic work, I take up arguments concerning masculinity and the middle classes: the links between Bohemia and the development of the theatrical West End, its complex cross-gendering of public and private, domestic and creative spaces are a vital part of a new understanding of performance in this society. Writing for the stage is considered here as a product of the Bohemian subculture, and its conflicts over gender are seen to cut both ways. I suggest that the anxieties of these writers circulate round the feminisation of the jobbing translator, the hack journalist and the dramatic writer, in their separation from the valorised poets and novelists

[13] Eve Kosofsky Sedgwick, *The Epistemology of the Closet* (Harmondsworth: Penguin, 1994), p. 193.

of the time, and that this anxiety has contributed to the pretended absence of women from that space.

PART II: MAKING

The dimensions of space and gender are further explored in the second part of the book, which turns to the theatre itself. I will employ genealogical and feminist methods to suggest new understandings of this despised culture, focussing on the parts played by women, not only on stage but also in management and creative entrepreneurship. Chapter 4 focusses first on the period from the first Parliamentary Select Committee on the Theatres in 1832 to the passing of the Theatres Act in 1843,[14] and consider the ways in which the theatres' period of doubt and turmoil played into the concurrent, larger disturbance in British culture. What Marjorie Garber has called 'category panic' is, she argues, endemic in the modern world, and reaches crisis pitch at periods of particular stress, when cultural and social dissonances result in the blurring of definitions and boundaries.[15] The deliberate transgression and ritual reassertion of gender divisions is a conspicuous result of such moments of high pressure, and the chapter explores the way in which, in the 1830s and 1840s, the London theatres obsessively represented and played out that testing of the line.

Chapters 5 and 6 move to include the post-1843 period, during which the new theatrical world, surveyed by a second select committee in 1866, took shape. Here the emphasis is upon the prominence, and in some cases the predominance, of women in the establishment of West End theatre. Despite continued reiteration even in the twenty-first century of the received wisdom that 'it was *only* as actresses that Victorian women could realistically hope to succeed in the theatre',[16] Katherine Newey has already shown us how rich a field of work the nineteenth-century theatre was for women writers,[17] and Tracy C. Davis gives us solid evidence that 'in nineteenth-century Britain, theatre is the only branch of industry or commerce where women, in significant numbers, were up-front business executives' and 'the emergence of hundreds of women in

---

[14] Properly 1843 6/7 Victoria c. 68, Theatres Regulation Act.
[15] Marjorie Garber, *Vested Interests: Cross-Dressing and Cultural Anxiety* (London: Routledge, 1992), p. 16 et seq.
[16] Kerry Powell, 'Gendering Victorian Theatre', in *The Cambridge History of British Theatre, vol. 2, 1660–1895*, ed. Joseph Donohue (Cambridge University Press, 2004), pp. 352–68, 361 (emphasis original).
[17] *Women's Theatre Writing in Victorian Britain* (London: Palgrave Macmillan, 2005).

the administration of Victorian theatre created a whole new challenge to the practices of "gentlemanly capitalism"'.[18]

Davis has very helpfully provided a detailed list of female contributors to management on the British stage up to 1914, and observes from her findings that the 'toughest market to break into was the West End of London' before the Victorian period; but adds that nevertheless we might see 'Eliza Vestris, Mrs Honey, Harriet Waylett and Madame Celeste, triumphant in the minors, as pathbreakers' while in the succeeding decades, as 'the industry grew, more and more names emerge' and 'Marie Wilton, famous for taking over the Prince of Wales's in 1865, was in good company as a London manageress in the 1860s'.[19] She lists Anne Dumarge, Louisa and Ruth Herbert, Alice Marriot and Harriet Pelham as managers and lessees at this point within the West End, and Anne Vagg just beyond at Collins's Music Hall in Islington. To these many more names of female impresarios may be added from Davis's list, beginning with Fanny Kelly, who built her own theatre, the Royalty, and managed it until 1849, where after her a series of other women took charge, including Harriet Pelham, Martha Oliver and Emily Fowler, before the long tenures of Henrietta Hodson between 1870 and 1887 and Kate Santley 1878–1902. Louisa Nisbett managed at the Queens (which later became the Prince of Wales's under Marie Wilton) in 1834 and the Adelphi in 1835; Elizabeth Yates managed the Adelphi after her husband's death in 1843; Mary Ann Keeley shared the management with her husband at the Lyceum 1844–7. The Olympic, Vestris's theatre, had several more women managers. Louisa and Mary Ann Swanborough took turns as lessees and managers in their family business at the Strand during the 1860s, and women of the Gatti clan held the lease at various dates of their music hall 'Under the Arches' in Villiers Street, as well as at their Lambeth Palace of Varieties. At the St James's a succession of women tenants and managers began with Jenny Vertpré managing the French players in 1835, to be followed by Laura Seymour in 1854, Fanny Wyndham, there in 1859–60, Leonora Wigan 1860–2, Ruth Herbert 1864–8, Mlle De la Ferte in 1868, and Mrs John Wood (by birth a Vining) between 1869 and 1874.

In Chapter 5 I focus on these directors, lessees and managers, including several important women who had authority in the theatres where they

---

[18] Tracy C. Davis, *The Economics of the British Stage 1800–1914* (Cambridge University Press 2000), pp. 273, 10.
[19] Tracy C. Davis, 'Female Managers, Lessees and Proprietors of the British Stage (to 1914)', *Nineteenth-Century Theatre* 28:2 (winter 2000), 115–44, 115–16.

worked with their partners or husbands, and who were widely acknowledged to be the actual moving force of the concern.[20] They operated not only as star performers but also in the role we would call director or artistic director: notably this was the case of Ellen Kean, neé Tree, whose work was vital to Charles Kean's venture at the Princess's; Celine Celeste, whose managerial abilities as well as her extraordinary stage gifts made her the equal and ally of Ben Webster, while between them they leased and managed at various points the Adelphi, the Olympic, the Lyceum and the Haymarket; and Priscilla Horton, aka Mrs German Reed, who invented the Gallery of Illustration in Regent's Street and whose cutting-edge importance is proposed in Chapter 2. Chapter 6 will conclude the argument for the importance of these women by offering a description and assessment of the theatrical work they actually did, the performances they staged and the importance of these to the Londoners for whom they were performed, and in the shaping of the West End as it is today.

The two parliamentary select committees I have mentioned frame the period of the formation of the West End. Much had happened between the two enquiries, in the development of London and indeed of Victorian Britain, but the preoccupations of the committee men remained remarkably constant. Since their reading of the history of London theatre has remained the basis of subsequent accounts, I will conclude this introduction with a consideration of what their questioning of witnesses suggests to have been their assumptions and intentions about the theatre of their times. This is a very different story from the one about the development of the West End that this book will attempt to tell.

THE SELECT COMMITTEES AND THE RECEIVED ACCOUNT, 1832–66

In 1831–2, which was of course also the time of the first parliamentary Reform Acts, the Select Committee on the Drama, chaired by Edward Bulwer Lytton, was chiefly concerned to introduce dramatic copyright for authors, and secondarily to reform theatrical licensing, abolishing the exclusive patent to perform Shakespeare and other 'legitimate' drama enjoyed by Covent Garden, Drury Lane and the Haymarket. The committee members asked their professional witnesses about the problems of the ancient patent houses, not only their old-established privileges and their hopelessly involved financial affairs but also their struggle to present

---

[20] Davis, *Economics*, p. 274.

straight plays in auditoria too large for them to be properly seen and heard. They clearly, from the tenor of their questioning, had a vision of smaller theatres where soft voices and unexaggerated facial expressions could make their points, and in which all sorts and conditions of men and women might become cultivated. They were hoping to encourage the widespread performance of the national poet and also the emergence of a new Shakespeare, to shape and to lead a new British way of life. Their focus on what James Glavin has called the 'monumental chimera of a national drama'[21] manifests a literary, rather than a theatrical, conception of the role of the stage, and one further disabled by its misunderstanding of theatre as being a tool of education, of social manipulation. The only immediate outcome of their recommendations was an abortive act which failed to give dramatists the copyright protection which the chairman of the committee (himself an aspirant dramatist) had chiefly aimed at.[22] It is by no means clear why it took the government until 1843 to bring in the legislation that freed the trade in theatricals;[23] but the consequence for the patent houses in the interim was a kind of planning blight, their owners and successive managements struggling desperately as they awaited the abolition of their so-called privileges, their crowd-pleasing expedients endlessly lamented by the frustrated dramatists who wrote for the contemporary press. Subsequent histories have normally accepted their account, and focussed almost exclusively, in considering this period, on the brief and unsuccessful managements of William Charles Macready at Covent Garden 1837–9 and Drury Lane 1841–3, writing them up as noble but doomed efforts to revive Shakespeare and encourage legitimate new writing for the stage.

But the vociferous partisanship of Macready's writer friends should not be allowed to eclipse the work of at least two other patent house managers of the time. One of these was Eliza Vestris, the importance of whose management of Covent Garden 1839–42 has been recognised by recent histories of Shakespearean production, and she figures here in Chapter 5; the other was Alfred Bunn, who in 1833 held the leases of both Drury Lane and Covent Garden. Bunn has been written of almost entirely as the enemy of 'the national drama', and of Macready its champion. His was a commercially spectacular career, culminating in this decade: he relinquished

[21] John Glavin, *After Dickens: Reading, Adaptation and Performance* (Cambridge University Press, 1999), p. 116.
[22] 1833 3 William IV c. 15, Dramatic Copyright Act.
[23] But see Tracy C. Davis's analysis in terms of the free trade debates, *Economics*, pp. 35–41.

Covent Garden in 1835, but remained manager of Drury Lane until 1839, while also leasing the English Opera House, a leading minor house, during 1837. He tried to make the large old theatres work by introducing spectacle and modern opera, investing in crowd-pullers like lion-taming acts – the young Queen Victoria adored these and went repeatedly to see them[24] – and paying unprecedented salaries for such international stars as the diva Malibran.[25] In 1838–9 Bunn's expenditure was over £44,000, his receipts were less than £29,000, and he was declared bankrupt. In October 1843 he leased Drury Lane again, and concentrated on spectacular presentations of opera and ballet. Macready's jealous scorn of Bunn, and the witty vilification of him as a philistine commercial manager by the would-be dramatists who operated in the pages of the satirical magazines like *Punch*, has tended to obscure the achievement of his staunch support and encouragement of English opera. As well as staging many operas by European composers, he produced eleven new operas by Balfe, Julius Benedict, Vincent Wallace, George Macfarren and Louis Henry Lavenu.[26] Madame Vestris, who had herself begun life as an opera singer at the Opera House in the Haymarket, also staged ground-breaking Shakespearean revivals and new opera at the patent theatres, having a great success in 1841 with Bellini's *Norma*, starring the last great Kemble, Adelaide.

From a perspective not determined by a concentration on the national drama, attempting instead to account for the dominant cultural trajectory in these years, it is vital to place the opera and its adjunct the ballet at the centre of an understanding of early and mid-Victorian theatre-going. These were the predominant performing arts in the 1840s, 1850s and 1860s, supported by fashionable people from Queen Victoria downwards, built into the elaborate rituals and hierarchical exchanges of the London Season and all it stood for in terms of social and cultural capital.[27] Before she came to the throne Victoria went to the Opera House frequently, adored Guilia Grisi and Marie Taglioni, and she continued to relish performances there after it took her name, as Her Majesty's Theatre.

Opera and ballet in these years are also highly significant to any understanding of the gender politics, as well as of the theatre, in Victoria's Britain. The Romantic ballet, springing from *La Sylphide* (Covent

[24] George Rowell, *Queen Victoria goes to the Theatre* (London: Elek, 1978).
[25] Alfred Bunn, *The Stage: Both Before and Behind the Curtain*, 3 vols. (London: Richard Bentley, 1840).
[26] *Dictionary of National Biography* consulted online; hereinafter cited as *DNB*.
[27] See Jennifer Lee Hall, 'The Re-fashioning of Fashionable Society – Opera-going and Sociability in Britain 1821–1861', Ph.D. thesis, Yale University (1996).

Garden 1832) danced *en pointe* by Taglioni, turning the idealised female into a disembodied spirit, and the Romantic opera, like Verdi's *La Traviata* (1853, Covent Garden 1856) dealing with the sale of sex, both embody the message that female sexuality is fascinating but fatal; *Traviata* at Covent Garden was deemed too inflammatory to be sung in English, and the Queen did not attend. She did see Verdi's *Rigoletto*, however; and her most passionate appreciation was reserved for the universal singing favourite Jenny Lind, who made her English début at Her Majesty's in May 1847, as Alice in Meyerbeer's *Robert le diable*, followed by hugely successful appearances in *La sonnambula, La fille du régiment* and *I masnadieri*. Compared to her excited following of the Swedish Nightingale, the Queen was only dutiful in her support of the national drama at Drury Lane and the Haymarket; on the other hand, she ventured to the minor theatres as early as 1836 to see Vestris and Charles Mathews, Buckstone, the Wigans, Frederick Robson and the Keeleys. In 1861 the death of Prince Albert ended her attendance at all public performances, but these comic favourites were welcomed to perform at Windsor for her, alongside the dutiful efforts of Charles Kean to bring her Shakespeare. Their work in the new West End theatres was often founded upon the 'higher' arts of opera and ballet, existing in a fruitful creative relationship encompassing both borrowing and burlesque.

THE AFTERLIFE OF THE NATIONAL DRAMA

The desire to improve and discipline a newly educated (and now a voting) public by means of a Shakespearean stage, conceived as national and educational, was still the dominating motive behind the questions put by the members of the 1866 Parliamentary Select Committee. They were convened when it became clear that the 1843 dispensation had by no means resulted in the renaissance of the Drama, but was rapidly leading to the development of sundry new, and alarming, theatrical forms. With the withdrawal of protectionism in the theatre, there was an influx of foreign performers, even dramatic companies playing in the French language at the St James's theatre in the heart of fashionable London, and a rash of new venues that were scarcely theatres at all, mounting concerts by Americans with blackened faces, or puzzling new crypto-dramatic shows; and there were insistent signs of the beginning of the music halls, where music and drama shared a space with eating and drinking. The committee's questions in 1866 imply that they feared the legitimate stage was being lost, swamped in the proliferation of novel entertainments without proper boundaries and with no discernable improving content.

The national drama, therefore, was still in need of rescuing. After they lost the supposed advantage of exclusively staging legitimate plays, both Covent Garden and Drury Lane seemed to managements in the 1850s only viable as opera venues or, in Drury Lane's case, hardly viable at all:[28] Macready's farewell there, in 1851, coincided with the year of the Great Exhibition, when performance of the nation shifted decisively to a different site. The Crystal Palace itself only stood in Hyde Park for a year, but its role was brilliantly assumed by the nearest theatre, the previously rather unimportant Princess's in Oxford Street. Davis and Emeljanow argue that in his management there between 1851 and 1859 Charles Kean made a 'concerted attempt to match in the theatre the Exhibition's image as a tourist site and redefine the role of the theatre as an element in the emerging West End "Theme Park"' where lavishly historicised Shakespeare, particularly, became the means whereby tourists 'could feel they were acquiring cultural capital'; he thereby annexed the idea of 'the national drama'.[29] Richard Schoch, accepting Kean's own version of these ambitions, claims that the Princess's in the 1850s 'possessed a nationalistic force because its audience, either actual or mythologized, was unique in regarding itself as the nation in microcosm' and made an 'inclusive appeal of a respectable and educational theatre' to high and low alike.[30] Clement Scott, who was a schoolboy in this decade, bears this out with the memory that he 'always managed to get to the Princess's Theatre, somehow or other' when home from Marlborough for the holidays, his orthodox clergyman father conniving at the boy's truancy because he was gaining a stage appreciation of the Bard. But Scott recalls the Princess's in close association with his wondering enjoyment of the Great Exhibition, and in retrospect is rather amused by Charles Kean's inclination to take himself very seriously; he gives much space in a chapter of his memoirs called 'The success of Charles Kean' to the witty and withering attacks upon the actor's pretensions by the Radical Douglas Jerrold.[31] The critics did not, on the whole, admire what

---

[28] Tracy C. Davis details the financial collapse of Drury Lane, and the equally precarious situation of Covent Garden, *Economics*, pp. 255–64.

[29] Davis and Emeljanow, *Reflecting the Audience*, pp. 199–200.

[30] Richard Schoch, 'Theatre and Mid-Victorian Society, 1851–1870', *Cambridge History of British Theatre, vol.* 2, ed. Donohue, pp. 331–51, p. 342.

[31] Clement Scott, *The Drama of Yesterday and Today*, 2 vols. (London: Macmillan, 1899), vol. 1, pp. 253–60.

Kean was doing in terms of showy modern melodramas, with stylish stage effects, like *The Corsican Brothers* (Princess's 1852) and productions of only those plays of Shakespeare susceptible of engineering into showcases for British history; and despite the full houses and socially inclusive audiences, Kean was not able to make the 'national drama' pay any more than the patent houses had done. The importance of Shakespeare at the Princess's in the modern account of the period seems to me to stem largely from its usefulness in subsequent arguments, which make it one more of the pillars of the bridge that carries us over the birth of the West End without engaging with the less accessible activities at the other theatres and venues south of Oxford Street. I intend to revisit Kean and, especially, his wife Ellen Tree, in Chapter 5, resituating their management within the context of their contemporaries rather than using it as an (anomalous) substitute for a consideration of early West End theatre.

   This, then, is the received account of the mid-Victorian stage; mine will be different. In Part I I hope to sketch a wider and deeper field of reference for my history, and in Part II to suggest some of the novel and still important ways in which its female professionals might be said to have shaped its modern face. My path will not be linear; like the walkers seeking the West End in Chapter 1, I will pass and repass certain theatres and key individuals, laying down successively, but without I hope with too much tedious repetition, some of the layers of historicisation that these women and their work have not so far been allowed.

Mapping

CHAPTER I

Why the West End?

London is the theatrical centre of Britain, time out of mind. When the 1843 Theatres Act was passed, there were three ancient patent houses in London and three new theatres with annual licences from the Lord Chamberlain's office, as well as a crowd – fluctuating between twenty-five and forty – of places which sometimes presented shows sufficiently conspicuously to be noticed by the press, or even to be prosecuted for exceeding their legal permission to play.[1] Responding to the increasing size of the city, there had been a boom in building and making over buildings for theatrical purposes through the first third of the century, which continued strongly through the 1830s, so that by the time the act came into force there were many potential places where the mushrooming population of the metropolis might be entertained. But 1843 was clearly a moment, obvious at the time as well as by hindsight, when a new dispensation in theatrical provision might be expected. All commentators who could spare time to consider the developing culture of Victorian Britain were looking for something to begin, in which theatre would be part of the new self-consciousness and self-definition of the British. Nobody knew at the time that this was to be the West End.

John Pick, in his incisive dissection and condemnation of the 'misman-agement and snobbery' of the West End, argues that the 1840s saw an opportunity missed, or even suppressed, when an explosion of entertain-ment provision across the whole city, for the benefit of the many, was not followed through, and the huge auditoria that had already been thrown up for spectacle and music at cheap prices were ignored, prosecuted or simply written off as *déclassé*. Instead, he suggests, theatre was allowed to remain in the hands of a few whose vested interests concentrated new

---

[1] See Jacky Bratton, *New Readings in Theatre History* (Cambridge University Press, 2003), pp. 40–66 for a discussion of the state of London theatre in 1832, and esp. n. 6, pp. 209–10, for the tally of theatres open around 1832.

development in the 'fashionable rectangle bounded by the Strand, Kingsway, Oxford Street and New Bond Street' despite the fact that such a theatre district was not really convenient of access for the many, and led to 'a highly ritualised theatre catering directly for the privileged' which led in turn to a 'near-monopoly of theatre practice' 'narrow in its social ambitions' but 'powerful in its creation of new managerial and artistic conventions to realise them'.[2] Tracy Davis, looking more closely at the operations of the licenser in the 1840s, notes the wavering and often obviously prejudiced or randomly political decisions about who should be granted theatre licences even within this central district, and concludes that 'what the Lord Chamberlain's office was having to go through in these years was not unlike the birth pangs of free market capitalism', especially when, from 1850, 'the picture was about to be complicated further by the emergence of music halls' and the consequent resurgence of attempts at protectionism by the theatre proprietors.[3]

Mary Poovey's analysis of the period 1830–64 provides a persuasive historical and epistemological overview of this 'moment of cultural formation'. Citing Adorno and Horkheimer, she argues that 'mass culture', 'organised by a "culture industry", a series of institutions that discipline desire and subordinate difference to homogeneity through technologies that reach (nearly) everyone' was the outcome of mid-nineteenth-century developments, and from the 1860s a notional national selfhood, the British Public, represented as a single culture,

competed with and then gradually replaced another representation which emphasised the differences among various groups within England. The image of a single culture had begun to seem plausible in 1860 – even though different subgroups continued to exist – because the technologies capable of materializing an aggregate known as the 'population' had been institutionalized for several decades.

These technologies – bureaucratic measures such as the census and the blue books of social statistics and reports which had been becoming institutionalised since the 1830s, and also new transport, cheap publications, national museums and so on – 'brought groups that had rarely mixed into physical proximity with each other and represented them as belonging to the same' whole.[4]

[2] John Pick, *The West End: Mismanagement and Snobbery* (Eastbourne: John Offord, 1983), p. 22.
[3] Davis, *Economics*, pp. 52, 53.
[4] Mary Poovey, *Making a Social Body: British Cultural Formation, 1830–1864* (University of Chicago Press, 1995), pp. 3–4.

On the ground, in the 1840s and 1850s, what seems to me to be the most important experience of becoming such a culture, for the citizens of the expanding city, was not gradual unification but, on the contrary, a sense of constant surprise and novelty. Like their own lives, the place they lived in was in a state of transformation, of rapid and all-engulfing change, and therefore of unprecedented complexity and differentiation. The old civic ideal of a multilayered but united London community for which the old patent theatres catered in box, pit and gallery fragmented as it grew, and there could be no single type of institution in which all the new, highly self-conscious classes of Londoner could easily be entertained together. They were, however, as Poovey suggests, not only all simultaneously present, but all highly conscious of each other, and the managers and capitalists catering for them sought ways of serving them all – if not all alike, still all, as far as possible, at once. As the city grew rapidly there were still many different grades of housing and work in and around the centre – London was still the workshop of the world, full of closely packed, small-scale manufacture; but it was also now the capital of empire, so that the expansion of bureaucracy, government and wholesale trade made for an enormous growth of its body of clerks and office workers. All of these workers, in addition, had many more layers of managers, who insisted upon recognition of their social status and their difference from those below, and also those above, them in the social scale.

The huge, simple popular audience that John Pick sees being sidelined in theatrical development was not therefore just the casualty of theatrical snobbery, but also of much larger social changes, and, from another perspective, of theoretical, sociological and cultural reconceptualisations then and now.[5] The drive to agglomeration and simultaneous differentiation, working within the expanding numbers of city dwellers, led, in topographical terms, to the initial urban overcrowding exploding outwards through urban clearances into, eventually, suburban expansion. An influx of millions into the old city was tackled by thrusting and funnelling

[5] There is a formidable tally of literature since the 1960s debating the understanding and realities of social change in this period, many voices which affirm and deny, explain and challenge and seek to understand the so-called Industrial Revolution and its consequences; but few deny that extreme, rapid physical and social changes took place between the 1790s and 1850, and that Britons for two generations were aware of their times as changing. See for a summary Dror Wahrmann, *Imagining the Middle Class: The Political Representation of Class in Britain, c. 1780–1840* (Cambridge University Press, 1995), especially the introduction and pp. 227–34 where he discusses 'the increasing awareness of the drama of social change', 'the realization of contemporaries that society around them was in irreversible flux', pp. 229, 234.

them out of the way, the demolition of central housing and the creation of many and various suburbs, so that the centre of London could be rescued, transformed, and, in some sense, made to serve them all. All these new Londoners did not constitute an undifferentiated 'popular audience', so much as the potential for huge profit, as well as huge influence, for anyone acute enough to find ways of catering for enough of them together, under the banner of the British Public. And, given the centralising and industrialising principles of the time, this might well happen most economically in a single district – though not in any one kind of institution. The question was where that should be, and which of the many faces of London it should reflect and take as its own. It was hardly likely to be the old entertainment district of Covent Garden, undermined as that was by its crumbling infrastructure, the outward migration of its wealthier inhabitants leaving old buildings at the mercy of pressure from surrounding slum and indeed criminal districts, notably the St Giles rookery immediately to the north. In the 1830s and 1840s this was not somewhere that a careful father would choose to take his family out for the evening. A new centre was bound to arise; somewhere with an attractive aura of comfort, luxury and excitement that would offer the visitor a sense of going somewhere special. This was to be the West End.

As Pick points out, the West End of 'the Town' (i.e. Westminster) was in origin the chosen residential and recreational quarter of the London elite. Its institutions began as the public expression of the life of the governing classes, who had the power and money to command their own leisure facilities, in the form of luxury shops, gentlemen's clubs, high-class gambling houses and brothels as well as the Opera House and the Theatre Royal Haymarket, and bookshops, libraries, galleries, concert-rooms and philanthropic and scientific institutions. As such, it was ready to be taken up by mass culture, the forces of commercial expansion, and made accessible and attractive to many of the newly stratified and defined layers of a general public who aspired to the experience of London as the metropolitan centre of the world.

The West End did not spring into existence as a unified commercial endeavour, of course. Pick's 'fashionable rectangle' of streets did not exist as such in 1840. Many of the streets themselves had not been built. Since the eighteenth century there had been New Bond Street, at the heart of the elite residential streets of the West End, flowing into Old Bond Street, which was an old-established centre for the luxury trades catering to the fashionable man, and thence to Oxford Street, more recently filling up with the feminised delights of middle-class shopping.

But Kingsway was not created until the first decade of twentieth century, after the Claire Market area had been flattened in the 1890s, making 3,700 working-class people homeless. Similarly Shaftsbury Avenue, which contains seven modern theatres, was not built until 1885, blasted through the St Giles slums and running roughly parallel to Drury Lane, from Piccadilly to Cambridge Circus on the Charing Cross Road – which was also a brand new thoroughfare. The Strand was an ancient road, and had long been a main artery of London retail trades, but its southern side turnings ran down straight into the river and, as the inhabitants of the city and their use of the newly invented water closet increased, the river side lived under a constant miasma of excrement, and the very real threat of cholera. Bazalguette, who was to be the architect of Shaftsbury Avenue, created the massive London sewers and riverside Embankments along the Strand from the 1860s onwards, in the face of endless argument and opposition. At ground level, therefore, what actually happened to create the West End as an entertainment centre was a random and piecemeal development of responses to needs and opportunities, often ill-conceived, delayed or undermined by ancient rights and time-honoured practices, and driven this way and that by conflicting motives, vested interests, public demands and private profit. The magic rectangle eventually contained a palimpsest of play-houses and pleasure houses of many kinds, all in the same place but each, by the customary cultural illusion of the modern world, only fully visible and known to the people for whom it was intended.

In surveying London theatre in 1832 in *New Readings in Theatre History*, I was able to characterise the London theatres – in the City, the East End and on the South Bank as well as in the West End – by a reading of their individual styles and assumptions as imaged by their bills, meaning both the actual performances they presented and their representation of them in daily print. By 1843 it is scarcely possible to be that comprehensive and at the same time discriminating in describing even the narrower target of the West End; and here I am also concerned not to isolate the entertainments offered in the theatres themselves from their teeming, heterogeneous context on the ground, in the streets and beside the other houses of resort. This chapter and the next will therefore employ different surveying tactics. Here the reader is invited to walk the streets and see what there was to be seen, over a period – a very long and rich period, in this context – of a generation, the thirty years from 1840 to 1870. Then, in the second part of this chapter, I attempt to fix and explore a single spot which characterises the West End experience, from its beginnings right up to the present day; characterises it not only physically, on the ground, but also in its less concrete, more conceptual existence, in all our minds.

Michel De Certeau's late-twentieth-century vision of the practices of everyday life includes the idea of 'walking in the city'. He contrasts a voyeuristic, ideal overview of New York from on high with the manifold experience of actually walking the streets, of many nameless individuals all blindly threading paths through the 'thicks and thins of the urban "text" below'. His argument is that while the conceptual Modernist city is totalitarian, the walker may slip through the meshes into a mythic and poetic experience of space at odds with the totalising intention.[6] To the average Victorian writer, however, the notion of walking the streets of London was textual in itself, and far from blind; it was a gesture of mastery and formation that imposed order and asserted his grasp of his city and its meanings. In the first half of the century the flâneur's detachment, his disenchanted observation of life from the shadows, had not yet occurred to the modern writer; his was a Victorian modernity, awestruck and excited, outraged or enthusiastic but above all engaged, possessive of the city in which he – or she[7] – may walk. London journalists glorified their daily walking or observing experiences in miles of news-paper column inches and expansive acres of articles in the huge periodical press, much as a twenty-first-century blogger writes and twitters con-stantly about her or his quotidian activities. The walk through the streets was one of Victorian journalism's familiar genres:

Of all the streets in London Bond-Street is my favourite. When a boy born in the bogs, I used to hear of walking down Bond-Street as something supremely pleasant, and to this very hour my morning walk down that street has lost none of its charms. It is a classic ground – fashionably classic ... What luxury of dress, furniture, equipage, or food is not found in Bond-Street in the utmost perfec-tion? Bought in Bond-Street, no matter what it is, whether a cheese or a chariot, a fish or fowling-piece, a chine of beef or a book, a pipe of wine or a proof print, it must of course be excellent exceedingly. Bond-Street, St James's-Street, Pall Mall,

---

[6] Michel De Certeau, *The Practice of Everyday Life*, trans. Steven Randall (Berkeley: University of California Press, 1984), p. 93.

[7] For the female Victorian journalists, see Hilary Fraser, Stephanie Green and Judith Johnston, *Gender and the Victorian Periodical* (Cambridge University Press, 2003), and on the freedom of women to walk in the streets see Lynda Nead, *Victorian Babylon: People, Streets and Images in Nineteenth-century London* (New Haven, CT: Yale University Press, 2000).

you are a whole world of delights to me, a paradise for peripatetic philosophers that can never pall, with your bookshops, picture-shops, army-clothiers, music-sellers, goldsmiths, wine-merchants, perfumiers, princely hotels, and Palace-like club-houses … Reader, if ever you find your mind inclined to grovelling pursuits or pleasures, walk from the office of *Bell's Life* in the Strand to the Tyburn end of the Edgware-Road, passing through the streets I named above into Oxford-Street, and if your taste does not become more elevated, and if you have not a higher sense of men and dignity, then I advise you to go and wallow in Wapping, for the west-end is not fit air for you to breathe.[8]

Where De Certeau's analysis applies to this and thousands of similar texts is in their bold and open appropriation of the culture they expound, the journalists' determination that they, not the planners, builders and owners of the city, really know what it all means, and are willing to share their wisdom with the other members of the public. They are writing the myth of the city, creating its legends and its stories, in the public press. Hundreds of anonymous men and women, as well as scores of known writers like Augustus Sala, Edmund Yates, the Mayhew brothers and the supreme Charles Dickens, beat out the map of the new city with their pens and their walking feet.[9] And while the artistic sketch writer – *après* Boz – may take a wry, chiaroscuro slant upon the phantasmagoric scene, the streetwise walker, knowingly leading the way, is a useful guide to the material landscape within which West End entertainment grew up sud-denly and flourished, as he would say, exceedingly. Borrowing that jaunty, nose-tapping, rather self-satisfied knowingness about the people and places they passed on their daily perambulations, therefore, we might imagine two of them, on a clement day any time between 1835 and 1865, setting out on two walking routes to pinpoint the new entertainment centre of their city.

Beginning with the female of the species: if she had a sense of history, and no great fear of the inevitable glimpses she would catch of her fallen sisters, one of whose ancient haunts this was, she might start at the old theatrical centre, the piazza of Covent Garden. The Garden was a liminal site, lying beside the legal district, half way between the old City, the financial district, and Westminster, the Town, the capital of fashion. There still stood the Theatres Royal Covent Garden and Drury Lane

---

[8] Anon., 'Lucid Intervals of a Lunatic no. 8', *Bell's Life in London*, 30 January 1842.
[9] For the most famous collections of these essays, see Charles Dickens, *Sketches by Boz*, collected 1836; George Augustus Sala, *Twice Around the Clock* and *Gaslight and Daylight*, 1859; Edmund Yates, *Fifty Years of London Life: Memoirs of a Man of the World* (title of the New York edition, 1885), and the Mayhews' *London Labour and the London Poor*, 1851.

(*map refs. 1* & *2*). But it would not be a promising place to seek new developments. As has already been suggested, the two old theatres were in desperate straits by 1832, with Covent Garden proprietor Charles Kemble's financial collapse coinciding with the Parliamentary Select Committee on the Theatres which reported in that year; and their situation really only deteriorated over the period between the committee and the 1843 legislation. Externally, they stood in a district rapidly going downhill, which reinforced the feeling of prospective audience members that the theatres were out of bounds because inextricably entwined with the drinking, gambling and prostitution that took place so conspicuously around and indeed within them. The worsening state of their affairs, the managers' conflicting aspirations, their weight of debt, their unshakeable encumbrances of tradition and expectation, have been much discussed, largely in terms of ideological conflict: see above, Introduction, pp. 9–12.

After 1843 the story of these vast theatres moves towards their modern role as the venue for spectacles, whether up- or down-market. Covent Garden became the Royal Opera House in 1847, successfully competing for the highest social levels of the audience with the old Italian opera house, the King's Theatre, now renamed Her Majesty's Theatre, in the Haymarket (*map ref. 33*), and this role was confirmed by the shape it took when it was once more burned down and rebuilt in 1856. Drury Lane, meanwhile, continued to scupper the pretensions of both the Drama and the opera until its future as the home of large-scale popular spectaculars clarified, under Augustus 'Druriolanus' Harris, who was not to arrive until 1879. There was a foretaste of his methods under the management of E. T. Smith in the 1850s, who opened in 1852 with the blockbuster *Uncle Tom's Cabin* and sought for successful shows in everything from Shakespeare to circus; but the solid success story of spectacular melodrama alternating with even more spectacular pantomime was not established for a very rocky twenty years more; our walker, at almost any time between 1835 and 1865, could well have found Drury Lane shuttered and dark. Neither house, therefore, was in a position to shape the new dispensation in public entertainment.

Nor was their geographical position right for widespread appeal. The district of Covent Garden was at least on the north side of the Thames, where the land rose more rapidly from the marshy, fetid tidal waters; but the two great patent theatres were surrounded by some of the most decrepit old building of London, housing some of the poorest inhabitants. The capital's major fruit and vegetable market was also there, and its houses of accommodation had been the night haunts of the more reckless pleasure seekers for generations; the hours of business of the nurserymen, porters and their buyers from the market overlapped with those of sex workers and their clients in the brothels, theatres, streets and gambling houses to keep its pubs very busy. In 1828–30 the squalid wooden sheds round the seventeenth-century Covent Garden piazza were replaced by the owner, the Duke of Bedford, with a graceful new market building – its Floral Hall was incorporated in the twenty-first century into Covent Garden theatre – but that purge, like other slum clearances of the mid century, did not make the surrounding area any more salubrious. The maze of surrounding streets housed many entertainment venues besides the two big theatres: looking out on the Piazza's north-west corner, for instance, in King Street, was Evans's (*map ref. 3*), the most famous of the proto-music-hall singing rooms, frequented by theatrical and writing professionals and their followers. Named for its proprietor W. C. Evans, comedian from Covent Garden theatre, it opened in the 1820s, was enlarged in 1855, on the crest of the invention of music hall, and shut down by the Licensing Act of 1872, which fixed the closing hour of public entertainments at 12.30 a.m. It became the National Sporting Club. Also in King Street were the first premises of the Garrick Club, opened in 1831, with which Evans's shared members and a certain attitude to life (*map ref. 4*).[10] Next door to Evans's, at no. 42 (*map ref. 5*), was Kilpack's Cigar Divan and bowling alley, established by Gliddon, a friend of Leigh Hunt's, in 1825 and used as an informal club, and a *poste-restante* by theatricals.[11]

Since we are at present imagining her as female, and Evans's, like the Garrick Club, was an exclusively masculine preserve, our pedestrian leaving Covent Garden behind would quickly pass them by. Seeking a place of entertainment particularly equipped to appeal to women, she could, in the second half of our period, cross Long Acre (not a leisured street but one devoted to manufacture, a centre of the carriage-making trade, running east–west from Drury Lane to St Martin's Lane) to St Martin's Hall (*map ref. 6*), at the top of Bow Street. Built as a concert hall for the singing teacher and concert-master Hullah in 1850, the imposing building was eminently respectable, and soon also used as a large auditorium for readings and similar entertainments: Mr and Mrs German Reed tried out their carefully pitched entertainments there in March 1855 (see Chapter 2), and Dickens began his reading career there in

[10] Christopher Pulling, *They Were Singing* (London: Harrap, 1952), pp. 173–5.
[11] See Robert Keeley to W. C. Macready, 12 April 1841, Harvard Theatre Collection.

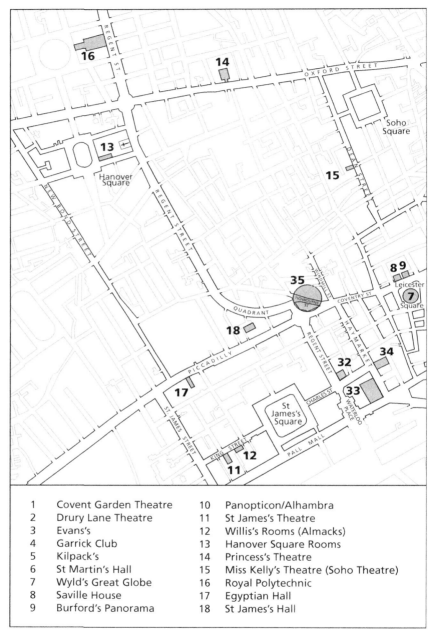

1	Covent Garden Theatre	10	Panopticon/Alhambra
2	Drury Lane Theatre	11	St James's Theatre
3	Evans's	12	Willis's Rooms (Almacks)
4	Garrick Club	13	Hanover Square Rooms
5	Kilpack's	14	Princess's Theatre
6	St Martin's Hall	15	Miss Kelly's Theatre (Soho Theatre)
7	Wyld's Great Globe	16	Royal Polytechnic
8	Saville House	17	Egyptian Hall
9	Burford's Panorama	18	St James's Hall

Map 1 Sketch of the mid-Victorian West End based upon Stanford's 'Library Map of London and its Suburbs', 1862.

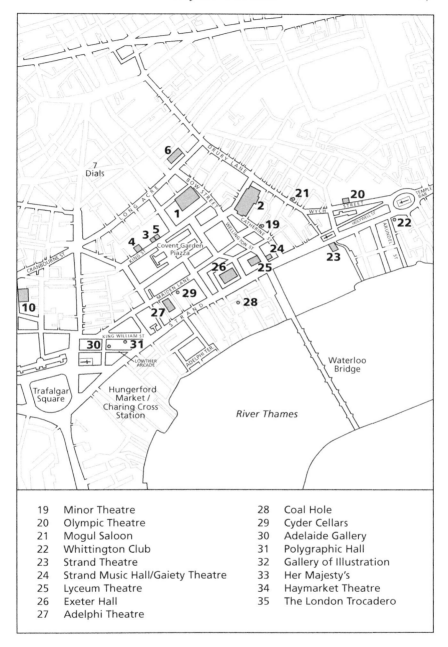

19 Minor Theatre	28 Coal Hole
20 Olympic Theatre	29 Cyder Cellars
21 Mogul Saloon	30 Adelaide Gallery
22 Whittington Club	31 Polygraphic Hall
23 Strand Theatre	32 Gallery of Illustration
24 Strand Music Hall/Gaiety Theatre	33 Her Majesty's
25 Lyceum Theatre	34 Haymarket Theatre
26 Exeter Hall	35 The London Trocadero
27 Adelphi Theatre	

1858. It seated an audience of more than 3,000 before it was rebuilt as the Queen's Theatre in 1867 by the famous Radical journalist and MP Henry Labouchere. In the Queen's first company was Henrietta Hodson, who rapidly formed a personal relationship with Labouchere which served her well as an opening into theatrical management, despite the efforts of her estranged husband to cash in on her ventures. I will return to these domestically supported West End managements in Chapter 5. The lady walker not actually bound for St Martin's Hall would need to take care not to cross Long Acre and walk north, where she would be in immediate danger of straying into St Giles, the fabled centre of London crime, a rat-trap confusion of decaying grand buildings inhabited by the poorest classes, whose evil reputation was relished and fostered by the popular press. The safer, and in some ways no less exciting, path was westwards, across St Martin's Lane and on into Leicester Square.

Here a much jollier myth was growing than the scandal of the St Giles slums: the myth of the great day (or night) out, the archetypal pleasure ground, the unpretentious, philistine face of the West End. By 1830 the Square was already, as Altick has it, 'the heart of the early and mid-Victorian mass amusement industry'[12] and an incongruous mixture of educational and eye-opening diversions was collected in and around it. In the mid-century its evolution was speeding up, overwhelming the now disgusting remains of the once green space called Leicester Fields. In 1851, stimulated and frustrated by the Great Exhibition, which was a strictly non-profit-making national show, commercial exhibitors sought places where they could sell as well as show their wares, and James Wyld, royal geographer, MP and retailer of maps, made himself into a 'monster showman' by having a Great Globe erected in Leicester Square (*map ref. 7*). Inside a brick rotunda 170 feet across was a zinc globe, 60 feet in diameter, blue and star-spangled outside, with stairs and viewing plat-forms inside where the spectator climbed and stopped to inspect a 'spherical relief map, made up of 6,000 plaster casts' of all the world, at 10 miles to the inch; and returned to ground level to purchase Wyld's cartographic wares. The visitor popularity of this unimpeachably respectable diversion came a very respectable second to that of the exhibition itself in 1851,[13] but its attractions wore thin over the ten years of its lease; it was then pulled down again, and rubbish and feral cats took over the central grass once more.

---

[12] Richard Altick, *The Shows of London* (Cambridge, MA: Harvard University Press, 1978), p. 229.
[13] ibid., p. 465.

The attractions mounted in the Square's surrounding buildings were more profitable and lasting, though in a constant state of evolution. Our walker would need to take care. The approach from Covent Garden lay through Cranbourne Alley, formed in 1677 as a mere footpath. This was the early headquarters of the popular music business in the shape of ballad printing and hawking, and she could buy broadsides of the latest songs, if she had a mind to them, but would find herself in 1843–4 shielding her skirts from deep holes, dust and disruption created by the process of widening the path into a road by pulling down all the shops and houses on one side. She would then have arrived on the northern edge of the Square just in time to visit a famous, if somewhat baffling, exhibition, Miss Linwood's embroidery.

This was a long-established exhibition for taking the children to, being safe, vaguely educational and very impressive. Victorian writers – Dickens, Thackeray, Sala – recalled it vividly from their childhood outings. From 1800 to Miss Linwood's death in 1845 it occupied the main space in a rebuilt mansion called Saville House (*map ref. 8*); her pictures, in woolwork, were mostly copies of old masters, but with some more modern subjects.[14] If our walker was indeed planning an outing for her children, and Miss Linwood's seemed a little dusty and passé, an alternative educational treat was a visit to one of Burford's Panoramas, next door (*map ref. 9*), which at Easter 1842 showed in its 'large circle' a new revised and historicised picture of the Battle of Waterloo, which had been the subject of the original panorama with which the showplace had opened in 1816. Upstairs the more robust youngsters could still be shown one of the original sensations, a huge picture of the bloody Battle of Acre, and, as a calming final experience, an architectural view of Jerusalem. Less child-safe diversions housed in the nooks and crannies of Saville House included concerts and balls and cheap and sensational exhibitions of all kinds. After 1845 in Miss Linwood's place came Mrs Wharton's 'Walhalla', which laid claim to the same unimpeachable artistic intent as her predecessor's pictures but actually involved foreign artistes posing in skin-tight pink fleshings and classical drapery, as near nude as, according to its critics, made no difference. There was a bar and a billiard room in the basement; the Salle Valentino held 2,000 dancers whose noisy polking and galloping competed with Mrs Wharton's music and the crack of rifles in the shooting gallery, the boxing match shouts from the

[14] ibid., pp. 401–2.

gymnasium and the thump of single-sticks from the fencing academy.[15] In 1865 the whole shooting match burned down, to be replaced by the Royal Denmark Theatre, which in 1880 took on its final form as the world-famous Empire Theatre of Varieties, which still stands in 2011, divided now down the middle into a cinema on the left and a casino to the right.

At right angles on the eastern side of the Square a London aunt planning a really up-to-date family treat at mid-century would find the Royal Panopticon of Science and Art (*map ref. 10*), an expensive venture in modern exhibition making, again after the manner of the Great Exhibition, built 1852–4 on the site of an earlier museum. Its central rotunda, 90 feet high, housed a floodlit fountain fed by an artesian well, and it hosted scientific lectures.[16] As with Wyld's globe, this high-minded and high-tech show ran out of steam and visitors very quickly, and the West End manager E. T. Smith took the decorative building over in 1857 and filled it first with a circus ring and then with its subsequently famous mixture of music hall stars, ballets and the higher classes of prostitution. As the Alhambra Theatre it encountered considerable opposition from all the other theatres of the West End, who successfully petitioned against Smith's application for a Lord Chamberlain's licence until 1871.[17] Seven theatres signed the petition against him in 1858, claiming they were all in 'close proximity'.[18] They would indeed be reached by a short walk, out of the western side of the Square, along Coventry Street, which our pedestrian might or might not know was a long-established centre of London gambling; but she could quickly pass by the casinos and arrive at Regent Circus, now called Piccadilly Circus: she had reached the heart of the West End.

If she were beguiled by the shops, our walker would now saunter northwards up Regent Street or Bond Street to Oxford Street. Her excuse could still be that she wished to buy tickets, available for most kinds of polite entertainment at one of the smart shops on her way: in Old Bond Street were at one time or another more than half a dozen bookshop/ticket offices, from the early example of John Ebers, bookseller and publisher who moved up from selling box tickets to managing the Opera House,[19] to the elegant man of business John Mitchell. Mitchell was a very modern figure, an agent and manager of individual celebrities as well

---

[15] ibid., pp. 230–1, 346–7.   [16] ibid., pp. 490–6.
[17] Diana Howard, *London Theatres and Music Halls 1850–1900* (London: Library Association, 1970), p. 10.
[18] Davis, *Economics*, pp. 54–5.
[19] See Jennifer Hall-Witt, *Fashionable Acts: Opera and Elite Culture in London, 1780–1880* (Durham: University of New Hampshire Press, 2007), pp. 156–7.

as theatres. Fanny Kemble turned to him when she decided to make her living from Shakespearean readings. She found him 'a Liberal, and honest man', an 'excellent and zealous manager' who 'could calculate the money value of my readings to me, [though] their inestimable value he knew nothing of'. She made jokes in her letters to friends about his pastel-coloured flyers for her readings: 'it really almost seems a pity to interfere with the elegancies of poor Mitchell, who is nothing if not elegant'; and mocked his way of referring to the audience he was aiming for, 'the British aristocracy, whom he idolized, and whom he thought fit ... to designate, collectively, under the title of my friend, Lord Lansdowne'.[20] Such genteel relationships were all part, as Kemble in her own terms fully understood, of the conversion of an old aristocratic system of deference and patronage into a modern middle-class purchasing of cultural capital for cash.

Ebers had had only his bookshop and the management of the Opera House by which to please his patrons, but Mitchell spread his nets further in the smart residential districts. He was lessee of the St James's Theatre (*map ref. 11*), a modern venue built in 1835 with pretensions to the highest fashion. Our walker would reach it by crossing back over Piccadilly from the Bond Street shop, and heading southwards towards St James's Palace, turning left into King Street. There, for a highly successful decade, 1843–54, Mitchell imported French acting companies to play in their own language to audiences able to understand the best of modern drama straight from the Parisian source, without the intervention of bowdlerising translation. There he also presented modern international celebrities like the street child turned tragedienne Rachel. He placed his fashionable readers and lecturers who preferred to avoid the theatre next door but one to the St James's, in Willis's Rooms (*map ref. 12*). There, in 1844, our walker would have found Charles Kemble, Fanny's father, financing his post-Covent Garden years by reading Shakespeare, under the patronage of the Queen Dowager, Adelaide, and her entourage. Built as 'Almacks' in 1765, Willis's Rooms was an imposing classical building housing a fashionable ballroom which, during its heyday in the early years of the century, was a society gathering place second only to the Opera boxes and ruled by the same ultra-exclusive clique of aristocratic ladies. By the 1840s public dancing was much less exclusive, and it was perhaps rather more to the point to be seen at expensive readings or lectures: in 1851 our walker could have attended Thackeray's series on the English Humorists there, in

---

[20] Frances Anne Butler, *Records of Later Life*, 3 vols. (London: Richard Bentley, 1882), vol. III, pp. 415, 345–6, 356.

company with all the literati of London, showing that they preferred intelligent lectures to vulgar Great Exhibitions. The London lecture-going culture, covering everything from literature and travel to popular science, grew strongly in the 1840s and 1850s, and was particularly aimed at audiences of women, appealing to the serious culture of self-improvement at every social level. Marianne Evans, for example, went to hear Faraday at the Royal Society (then still meeting in Somerset House on the Strand) in January 1851, and remarked in a letter that his lectures were 'as fashionable as the Opera' and so were frequented by 'store of ladies' who reputedly lowered the intellectual level.[21]

There were other attractions in St James's Square: in 1844 Charles Kemble's audience could have visited Christie's auction rooms opposite Willis's, or popped in to see the decorative scheme planned for the new Houses of Parliament in Crockford's exhibition rooms on the corner of King Street. Crockford himself, a fishmonger from the City who had made a fortune by building a splendid gambling club round the corner off St James's Street in 1827, died in 1844. Our walker would probably not be drawn down St James's Street to Pall Mall, since gentlemen's clubs were of no use to her. If she had a mind to the most exclusive serious music, she could go back up Bond Street all the way to Brooke Street, which would take her into Hanover Square. There stood another imposing set of eighteenth-century rooms (*map ref. 13*), where the Concerts of Ancient Music took place until 1848 and were succeeded by those of the Philharmonic Society, and where the celebrities she might hear included Liszt, Mendelssohn, Paganini and Jenny Lind; or indeed, in 1846, the first black-face American troupe called the Ethiopian Serenaders. From here she could cross to the Princess's in Oxford Street (*map ref 14*), a West End theatre somewhat out on the edge, as also were Fanny Kelly's little theatre in Dean Street Soho (*map ref. 15*), the Queen's in Tottenham Court Road, which was to become the famous Prince of Wales's, and the aspirational but never very successful Marylebone, up the Edgware Road in Paddington: these last two are not even physically on the map, and our walker will not go that far. She might have ventured, if she were intent upon a very improving day out, as far as the northern extension of Regent's Street, where stood an important large hall dedicated to popular science, the Royal Polytechnic (*map ref. 16*), patronised by Prince Albert. It had august support, but it was never able to convince the public of its entertainment

[21] George Eliot to Mr and Mrs Charles Bray, *The George Eliot Letters*, ed. Gordon S. Haight (Oxford University Press, 1954), vol. 1 *1836–1851*, p. 342.

value: see Chapter 2. Our walker would find more successful and appealing exhibitions, music and lecture rooms right in the heart of Piccadilly.

She and all her guests could find something to interest each of them there, compendiously collected behind the curious façade of the Egyptian Hall (*map ref. 17*). Through the 1850s, while Charles Kean up at the Princess's was busy constructing a national sense of self through his seasons of Shakespeare (see Introduction, p. 13) there was a series of ethnographic exhibitions in London that performed the same discursive task of urgent cultural self-definition from the other side, by marking what was not British. Appearing all over town, but especially at the Egyptian Hall, 'native' people on display fed the British Public a sense of themselves, as distinct from the world's 'savages', noble or debased: in 1843 came the Ojibbeways and then the Ioways; in 1845 the Bosjesmen; in 1850 the Kaffirs; and in 1853 the Aztec Lilliputians and the Earthmen were paraded through the capital's exhibition rooms.[22] If she happened to arrive at the Egyptian Hall when no such group were there, our walker could still have relied upon finding, from 1851 until his death, a performance which also fulfilled part of the national agenda: Albert Smith's solo entertainment, which offered not a view of the other, but of the modern Londoner himself, real and unvarnished. Smith's *Ascent of Mont Blanc* was the first long-running West End show: see Chapter 2.

If our pleasure seeker and her family had already seen Smith's current show, or would perhaps prefer some music, she could from 1858 have walked a few yards eastwards and crossed Piccadilly to find the major London concert room, the St James's Hall (*map ref. 18*), beside the Quadrant in Regent's Circus. We may leave her there, deciding whether her visitors' musical tastes are for the main room, where they might hear the great music makers of her time, or the Little St James's Hall below, where they could instead enjoy the Christy's Minstrels' show, 'replete' as the advertisements said, 'with mirth and fun'.

DOWN THE STRAND

There were other routes from Covent Garden to Regent's Circus and the heart of the West End. Imagining our walker this time as a man, perhaps not simply a potential audience member but a would-be creator of theatre, say a writer, we could follow him as he walked from Covent

---

[22] See Altick, *Shows of London*, pp. 273–87.

Garden south, this time, towards the river, where he could reach the West
End by walking along the Strand. Setting out from the east side of the
Piazza towards Drury Lane, he would pass not only the other patent house
but also a theatre at the opposite end of the scale, the Minor in Catherine
Street (*map ref. 19*), an exhibition room turned raffish 'private' playhouse,
which had been established in an upper room there since 1807. Very near,
at 197 Drury Lane (*map ref. 21*), there also stood the venerable entertainment venue known as the Mogul Saloon, already long established when it
applied for a theatre licence in 1849, on the reasonable pretext that Covent
Garden was only offering opera and Drury Lane was closed; but the Lord
Chamberlain's office was not yet prepared to accept the death of hope for
the old national theatres, and it was refused.[23] In 1851 the Mogul became
the Middlesex Music Hall and is now the site of the New London
Theatre. Next to it was then the turning into Wych Street, where at the
Olympic Madame Vestris's first management began in 1831 (*map ref. 20*).
The Olympic was burnt down in 1849 (another reason why the Mogul
should have received its licence that year). Rebuilt, the Olympic is one of
the West End theatres that will figure in the following chapters. When
Lyon's Inn, just across the road, was demolished, the new buildings on
that site included another theatre, the Globe, opened in 1868.

Overlaid on the market and the houses of entertainment here and
down into the Strand was the office district of the Victorian periodical
press. Our writer-pedestrian would be familiar with these premises, since
most Victorian artists of the pen and pencil made a daily living by
working in this world. Walking out of Covent Garden down Catherine
Street would take him past the offices of the *Court Gazette* and *Court
Journal*, the *Naval and Military Gazette*, the *Racing Times*, the *London
Herald*, the *Illustrated Times*, the *Literary Gazette* and, most importantly,
The Era, the show business trade paper, for which see Chapter 2. In 1868
the *Echo*, the first halfpenny daily paper in London, also began here. The
officers of *The Morning Post* were on the next block, Wellington Street.
Joseph Moses Levy's *Daily Telegraph*, the first low-priced (1d), quality
broadsheet newspaper, was first issued on 16 September 1855 from small
offices at 253 Strand. Heading eastwards from the Olympic towards those
offices, in what became the centre of the print and publishing world, and
perhaps seeking to stay clear of the dangerous traffic backing up from the
bottleneck at old Temple Bar, our perambulating man of letters could
pass through Holywell Street, where antiquarian books and modern

---

[23] Davis, *Economics*, p. 53.

pornography were offered from some of the oldest surviving shops in London. Even our female pleasure seeker would not necessarily be put off by the prints of bare-legged actresses in these little dusty windows: Lynda Nead, in her analysis of the history of the old street as 'the topographical embodiment of debates throughout the nineteenth century concerning the look of modernity, its special articulation and its relationship to the past'[24] has noted that much journalistic anxiety about its displays of indecent material focussed on its attractions to young middle-class people, including girls and young women.

Neither she nor the journalist who is our current avatar would be likely to carry on from that point through Temple Bar; we will have him brave the snarled traffic and turn back westwards along the Strand, the old road linking the City and the Town. W. S. Gilbert, who could be our man – he was one of the young hopefuls writing for the stage and the press, and he produced journalistic accounts of the town – characterises the Strand at this point as having 'a theatrical tone which there is no mistaking', thronged with actors between Wellington Street and Lacy's, the theatrical booksellers, close-shaven men you feel you have met somewhere and young ladies whose faces you seem to know, bound for 'afternoon coffee and buns at Creighton's'. Gilbert and his like, the young men 'who pretend to be at all *au fait* with literary or theatrical affairs', were, he claimed, bound to meet someone they knew in 'the short distance between Southampton-street and the Adelphi', if only because all the 'well-known literary and theatrical clubs are within a few hundred yards of this classic spot'.[25]

The next turning, Arundel Street, held two of them. The Crown and Anchor Tavern, whose large meeting room had been a famous concert venue in the previous century and the scene of many political banquets, was taken over in 1848 by a hopeful band of Radicals, led by Douglas Jerrold, to be a new kind of social club, the Whittington (*map ref. 22*), offering all the benefits of a London club with the unusual and adventurous difference that it was open to both men and women to be members. The idealistic leaders found it difficult to get the members, who were mostly very young, to understand the function of the place as they intended, and there was a perpetual struggle between high-minded educational offerings and a craving for the polka. Socially ahead of its time, the Whittington struggled to find a profitable and at the same time

[24] Nead, *Victorian Babylon*, p. 168.
[25] W. S. Gilbert, 'From St Paul's to Piccadilly', *Belgravia* 2 (March 1867), 69–74, 71–2.

respectable niche in the entertainment world, swinging from Shakespearean readings, popular preaching and scientific lectures to assaults at arms.[26] Further down the same side street towards the Thames were the first rooms of the journalists' meeting place the Arundel, particularly haunted by dramatic critics; it is discussed in Chapter 3. Another block to the west (where the Aldwych tube station was to be built) were the offices of the sporting newspaper *Bell's Life*, and next door the Strand Theatre (*map ref. 23*), created in the heat of the licensing wars of 1831 out of the older premises of Burford's Panorama, an exhibition which had occupied the spot since 1806; the Strand is important amongst the West End theatres to be considered in this book.

Crossing back to the north side of the road the walker would return to the foot of Catherine Street, where stood Doyley's, a large clothing warehouse famous for fashionable casual wear, which survived until the 1840s. At no. 332 were the offices of the daily newspaper *The Morning Chronicle*, which was coming to the end of a long and fashionable life in 1861. By 1863 the Strand Music Hall occupied the best part of this site, fronting on to the Strand, and by 1868 that too had been superseded, by the Gaiety Theatre and restaurant (*map ref. 24*). Next door, across the side turning of Wellington Street, was an older theatre, the Lyceum (*map ref. 25*), which like the Strand Theatre had started life as an exhibition space, many times rebuilt after its opening in 1765. It was rebuilt and opened once more on this new site in 1834, after a fire and the first burst of street remodelling along the river, as the English Opera House. Despite its vicissitudes, the Lyceum was always closer to legitimacy than the Gaiety or the Strand, and was of course eventually to become the epitome of high Victorian theatrical style, under the auspices of Henry Irving and Ellen Terry. One sign of its status was that until 1869 its back rooms housed the Beefsteak Club, a convivial gathering founded in 1735 by John Rich, the patentee of Covent Garden Theatre, and George Lambert the scenic artist. Irving was to revive it in high style. In the 1840s the Lyceum's most successful licensees were Robert and Mary Ann Keeley; in 1847–55 the Mathews's had their 'alert and intelligent' management there, and in the 1860s came Madame Celeste; it figures largely in Chapters 5 and 6.

The next block along the northern side of the Strand had comprised another ancient exhibition building, the Exeter 'Change, which developed

[26] See Christopher Kent, 'The Whittington Club: A Bohemian Experiment in Middle-Class Social Reform', *Victorian Studies* 18:1 (September 1974), 31–55. The assault at arms is advertised in *Bell's Life*, 26 June 1850.

during the eighteenth century from an arcade of fashionable boutiques into the best-known exhibition of wild animals in England. It persisted (presumably adding an exotic touch to the smell of the drains and the fetid river) until 1828, when it was displaced by the same road improvement works that relocated the Lyceum. Human performers, notably Charles Dibdin the elder, had also run seasons there in its large upper room.[27] After the road-works a 'Society for Erecting and Maintaining a Building in the Metropolis for the Meeting of Religious, Charitable, and Scientific Institutions' got together and created the Exeter Hall on the site (*map ref. 26*). The lurid reputation that the old building had derived from the sensational show cloths of the animals that used to enliven the façade, and from the dramatic and bloody end of its rutting elephant Chunee, shot by a platoon of Guardsmen, was continued on a less material level as the Hall became a byword for mass agitation and sensational preaching, ranging from fervent anti-slavery campaigns to bigoted evangelical denunciation of Catholic emancipation. By the 1860s the comic singer G. W. Mackney could make fun of the serious business of the hall, singing, in his invariable black-face makeup, about wooing a young woman: 'Down on my knees in the Strand I did fall, / Slap on my knees by the Exeter Hall' and collapsing into the famous pose of the chained slave in the Wedgwood medallion, appealing for recognition as a man and a brother. Evangelical meeting and preaching had continued there after the anti-slavery campaigns came to a triumphant end in 1833; serious but less extreme middle-class audiences frequented the Hall on other nights for the concerts of the Sacred Harmonic and National Choral Societies, which filled its large central space (131 feet × 77 feet) uncomfortably full; it was provided with a huge orchestra seating up to 750 performers, and audiences could reach 3,000.[28]

Just beyond the Exeter Hall was the Adelphi (*map ref. 27*), another theatre which had anticipated the emancipation of the 1843 act, the Scotts, its proprietors, having been granted a Lord Chamberlain's licence for burletta at the Sans Pareil in 1806. It was renamed in 1819 to borrow the cachet of Adelphi Terrace, the Adam development of houses across the road from it, facing the river, one of which had been Garrick's last home and the centre of a glittering theatrical and literary circle, still echoed in the inhabitants of the gentlemen's chambers that were there in the

---

[27] Altick, *Shows of London*, pp. 38–9, 307–16.
[28] The dimensions of the hall come from Walter Thornbury, *Old and New London*, vol. III (1878), p. 119, available online at www.british-history.ac.uk/source.aspx?pubid=341 (visited 30.11.2010).

nineteenth century. Climbing steadily to become an important West End theatre (see Chapters 5 and 6), Scott's building was renewed in 1858 to a design by Samuel Beazley, built under the management (and on the occasion of the foundation stone laying, the Masonic trowel) of Benjamin Webster.

It would be a mistake to assume that the audiences of the Lyceum and the Adelphi would not include people who on other occasions frequented the serious meeting and concert rooms that loomed so large between the two theatres. In, for example, the diary of Henrietta Thornhill, born 1847, a young lady with a brother at Eton and a family that kept its own carriage, we may see a middle-class London life that included many of these available diversions: in 1873 she records services in Westminster Abbey and concerts in the Exeter Hall, alongside plays at the Strand and the Globe, home readings of Shakespeare, a party at Lady Young's and the Boat Race seen at Putney.[29] If anyone in the Thornhill family had frequented the next nearest places of entertainment, however, Henrietta would not have been likely to know or record the fact. The Coal Hole, which lay in Fountain Court opposite Exeter Hall (*map ref. 28*), down an alley towards the river, and the Cyder Cellars, behind the Adelphi in Maiden Lane (*map ref. 29*), both dated back to the beginning of the century, and both offered entertainments in the 1840s and 1850s which are represented with head-shaking as well as nostalgia in the memoirs of respectable high Victorian gentlemen. These were tavern song and supper rooms, where Thackeray and his contemporaries had witnessed the performances of early music hall singers much as George Hodson (Henrietta Hodson's father), Sam Cowell and J. W. Sharp, and especially, as they recall it, W. G. Ross singing the blood-curdling ballad of Sam Hall, the unrepentant murderer. Fast men that the reminiscent writers knew of – rarely they themselves – had enjoyed the louche and smoky excitements of these places, and of the cross-dressed burlesque trials for adultery conducted by Renton Nicholson. Having pushed free of the congested traffic at the Temple Bar end of the street, and inspected the transformations of these various centres of the culture of the town, the nineteenth-century pedestrian who reached the western end of the Strand would, for many years, have found himself approaching a wilderness of building sites surrounded by hoardings. Charing Cross was once an open space, from which Whitehall, Cockspur Street and St Martin's Lane branched. It had large inns – the Bull's Head Tavern, the Golden Cross – used as stage

---

[29] See 'Diaries of Henrietta Thornhill', catalogue ref. IV/81, London Metropolitan Archives.

coach termini, and was a place where proclamations were read and itinerant shows and entertainments set up. In 1812, after the famous sea battle and during the grand design period of Regency London, the idea for Trafalgar Square was conceived by the leading architect John Nash, intending to do away with the inelegant, sprawling royal stables on the northern side of the space. The National Gallery was eventually completed on that site in 1838, but the rest of the square itself took decades more.

Alterations at the southern edge near the Strand, however, got under way quickly. On the southern side, behind the house where Charles Mathews senior was born, the old Hungerford fish and vegetable market extended down to the river. It was rebuilt in 1831 and included a riverside pub, the Swan, with an entertainment licence, which may have been the continuation of one granted to a room upstairs over the old market, which started as a French church, became a pauper school and ended its days as some sort of music hall. In 1862 the whole area was cleared to make way for Charing Cross railway terminus and hotel. Under the arches of the railway bridge behind, however, the famous music hall called Gatti's Under the Arches sprang up in 1866.

The northern side of the street was more fashionably developed. In the early 1830s a wedge of new public buildings opened there, including Decimus Burton's Charing Cross Hospital, and the highly successful Lowther Arcade, described enthusiastically by George Sala as

a tube of shops running from St Martin's churchyard into the Strand very nearly opposite Hungerford market . . . light and airy, and roofed with glass . . . resonant with the pattering of feet, the humming of voices, the laughter of children, the rustling of silk dresses, and buying, selling, bargaining, and chaffering.[30]

Entertainment venues followed: the Adelaide Gallery Exhibition Rooms, (*map ref. 30*), built in 1830 as part of the Lowther Arcade development, acquired a theatrical licence in 1850 but was eventually refused a licence in 1862. In 1854 a cigar divan in King William Street, which runs parallel to the arcade, was turned into the Polygraphic Hall for exhibitions and then shows (*map ref. 31*). In 1850 Dr Newman delivered there his celebrated 'Lectures on Anglican Difficulties'. In 1869 it was converted into the Charing Cross Theatre, later to become Toole's, with a frontage on the Strand.

The developments here offer, perhaps, some sort of London equivalent of the Parisian arcades. All built before 1848, Paris's fourteen arcades were

[30] George Augustus Sala, *Gaslight and Daylight* (London: Chapman, & Hall, (1859), pp. 198–9.

for Walter Benjamin prototypical manifestations of modern life. Their three-storey-high iron and glass roofs enabled the blending of the private domestic interior and the public street system in a way that emblematised the period of bourgeois ascendancy, and that was swept away, after the proletarian challenge of 1848, by the Hausemannising of the capital, the creation of a new and more belligerent capitalist city. No such political challenge moved the development of London; but the threat posed by its sheer size proved both formative and disruptive of the Strand's shops, its serious and frivolous entertainments, the arcades and markets and halls in their mission to generate and consume money and cultural capital. Three decades of development, culminating in the creation of the Embankments, of major rail links to the suburbs and the whole of the south of England, and of Trafalgar Square, transformed the old shopping street behind the medieval palaces along the Thames, which was by the nineteenth century beset by urban nuisances, into a main artery of the West End.

Having arrived in Trafalgar Square, our pedestrian writer had reached the fashionable districts. He could stroll along Pall Mall and up Regent's Street to number 14, the Gallery of Illustration (*map ref. 32*), a house built for his own use by John Nash, but now a fashionable rendezvous for viewing topical panoramas or being dramatically entertained without entering a theatre, discussed in Chapter 2; or he could choose the classic ground of the Haymarket. Passing the Opera House (*map ref. 33*), renamed Her Majesty's on the accession of Queen Victoria, but seriously challenged in the late 1840s by the operas at Covent Garden, he would arrive on his right hand at the third patent theatre, the Haymarket summer theatre (*map ref. 34*), which was the preserve of Benjamin Webster in 1843 when the patents were abolished. Perhaps this was his goal; maybe our hopeful writer-pedestrian was taking his latest script for consideration where he could expect a friendly reception from the old man and might even cherish the possibility that he would be paid a trifle on account – though his chances of getting an actual production of his drama were very slim.[31] Webster modernised the house as a response to the 1843 act, cutting back the old forestage and putting in gas lighting and stalls, and launched into year-round production of the Drama; even he,

---

[31] In his farewell speech at the Haymarket, Webster asserted that he had paid authors at least £30,000 – sometimes for a script containing nothing but a title page and blank sheets. See Margaret Webster, *The Same only Different: Five Generations of a Theatre Family* (London: Victor Gollancz, 1969), pp. 88, 95.

however, who had been one of the leading agitators for the freedom of the stage, found his concept of what the public wanted severely challenged by the newer caterers, and by the time he came to give his evidence before the 1866 Parliamentary Select Committee was all for the reinstatement of some kind of protection, against the inroads of music halls and foreign stars.[32] Successful or not in seeing the manager, our walker would soon be on his way. At the top of the street his walk would bring him to Regent's Circus, where he could join our lady pedestrian, at the heart of the West End: in its central and essential place, which the final section of this chapter will seek to understand.

THE PERSISTENCE OF PLEASURE

The West End remains so far elusive, as an idea. Perhaps the problem is the concrete, the ultra-materialist perspective of these walks into the territory. Maybe the map required cannot be traced with feet upon the ground, but is mythological, like those created by twenty-first-century performance artists such as Wrights & Sites, who offer 'a Mis-guide to anywhere'[33] and actually expect you to find your way into your own imagination. The West End on the ground is less real, perhaps, than the one in all our heads; it is an idea, one that maps not streets and passage-ways but youth and age, past and future, inheritance and novelty. To get a sense of that theatre, we need to look beyond the concrete, to developments less explicit, more suggestive. Maybe the aspect of Victorian modernity we are seeking is not the Crystal Palace exhibition of the latest information and education, seen in the light of bright shiny realism, claims of truth, sparkling lamps and spectacular visuality, as taken over by Charles Kean's spectacular modern Shakespeare productions at the Princess's, but another facet of the Victorian Glassworld described by Isobel Armstrong: the phantasmatic.[34] I would suggest that the bright allure of the West End may be better epitomised as a less concrete manifestation of Victorian wizardry with glass – not transparency, lucid information and bright illumination, but smoke and mirrors. This place promises not education and authenticity, but illusion and excitement; it is

---

[32] See Scott, *Drama of Yesterday and Today*, vol. I, pp. 472–3 for Webster as protectionist, and his answers to the 1866 Select Committee, 2903 et seq.
[33] www.mis-guide.com/anywhere.html (visited 08.10.2009).
[34] Isobel Armstrong, *Victorian Glassworlds: Glass Culture and the Imagination 1830–1880* (Oxford University Press, 2008), pp. 110–12, 204–50.

glittering but not gold, fantastic, lit by fairy-light rather than sunshine, and leads willing folk astray.

One of the difficult aspects of writing the two walks I have just offered was that it was impossible to fix upon a single time at which to set them. Imagining my two pedestrians walking on any given day would have excluded most of what I wanted to notice about the fabric of the West End, because there was no one date on which it was a finished creation. It was constantly being made and remade, demolished and made over, abolished and renewed; but always upon the same, or almost the same, acre of ground. This leads me to ask why some spots, certain places, were repeatedly used, in this way, in spite of the physical and often legal difficulties faced by their developers – why not start over somewhere else? After the accretion of trouble around the patent houses finally sank the attraction of their historical significance, why would another theatrical centre be developed that carried a similar double meaning, of both infinite promise and endless disappointment? The question put in that way suggests its own answer: promise and disappointment are two sides of the same coin. You can't have one without the other. What remains to be explored is how this truism relates to the history of entertainment in London. Focussing on a single spot, therefore, this final brief section attempts to show the complex and contradictory power of the very idea of the West End.

Our two pedestrians have met in Regent's Circus, now called Piccadilly Circus; and there stands what is now called the London Trocadero (*map ref. 35*). This is the odd, triangular block of tall buildings that points towards the winged statue, actually a memorial to Lord Shaftsbury but known as Eros, the god of love. This place could well be dubbed the quintessence of the West End; and it is, appropriately, in redevelopment; even its website, Londontrocadero.com, is currently (November 2010) in redevelopment.[35] This is because its present owner, a young entrepreneur called Asif Aziz, has met with repeated civic rejection of his plans for rebuilding and reopening the attractions there. In 2009 the website explained that his proposed glass façade was felt to compromise the 'heritage' of a site which has seen so many changes that even the road layout through, around and in front of it would not be recognisable to a traveller from 1840. At that moment it offered a wilderness of scaffolding and semi-deserted building projects, surrounding a casino, a large

---

[35] In redevelopment again, one should say, since the information that follows here was taken from its previous temporary manifestation (visited 08.10 2009), and is no longer to be seen.

basement eating place for tourists called the Rain Forest Café, several bars, two cinemas – one closed, and according to the plans destined to become a community theatre – a West End ticket office, Ripley's 'Believe it or Not' Museum, and an indoor fair, 'Funland', complete with a bowling alley and dodgem cars. Through the site runs a stub of Windmill Street, separating what was the old London Pavilion – its 1880 façade can still be seen, and its handsome passageway lamps – from the back-block house of entertainment that was called the Trocadero when it closed in 1965. The place has previously passed through two prolonged periods of planning blight, in the 1870s before the construction of Shaftsbury Avenue, which now forms its westerly boundary, and in the 1960s, over the protracted and agonising remodelling of Piccadilly itself, which finally deposited Eros immediately on the doorstep. But every failure somehow seems about to be a success; every closure provokes another speculator to buy the place and open it again. The history is long, even if one discounts the unproven gambling hell called Piccadilly Hall, standing in the fields some time in the seventeenth century. It could begin with a tennis court and wine vaults fronting on to Windmill Street in 1744, which became Cooke's Circus, then the Royal Albion Theatre, then an exhibition room with mechanical waxworks and a 'Grand Centrifugal Railway', descending by 1846 to a programme of *tableaux vivants* and in 1851 a dance hall called the Argyll Rooms, famous for prostitution, which lost its licence in 1878. In 1882 one Robert Bignall reopened it as the Trocadero Palace, a music hall, which it remained, premiering 'Two Lovely Black Eyes' and being at one point run by Albert Chevalier, until 1895, when it was let to J. Lyons on a 99-year lease, and it became a glamorous restaurant, its men-only Long Bar enthusiastically dubbed 'the hub of the Empire'. Novelties blossomed there like Concert Teas in the Empire Room, ballet in the grill room, telephone ordering in the restaurant, and Charles Cochran's late-night cabarets where Anna Neagle began her career as a dancer.

In front of this, across the street, the London Pavilion evolved through even more dubious speculative building and showmanship. First there was, straightforwardly, the Black Horse Inn, with a yard behind it, fronting on to the now disappeared Tichbourne Street. In the 1790s a long room was erected behind that, over the coach houses and standing on legs half way across the yard; into this moved an exhibition, belonging to one Weeks, showing huge glittering clocks disguised as temples and carried by sixteen elephants, and a mechanical bird of paradise and a tarantula spider; it cost half a crown to see the clocks and a further shilling each for the bird and the spider, high prices by the standards of 1790, when a seat in the pit at one of the theatres royal would cost 3s for the whole evening.[36] From 1834 the place was let for concerts, balls, exhibitions of pictures; then in 1851, on the rising crest of the first music hall building boom, Henry Robin adapted it for use as a Theatre or Room for public diversion. A raised platform, boxes and a gallery were constructed, and the Office of Metropolitan Buildings, desperate as they were about all the dangerous speculative building that was going on, required the supports in the yard to be strengthened. The room had seating capacity for about 170 persons and was known as the Salle Robin. It soon reverted to exhibition use, however, from 1859 housing Dr Kahn's Anatomical Museum: his chief exhibition piece was a waxwork entitled 'Marriage'.

At the same time Loibl and Sonnhammer, two of the new breed of music hall magnates, got hold of the lease to the Black Horse and created the London Pavilion, by the simple expedient of painting the stable walls and putting a glass roof over the yard. They included a six-lane American bowling alley and a rifle range, installed a piano and hired a chairman: they announced 'The Finest Rooms in London. Open Every Evening at 7 o'clock. Operatic Selection from all the favourite Operas ... Admission: By Refreshment Ticket, 6d'. By 1862 they had made enough to build a two-sided gallery on Dr Kahn's level; the engulfed and presumably disastrously darkened exhibition room went downhill, though it had a noisy moment of fashionablity as the Empress Rink – roller-skating, under the auspices of a granite merchant – in 1876. The song 'By Jingo', the emblem of their otherwise invisible, but arguably immense, contribution to political history got its first performance at the old 'Pav.' in 1871 and was celebrated ever after.

Contemplating the Shaftsbury Avenue redevelopment, the Metropolitan Board of Works then bought up the hall and the next-door venue. The city fathers were no doubt pleased at the possibility of extirpating this variously perilous place, which was in danger of falling on its patrons' heads, breaking their legs, corrupting their morals, sending them out drunken and brawling, or any combination of the above. However, they found themselves instead waiting an indefinite time for the new road to materialise, during which they embarrassingly had a rackety music hall to let. Loibl refused their terms, which were not only expensive but also very dictatorial in respect of the proper conduct of the place. R. E. Villiers, the proprietor of the Canterbury Music Hall, was a wiser man, and took it, for £7,000 per annum – plus an annual £50 back-hander, for turning a

---

[36] On the high quality of Weeks's mechanisms, see Altick, *Shows of London*, pp. 350–1.

blind eye, to the MBW's valuer F. W. Goddard. This was only the first step in the urbanely corrupt acquisition of the triangle of land that eventually resulted from the new street pattern, on which Villiers built the New London Pavilion in 1881. The scandal eventually brought down the local authority, but the 'Pav.' lived on to become one more of the cultural cornerstones of the masculinity of the British Empire.[37] In 2009, as in 1880, there was public ferment over the clash on this site between modernisation and history in the West End; in the twenty-first century, as 130 years ago, all of its transformations, aspirations, advertising and self-aggrandisement are actually about satisfying a huge market of pleasure seekers – who all, still, come here. They come, from everywhere – the suburbs, the provinces, the world – to a special place, a spot that promises everything, which they imagine will be the way in to their own potential experience of metropolitan high life, because it has been dedicated to that purpose by its very embeddedness in a history of looking and consuming, becoming the repository of the experience of countless others.

There is potency in the imagined memory of all those others, whom we do not know, all hitting this same spot. The West End is a portal, a gateway to elsewhere, exultation, transfiguration – pleasure. People – audiences – are drawn like moths to the music, the lights bright or dim, the show, the special occasion, the champagne, the oysters, the thrill of it all. This is the reality – the evanescent, here now and gone again, reality of the West End: theatre, and music, light and heat, a good night out. And, pace John McGrath, it is in its very essence unimproving. If we are lucky, we find it there; but never for long. It is an ecstasy of the moment, and we cannot hold on to it. It lives, therefore, in the imagination of each and all of us.

---

[37] The information in this description of the two venues is derived from the files on them at the Victoria and Albert Theatre Collection.

CHAPTER 2

The Era: *hierarchies, seriousness and the organ of the profession*

INTRODUCTION: SOME ARE MORE EQUAL THAN OTHERS

Having rejected the hostile characterisation of mid-century entertainment generated and transmitted by contemporary intellectual and subsequent academic critique, and adopted instead the practical strategy of walking the city streets in the wake of less pretentious Victorian pleasure seekers and journalists, the previous chapter concluded that the essence of the West End was not to be comprehended on the ground. It is not simply a site, but a complex text; its existence is discursive, and a key, a lexicon of that discourse is required. This chapter, therefore, turns once more to the Victorian press, but endeavours this time to understand it as a guide to pleasure and leisure through its articulation of self and culture, by means of one of its own major analytical and taxonomic tools: the notion of class.

In 1878 Matthew Arnold, by then a senior public figure, a noted social and religious critic as well as an established poet, lectured on the subject of 'Equality', which he assumed his auditors would regard as a chimera pursued only by the French and the otherwise misguided. His argument in its favour rests upon his characterisation of English class society, in a taxonomy he had refined upon since his description of the 'Philistines' and 'Barbarians' in *Culture and Anarchy* in 1869. The published version of the lecture appeared in the intellectual journal *The Fortnightly Review*, and it includes the following passages:

our middle class divides itself into a serious portion, and a gay or rowdy portion ... With the gay or rowdy portion we need not much concern ourselves; we shall figure it to our minds sufficiently if we conceive it as the source of that war-song produced in these recent days of excitement –

'We don't want to fight, but by jingo, if we do,
We've got the ships, we've got the men, and we've got the money too.'

We may also partly judge its standard of life, and the needs of its nature, by the modern English theatre, perhaps the most contemptible in Europe. But the real strength of the English middle class is in its serious portion.

This 'serious portion' of the English, he goes on,

driven by its sense for the power of conduct, in the beginning of the seventeenth century ... *entered the prison of Puritanism, and had the key turned upon its spirit there for two hundred years* ... they created a type of life and manners, of which they themselves indeed are slow to recognise the faults, but which is fatally condemned by its hideousness, its immense ennui, and against which the instinct of self-preservation in humanity rebels.

The 200 years he specifies had passed, when he spoke, and Arnold understood that these Puritan prisoners were seeking to break out; but they have no model, he suggests, for a new idea of conduct, since the cultivated and refined gentry (amongst whom he presumably counts himself) have little impact upon the middle classes.

What the middle class sees is that splendid piece of materialism, the aristocratic class, with a wealth and luxury utterly out of their reach ... and thus they are thrown back upon themselves – upon a defective type of religion, a narrow range of intellect and knowledge, a stunted sense of beauty, a low standard of manners. And the lower class ... too are thrown back upon themselves; upon their beer, their gin, and their *fun*.[1]

Another hundred years on, over the last decades of the twentieth century, grand narratives like the supposedly Marxist analytic tool of class went out of fashion. Now, however, historians are urged to attend closely to the self-perceptions of the people about whom they write; and Arnold is by no means the only Victorian to be deeply concerned with the complexities of class.[2] It is appropriate in attending to the dilemma he perceives to return to the best twentieth-century commentator upon nineteenth-century leisure history, Peter Bailey, who in 1977 once more identified leisure as a problem for the mid-Victorian middle class.

[1] Matthew Arnold, 'Equality', *Fortnightly Review* 23:135 (March 1878), 313–26, 326–7, 332 (emphasis original).
[2] A good summary of the changes in academic fashion with regard to the use of the term is to be found in David Cannadine, *Class in Britain* (Harmondsworth: Penguin, 1998), where he explains (p. 12) the supersedure of a Marxist economic analysis by the linguistic turn, which asserted that social history is now 'the history of a limitless number of individual self-categorisations and subjective social descriptions – of which class is only one among a multitude of competing and frequently changing vocabularies'; but asserts (p. 2) that 'class is still essential to a proper understanding of British history and of Britain today – provided it is appropriately defined, properly understood, imaginatively treated and openly approached'.

He suggests that for them the new idea of leisure played painfully into 'endemic status anxiety ... for leisure represented a new and relatively unstructured area in the life-space where social distinctions were particularly vulnerable'.[3]

The problem was held at bay, Bailey suggests, through the early, hard-working and often crisis-ridden years of Victoria's reign. Few aspirant businessmen had much time away from their strenuous working lives until after the 1840s; and had they had the time, evangelical Christian prescriptions – Arnold's Puritanism – about conduct made most recreations simply unthinkable for many of them. But thereafter successful men relaxed their previous habits, whether of unremitting work or homosocial after-hours practices such as heavy drinking, and created a space for new recreations, for both men and women, that 'had to be filled, but each of the components in this necessarily ad hoc creation had to meet demanding standards of probity to conform with the middle classes' self-image as the moral arbiters of society'. Still looking to 'their churches and other leaders of opinion' for guidance, and holding on to the conception of themselves as well-conducted, they nevertheless found leisure 'a fluid and open territory which offered a freedom that outstripped the reach of traditional social controls. To middle-class sensibilities, leisure represented a normative as well as a cultural void and placed alarming new responsibilities upon the individual's capacity for self-direction.'[4] Bailey quotes the many serious journals where the ban Arnold deplores on most possible leisure occupations – not only drinking and gambling, theatre and concert-going, but also singing, playing indoor or outdoor games, dancing – was slowly and partially relaxed in the search for admissible forms of holiday that imperilled neither social status nor the immortal soul. Bailey repeatedly uses spatial, territorial images to convey his understanding of this dilemma: 'leisure was less the bountiful land in which to site Utopia, than some dangerous frontier zone which outran the writ of established law and order'.[5] London's West End at the mid-century is the material realisation of that zone, and both its Utopian and its dangerous aspects are clearly to be discerned.

---

[3] Peter Bailey, 'The Victorian Middle Class and the Problem of Leisure', *Victorian Studies* 21 (autumn 1977), reprinted in *Popular Culture and Performance in the Victorian City* (Cambridge University Press, 1998), pp. 13–29, p. 17.
[4] ibid., pp. 19, 20.   [5] ibid, p. 21.

THE ORGAN OF THE PROFESSION

For the newly and busily leisured, the most up-to-date guidance to the territory I sketched in Chapter 1 appeared in the popular press. The new journalism and fiction offered a huge quantity of earnest, jocular and knowing help in understanding others and positioning oneself in the modern world. Alongside the spiritual and emotional advice abundantly available in popular philosophy and in the rapidly developing realist novel, factual guides explained everything from good handwriting and the new scientific taxonomies to the rapidly expanding railway timetable. Travelling by train was, in itself, an opportunity for reading, a new market immediately supplied; and helpful advice about what to do and where to go when you arrived at your holiday destination, in this case London, was available in quantity. Outstanding amongst these guides was *The Era*. Most mid-Victorian periodicals concerned themselves to some degree with the worlds of performance. A few simply deplored the spread of entertainment beyond the idle classes, some offered intellectual engagement with new cultural forms, and a few cheap and fugitive rags still peddled gossip and sensation about celebrities almost as eagerly as *The Age* or *The Satirist* had done;[6] but *The Era* was different. It was, as many people put it, 'the organ of the Profession'. At a substantial 6d weekly, available for the early trains to deliver to the country publican on Saturdays and on sale in updated town editions for the professional and pleasure-seeking traveller all weekend, it sought to provide an accurate guide to the entertainment scene countrywide, together with a detailed exposition of each week in the West End. This was obviously a paper for the fun-loving middle classes, then; but, as I hope to show, it also sought to cater for a wider and more inclusive middle-class audience, and, in doing so, precisely reflected the growth of the new West End.

    The Era began publication in 1837 or 1838.[7] In 1853, under the leadership of its long-time editor Frederick Ledger, the paper claims it is the 'best political, social, sporting, theatrical, literary, commercial, agricultural, and general family journal published, and contains more original matter than any other Weekly paper. It is the Country Gentleman's *vade mecum*,

---

[6] See for example *The Little Wonder, the journal for fast and funny people*, described in Nead, *Victorian Babylon*, p. 116.

[7] *The Waterloo Directory of English Newspapers* (www.victorianperiodicals.com) gives September 1838 as the starting date; 1837 is claimed in the paper itself.

and the only acknowledged weekly organ of the Freemasons, Licensed Victuallers, Odd Fellows, and Foresters.'[8] The description is part of an 1853 advertisement for a Derby sweepstake that the paper proposed to run. In 1849 the paper's proprietor, George Davis, had felt such dubiously legal betting activity was undignified and would harm circulation, and tried to take out an injunction stopping Ledger and his fellow lessee John Strutt from running it; but the advertisement shows they were still using the scheme to boost yearly subscriptions four years later. As the organ of the Masonic and various other social fellowships, and especially the public house trade, it was hardly possible to distance the paper from betting, and the early decades are unblushing in their coverage of every kind of racing, hunting and coursing as well as more apparently innocent games like chess and cricket; but it was, increasingly, as the place to learn about theatrical and musical entertainments that *The Era* became the leading publication.

Clearly this is an organ of the 'gay and rowdy' middle classes, as understood by Arnold. But it aspires to take the other camp by the hand, and to lead them to participate too – beginning by reading a paper published on a Sunday. Despite the inevitable whiff within its pages of drink and betting, Ledger was himself very concerned with the probity and elevation of his journal and all it represented; and for him the theatre and certain other entertainments appear to have represented that higher ground. Serious artistic and intellectual events are reviewed and advertised. Ledger's editorials, the language of his reviewers and of his advertisers, insist upon the dignity of the Drama, and the gentility of its patrons. But the reviews and, even more, the advertisement columns nevertheless need to attract and inform all levels of audience for all kinds of show, as well as to inform the professional world what opportunities there are each week to rent a concert hall, hire a tragedian, or sell a lion to a travelling circus. This makes for a complicated read.

The configuration of *The Era* maps on to and glosses the many layers of the West End world. The paper itself has its highways and byways, its popular destinations and specialist backyards, its first points of call and its shadowy doorways; it is a labyrinth or rookery of many meanings, each item within its text only clearly legible to that particular kind of reader to whom it is addressed. Those contemporary readers were well aware that the paper spoke several languages. By the 1860s it had began to attract piqued, amused or condescending attention from writers in other

---

[8] *York Herald*, 3 December 1853.

journals. The less thoughtful proclaim the language of the stage's 'recognised organ' to be 'calculated to excite the astonishment or mirth of
outsiders': 'what in the world does a manager mean when he advertises
for a corner man?'[9] while the more knowing, like the *Saturday Review*
author who may be Edmund Yates, are fascinated by the differential
address and the cryptic abbreviation of many of its advertisements. 'In
one part of the newspaper, actors and managers speak among themselves,
while in another they address expected audiences', he says wisely. He
quotes the 'wanted' ads seeking 'heavy', 'juvenile' and 'utility' actors and
suggests the experienced reader can imagine the 'sumptuousness of the
epithets' to be used for these same folk on a playbill; knowingly he hints
that the more that individual advertisers claim for themselves the less
impressive they really are; and waggishly interprets the request that
perhaps a performing bitch called Octar Evans 'will write' as actually
addressed to its owner – since Octar is hardly a female name.[10] For the
twenty-first-century reader, *The Era* is therefore far more than a mine of
detailed factual information; close attention to its columns, the signals of
its layout as well as of the content of its many advertisements and notices
reveals a cryptic web of interpellation addressed to the many-faceted
middle classes – serious as well as gay.

THE TREATY OF PARIS AND THE DESTRUCTION
OF COVENT GARDEN

I will take *The Era* of 6 April 1856 as my example.[11] The paper, a typical
sample, consists of four sheets, making sixteen broadsheet pages. It has
two centrally placed editorials, on this day a leader concerning the
national news of the signing of the Treaty of Paris that ended the Crimean
War, and another on a theatrical matter, the burning down of Covent
Garden Theatre; both had happened at the end of the previous month.
The national issue is relatively little discussed elsewhere in the paper, but
Covent Garden is lamented in a long and very bad poem by the veteran
dramatist Fitzball, and articles cover both the legal investigation of the fire
and the praiseworthy efforts of the lessee Gye to mount his English Opera
season at the Lyceum instead: readers learn that the theatre in the Strand
is being equipped with private boxes, and stalls in place of its pit, for this

---

[9] 'Theatrical advertisements', *London Review*, 16 December 1865, 673.
[10] *Saturday Review*, 7 March 1863, 304.
[11] Page numbers relating to this paper are given in brackets in the text.

purpose, and that a company has been hired already so as to stave off the advances of the rival Italian Opera company, which opens next month at Her Majesty's in the Haymarket. The paper exhorts the other sufferers in the surrounding properties affected by the disaster not to resort to blaming others, but to get on with business, facing their losses 'manfully and hopefully' (p. 9).

Meanwhile the non-professional reader is informed about the rather quiet start to the post-Easter theatrical season in London and offered reviews of two concerts of modern music, one of which, Benedict's at the Hanover Square Rooms, is stimulating but too long, while the other, by Hullah at St Martin's Hall, is praiseworthy in its 'liberal arrangements', which is *Era* language for low admission prices. A belief of the liberal wing of the serious classes was that the masses could be civilised by music, and inexpensive access to good concerts was one prong of their attack upon ignorance. Less 'seriously', *The Era* often runs specialist sports listings according to the season of the year, and on this day, just after Easter, they publish a two-page guide, under the heading 'Sportsman's Gazette', decorated with rods and game bags but actually calendaring the new season's flat-racing meetings. There are two further pages of sports reporting, some miscellaneous titbits including a detailed description of a bungled execution for murder, a professional information column on the outcomes of the latest licensing sessions of the London magistrates, and a concluding report on Freemasonry.

THE FRONT PAGE: RESIDUAL HIGH CULTURE[12]

The letterpress, therefore, is varied and wide-reaching; but the main matter of the paper is the advertisement columns. These cover the back and front outside pages and spill on to the inside of each (see Figures 1, 2 and 3). The display ads for the theatres, running from the announcement of the forthcoming Italian Opera season at Her Majesty's to tonight's programme at the Standard in Shoreditch, form the first column in prime position on the front (Figure 1). At the foot of this page here is a small puff for the Royal Victoria Saloon in Catherine Street, which opens every day at 10 p.m., for 'wines suppers etc.', claiming that 'Visitors to London should not leave without seeing this most elegant room'. This is in fact

---

[12] The terms 'residual', 'emerging' and 'dominant', used of strains in the culture of the day, are drawn from Raymond Williams, *Marxism and Literature* (Oxford University Press, 1977).

Figure 1   Front page advertisement columns from *The Era*, 6 April 1856

a late stage in the history of the oldest and best-known private theatre, the Minor, where many stage aspirants had bought their first Shakespearean roles. It was to be taken up by the amateur actors in the early 1860s and then cleared for redevelopment, but meanwhile various dubious ventures, such as Jessop's coffee house for young gents and then this dancing saloon, were tried and forced to close. The reputation of the place was shady, generations-deep, and in any case such public dancing saloons, called Casinos or *Bals*, were widely regarded as existing for the purposes of prostitution.

Dancing in public was very much a contested recreation, unlikely to meet the views of even the moderately serious, though it was very widely practised: there was a 'mania' for quadrilles and polkas. In the third column on the front page is an advertisement for the Royal Cremorne Gardens, described by Lynda Nead as 'a testing ground for metropolitan identities and behaviours' where social dancing – on a decorated and glittering platform, constantly upgraded and refurbished – 'choreographed a performance of modern street behaviour' and epitomised the fact that in the 1860s respectability was 'up for grabs: there were different definitions of what constituted respectable behaviour and of the limits to acceptable public behaviour'.[13] Cremorne was both the most conspicuously successful arena for public dancing and the limit case for its public exposure; dotted about the *Era* columns the indoor, more discreet – or at least more hidden – places for dancing offered alternatives, to those who knew how to read them.

The Cremorne advertisement, and several others for outdoor entertainment venues in the immediate suburbs, are placed after the theatres on the front page, and mingle with various professional and quasiprofessional notices. Performers seek engagements, teachers of acting seek pupils, waxworks want to hire musicians, concert halls look for attractions and bars advertise those they have already hired, like the 'young giant' 7 feet 5½ inches tall and weighing 20 stone to be seen serving in a tavern at 69 Drury Lane. The front is therefore in effect a restatement of tradition:

---

[13] Nead, *Victorian Babylon*, pp. 120, 128; see at length pp. 118–36 for a finely nuanced exploration of Cremorne's dancing and its implications; but see also Albert Smith, *The Natural History of the Ballet Girl* and *The Natural History of the Gent*, both 1847, for a close-up insider's vision of the London culture of social dance. Smith is clearly discussing a wide range of social placement and acceptability in his survey of the places where people danced in public, everyone from the aristocrat to the 'gent' – what in the 1990s would have been called the Chav – and the professional dancer, the ballet girl, in her time off from the theatres.

it works for the residual culture, the old world of entertainment, from Italian Opera to freak shows.

Page two is for the consumers' needs in their private lives. Set out opposite the 'Sportsman's Gazette' that lists the race meetings, these ads are clearly aimed at the rowdy racing gent. Starting with patent medicines for dealing with 'family problems' including female 'obstructions' – that is, abortifacients – they go on to cures for 'spermatorroea' and other diseases brought on by 'early abuse', then cover remedies for gout and ruptures and falling hair before reaching trousers and shirts for sale, cigars and fancy pipes, a versifying hatter, hair dyes, Holloway's pills and timetables for steamship sailings. The final column, lying next to the race meetings, is given over to tipsters, bookies and dining rooms. Here are the rowdy middle classes revealed in unflattering detail at home and at play; this page, if they looked at it, would have confirmed the serious in their condemnation of worldly recreation.

THE BACK PAGE: THE EMERGENT MUSIC HALL

Elsewhere the new middle classes as consumers are shown in a better, or perhaps simply a more prosperous, light. On the back page, gentlemen's relatively innocent personal needs – tooth enamel and hair oil, books about gardening – are mingled with more expensive purchases, in display ads for forthcoming auctions of houses, as well as of businesses such as pubs. But here, on the back of the closed paper, the first column in the equivalent position to the traditional theatre ads on the front is once more about entertainment venues – but a different group of them, and one which signals a striking new development (see Figure 2). It has two lengthy personal communications which are addressed to the fellow professional, but which also perform in public the role of the struggling professional man behaving 'manfully and hopefully' as adjured by the editorial. George Payne of the White Hart Tavern in Catherine Street and Dicky Dunn formerly of the Nell Gwynne thank patrons for support after the Covent Garden fire, and give their new business addresses and opening plans. Other ex-entertainer publicans – the clown Harry Boleno, equestrian Tom Barry – get in on the sympathy to let the public know they too have new licences in West End taverns, where they each have 'harmonic meetings' or 'reunions' once or twice a week. Other dining rooms and also taverns advertise. The City Concert Room, Dr Johnson's, Fleet Street, has not only 'chops, steaks, kidneys' at a reasonable rate but also 'glees, madrigals, duets' absolutely free. The Cyder Cellars in Maiden Lane has a headline demanding 'Have you seen Gus Grant? Because he is the most Highly Talented comic singer of the day' while the Coal Hole nearby relies on its known attractions – the 'usual' poses plastiques, followed by Lord Chief Baron Nicholson and the 'judge and jury' show: 'the Judge's cigar will be lighted at half past nine o'clock'. The Coal Hole is described, for the amusement of the knowing, as standing in Fountain Court, Strand, 'opposite Exeter Hall' – opposite to that hyper-respectable venue in more ways than one. At the bottom of the page the programme for the Lord Raglan Music Hall, Theobald's Road, is given at length, and rather surprisingly to modern eyes this includes daily selections from 'standard operas', *The Bohemian Girl* on Tuesday and *La Sonnambula* on Thursday, as well as a star turn who is a mime and 'protean illustrator', daily. Like the other concert rooms, the Raglan lists no charge for admission, and its programme clearly includes 'music' in the high art sense; but it is, and will more firmly become, a music hall in the other, the popular, sense.

The back page, then, is the harbinger of the coming thing – the music hall. An exemplary trajectory of such an establishment can be traced in the development of Weston's Music Hall in High Holborn, converted in the next year, 1857, from the National Hall where previously, as *The Era* puts it, 'social crotchet-mongers ventilated their wild theories, and infidel lecturers sowed broad-cast among the unthinking the seeds of political discontent and cheerless Atheism, into a well-appointed and wellcon-ducted concert-room'. This public-spirited enterprise was, according to Mr Huggins of the sponsoring brewery who took the chair at its opening, to be 'a great boon to the multitude … a home to the weary and tired, after the avocations of the day. There was no dissipation – at least, there should not be – in any of the entertainments provided' – a restraint the brewer ingenuously confirmed was in the best interests of the proprietor, in keeping up the value of his property, and therefore would be strenuously observed. By 1860, large profits meant the young entrepreneur Weston had been able to rebuild the hall on a grand scale, exorcising any ghosts of the earlier political and educational mission that might have hung around by wrapping large mirrors round the auditorium, adding brilliant lights and private stage boxes, hiring liveried attendants and full-dress waiters, and offering a programme combining selections from the Bishop's ballad music and from operas and melodramatic music of the whole century with the latest comic attractions such as J. H. Stead, 'the Cure' (for melancholy), who sang while jumping up and down,

Figures 2 and 3   Back and centre page advertisement columns from *The Era*,
6 April 1856

and Sam Collins, the make-believe Irishman.[14] Similarly in 1862 it could be reported that the Oxford Music Hall in Oxford Street 'keeps up its stately reputation and high character for good and original opera music, the lighter portions of the evening being devoted to the drolleries of Mr Randall' while at the Canterbury there is a flying trapeze and for this audience there is the advantage of not being moved from the seats for the performance; 'for, no doubt at a considerable sacrifice, the necessary space is withheld from the public. Here is "Old Bob Ridley and His Son", showing how strangely originality gives way to imitation. The "Sly glance" is taken from the Swiss singers; the "Young Man" is an alteration from Mrs German Reed.'[15]

Thus the music hall claimed in these early days to take part in the middle-class project to civilise the masses by providing worthwhile leisure pursuits; its programmes include music shared with other current entertainments, which gave countenance to participation in its innocent fun by young people in higher ranks of society. This wide range is exemplified by such a song as 'Old Bob Ridley', above, which is drawn from the newly imported genre of blackface minstrelsy.[16] There is a considerable body of modern academic scrutiny of minstrelsy, especially in its original American context, and Tracy Davis's compilation of the nineteenth-century repertoire has a focus upon exemplifying the 1860s through the British work of the Christy Minstrels.[17] I shall not describe them, therefore, but note here the pervasive presence at mid-century of various kinds of blackface performance, which was adapted for every kind of audience in Britain. The main influx of minstrel singing began in London with the Ethiopian Serenaders, whose concerts were held at polite venues such as the Hanover Square Rooms in 1846, and Christy's troupe became a fixture at the St James's Hall; but a broader blackface clowning, with rumbustious slapstick and catchy chorus-led singing, had been shaped

[14] *Era*, 15 November 1857 and 26 August 1860. [15] *Lloyd's Weekly Newspaper*, 19 January 1862.
[16] It was already enmeshed in the web of popular song 'origins' by this point, having been published as a Christy Minstrel song in 1854 and as one written by Charles White in 1855, before this, presumably British, plagiarist/parodist served it up as something else again in 1862; among other vicissitudes, it has subsequently been recorded by Ewan McColl as a folksong and recently transmogrified into a real ale, whose name was then appropriated by a commercial brewery.
[17] See Tracy C. Davis, *The Broadview Anthology of Nineteenth-century British Performance* (Peterborough, Ont.: Broadview Press, 2011) and '"I long for my home in Kentuck": Christy's Minstrels in Britain (1857–64)', conference paper in progress, delivered first at TaPRA in 2010. Earlier discussion is accessible through Sarah Meer, *Uncle Tom Mania: Slavery, Minstrelsy and Transatlantic Culture in the 1850s* (Athens: University of Georgia Press, 2005).

for the stage in Britain by T. D. Rice in the early 1830s, taken root, and was to become a staple part of every music hall bill from top to bottom of the trade.

While Christy's at the St James's Hall continued to attract audiences of well-intentioned middle-class folk, including those who would not feel at home in a theatre, frequenting the nascent music halls was not long regarded as socially acceptable. By the 1860s periodicals such as *Punch* were beginning to warn the middle-class youth to avoid seeking music and company, especially female company, in such places: the music is drowned by the noise, or displaced by 'silly, coarse and vulgar comic songs' with 'clap-trap chorusses', and the attached bars are not somewhere a decent boy would want his beloved to know that he spent his leisure time.[18] This was in 1862; by 1866 both the ubiquitous blackface minstrelsy and the growth of the halls, offering the combined consumption of drink, tobacco, song and comic entertainment, were sufficiently alarming to old vested interests in the entertainment world and also to the serious middle classes concerned about their own and their children's conduct to provoke the anxious interrogation of the Parliamentary Select Committee.

Returning to *The Era* back page in 1856, however, it seems that the rowdy middle classes and the lower-class seekers of beer and fun are interpellated simultaneously there as good fellows and generous patrons. In these advertisements it is still possible to evoke – or perhaps better to perform – a sense of camaraderie, community and personal knowledge man to man, the respected servants of the public speaking to their friends and patrons, and music with one's supper is advertised as a shared pleasure rather than necessarily as a commodity. But change is clearly on its way; the West End was in the process of winnowing the range of possible attractions to exactly the right mix. As the music hall of the second half of the century developed its dominant, class-segregated forms the Oxford, like the Pavilion, became a resort for the broadly middle-class sons of the Empire, the Raglan in Theobald's Road was excluded from the West End map, consigned to the amusement of city workers; but the Coal Hole, firmly within the magic rectangle, was wiped out, as its overtly sexualised, late-night kind of entertainment became more obviously unacceptable. In 1862 it was refused a licence and closed, and by 1887 it had been demolished and replaced by Terry's Theatre.

---

[18] *Punch*, 23 August 1862, 79.

If the *Era* front page represents the traditional culture of the theatres, and the back the challenge from the future forms of music hall, one might look for the expression of current taste elsewhere: and the paper's advertising includes one more important division. Inside, on page 8, in prime position alongside the editorial on the peace treaty, there are four more columns of display advertisements. They include most of a column announcing the credentials and products of large assurance companies; several day excursions by train, to the races or to the seaside; and advertisements for the Grand Naval Review, military tailoring, Schweppes Malvern Seltzer Water, a liqueur ginger brandy, and for graves in the new necropolis at Woking. These relatively serious, certainly not inexpensive purchases, for the heads of families rather than for gents about town, are offered between the paper's political leader on their right, and a very interesting first column in the left-hand prime position (see Figure 3). The advertisements there occupy the position which, on the front, belongs to the old theatres and, on the back, to the rising music halls. In the middle, this prime site on the page lists the week's shows that are, I would argue, to be regarded as the dominant, the cultural mainstream of the day; and they are aimed at serious people. Whereas the shows advertised on back and front stretch right across London, and across all classes, these are all in the new West End. Moreover, they are entertainments asserting themselves to be free from the taint of the theatrical, whether high or low; meant for those who buy graves and insurance and go to the Naval Review, to guide them on the occasions when they seek diversion in town.

The most traditional is the concert at Willis's Concert Rooms 'Under the Patronage of the Dowager Lady Willoughby de Broke', an unimpeachably polite Welsh lady, daughter of Sir John Williams, Bart., who presents 'the Celebrated WELSH NIGHTINGALE' Miss R. I. Williams. The attraction of the singer does not seem to be chiefly musical, however, since her programme is not listed in detail, apart from one piece expressly written for her; otherwise we are told only that she will appear in 'Twelve Characters': – a quasi-dramatic assumption, then, under the guise of an aristocratic meeting for music. Its elite credentials are somewhat undermined by the sale of tickets, which, while they are at the exclusive single price of five shillings, are not to be had only by application to the lady patrons, which would have been the gatekeeping practice of an old-fashioned elite event, but are available at the door. So the concert is a luxury endorsed by the remote aristocracy, but available to the middle classes. Similarly, the announcement that 'The Misses Marshall have the honour to announce to the Nobility, Gentry, their pupils, and friends' that their first 'GRAND FULL DRESS BALL' of the season will take place at the Princess's Concert Room (that is, within the Oxford Street theatre) is dressed up carefully so as to lend it as much aristocratic countenance as possible. To disguise the fact that this is a public dance, to which anyone can gain admittance by paying at the door, we are told that tickets are on sale at the libraries, in elite style, and the price is not given in the advertisement, which is also a mark of exclusivity. Thus the middle classes, with pretensions to the utmost respectability, are being wooed into the leisure culture by association, as Arnold notes, with the activities of the aristocratic world.

Then there are advertisements on this page for five exhibitions, of various sorts; here the association invoked is with the world of rational recreation, the lecture circuit and the scientific demonstration of modern inventions and topical information. The least innocuous of these is Dr Kahn's, in Coventry Street, an old-established venue which announces refurbishment and 'important additions to the scientific department', only one of which, however, is described, and that is 'a magnificent full-length model of Venus'.[19] A lecture on these models and displays of anatomical mysteries is delivered by Kahn every evening at 8.30, admission 1s, 'for Gentlemen only'. This last is an assertion of propriety, but hardly one that most parents and guardians would find completely reassuring. Kahn's exhibition room eventually disappeared under the foundations of the Pavilion music hall, the venue at which the Jingo song excoriated by Arnold made its first appearance; see Chapter 1. A safer shillingsworth in 1856 was the French Exhibition Gallery in Pall Mall, where from 10 a.m. till dusk one could see the work of several war artists, a new breed of painters, exhibiting 'Authentic Sketches' from the Crimea. Seeking a similarly tasteful and instructive evening entertainment, one could visit the exhibition room at the Egyptian Hall in Piccadilly, prices ranging from 1s to 3s, where innovative mechanical figures from the previous year's Paris Exhibition were set working from 11 a.m. to 5 p.m. and also from 7 p.m. to 10 p.m.; or go to see a similar show at 8 p.m. on weeknights, at a slightly cheaper price, at the Regent Gallery in the Quadrant, Regent Street.

[19] For an exploration of the waxworks' combination of surgery, celebrity and soft porn, see Pamela Pilbeam, *Madame Tussaud and the History of Waxworks*, (London: Hambledon & London, 2003), pp. 1–16, and Altick, *Shows of London*, pp. 55–6, 338–42.

A more exciting exhibition, however, combining the educational with the theatrical/spectacular, was the 'Grand Historical, Romantic, and Musical Entertainment, entitled KENILWORTH and the VISIT OF QUEEN ELIZABETH TO THE EARL OF LEICESTER, with SPLENDID DIORAMIC ILLUS-TRATIONS' to be seen at the Royal Polytechnic, under the patronage of Prince Albert. The advertisement for this promises a specially written text, and vocal illustrations sung by the Misses Mascall. A diorama of the destruction of Covent Garden theatre was offered for good measure. The Polytechnic, built in Regent Street in 1838 to provide the public with 'a practical knowledge of the various arts and branches of science con-nected with Manufactures, Mining Operations, and Rural Economy',[20] was by 1856 torn between education – it inaugurated evening classes in this year, appealing therefore to a wider audience who worked during the day – and quasi-informative, visually spectacular showmanship of this kind, a division of focus which probably contributed to its failure over the coming two decades. Similar educational and scientific pretensions struggled at the Royal Panopticon of Science and Art in Leicester Square, which a couple of weeks later, on 20 April, was advertising two scientific demonstrations – of the rotation of the moon, and of the manufacture of aluminium – and Mendelssohn's oratorio *Elijah*. Within the year such odd mixtures were to give way to straightforward entertainment. As with the Alhambra, the Panopticon became a highly profitable venue for spectacular ballet and music hall for the gay and rowdy, frequented by expensive sex workers and their clients. Its success greatly exercised first the 1866 Parliamentary Select Committee and then the moral campaign-ers of the end of the century. Meanwhile the Polytechnic, despite its royal tag, was to wither away, not having found its own plausible and enter-prising entrepreneur.

BY ANY OTHER NAME: DRAMATIC READERS
AND MODERN ENTERTAINMENTS

Having already seen, or decided against, the exhibitions, the serious *Era* reader scanning the inside column had a choice of five other attractions which had much in common. Most importantly, they were not the theatre; but they were at least as good as. Each one a different kind of disguised dramatic fiction, each is billed under the name of a

---

[20] *Prospectus*, 1837, at www.aim25.ac.uk/cats/15/5141.htm from the records of the Royal Polytechnic Institution held by the University of Westminster (visited 5.12.2010).

single individual celebrity. The most obviously demi-theatrical is
Mr Adolphus Francis's Dramatic Declamations, which are the Saturday
evening attraction at the Regent Gallery in the Quadrant. He is doing
Macbeth this week, and *King Lear* next. Dramatic readings were an
established part of the rational recreation movement,[21] got up at every
level from the village penny reading, intended to elevate the poor by
contact with Shakespeare and the classics, to the lecture programmes of
the prestigious and socially exclusive scientific or literary and philo-
sophical institutions established over the foregoing half century in the
leading manufacturing towns, including London. Since some time in
the 1830s their strictly utilitarian fare had been relieved with lectures on
the arts and variegated with music, and dramatic readings served to
illuminate and soften the rectitude of the serious and successful without, it was hoped, undermining it, and to admit them to the appreciation of the national poet without the risk of contamination from
entering the purlieus of a theatre.

Such events could be large and grand social occasions. In May 1863,
for example, this same Adolphus Francis was to be the male reader,
opposite Edith Heraud declaiming all the female parts, in a reading of
Antigone complemented by Mendelssohn's entire score, before nearly
2,000 people at the Suffolk Street Gallery (presumably that of the
Royal Society of British Artists) under the auspices of the Society for
the Encouragement of the Fine Arts. Even more ambitious, although
purely commercial, was Mrs Fanny Kemble's reading of *A Midsummer
Night's Dream*, in which she read – or rather, played – all the parts
from Hippolyta to Bottom, in a version of the text that she had created
to suit her own exalted vision of Shakespeare, based on a scholarly
rather than a theatrical edition of the play. In this virtuoso performance she too was supported by Mendelssohn's music, his overture and
entire incidental music for the play being performed all round her by a
large orchestra and a chorus of up to 300 singers. She originated this
prodigious production in New York and returning to England tried it
out at the fashionable St James's Theatre before taking it to its natural
homes, filling Manchester's Concert Hall with it in March 1853, after
which event the secretaries of six other northern cultural institutions
hastened backstage to offer her engagements. In February 1855 she

[21] For rational recreation, see Peter Bailey, *Leisure and Class in Victorian England: Rational Recreation and the Contest for Control, 1830–1885* (London: Routledge & Kegan Paul, 1978).

returned to London and on two nights filled the largest of the Exeter Halls with 'this marvellous reading' as the *Ladies Newspaper* called it, 'incomparably great'.[22]

Adolphus Francis, the particular 'dramatic illustrator' in this edition of *The Era*, was not such a long-lasting success as Fanny Kemble, but there were more famous and personally influential solo entertainers to be found on that day in 1856: Albert Smith, W. L. Woodin, Emma Stanley and Priscilla Horton were all advertising. These four, and a varying and increasing number who imitated them, were at the heart of the new 'entertainer' business, which *The Era* described thus, at its height in 1866:

The modern 'entertainer' surrounds himself with the most elaborate appliances, and maintains his position all the year round. Formerly the assumption of a character in front of a scene would have been deemed by many an objectionable approach to theatrical representation. Now those conscientious scruples which deter some members of the community from visiting the Theatre only seem to give a greater relish to their enjoyment of that entertainment, which is found to approximate most closely to the drama in construction. An audience more exclusively select, and earlier hour at which they can withdraw, and an assurance of the programme containing nothing to ruffle the smoothness of even the primmest sense of propriety, have been received as recommendations which have turned in this direction the favour of a very large class. The 'entertainers' have passed through the fiery ordeal of Clapham and Stoke Newington and come forth unscathed, and their programmes are peacefully permitted to rest on the table, even in those families where the syllabus of a secular concert would be most severely scrutinised.[23]

These 'entertainments' were the first really successful efforts at recreating the theatrical to satisfy a broad spectrum of middle-class taste. They built upon one of the most spectacular elements of rational recreation, the panoramas or dioramas such as those exhibited at the Royal Polytechnic discussed above. Such modern spectacles were normally exhibited either without commentary or with the accompaniment of factual, informative and inevitably rather tedious lecturing. The new departure was the addition of the skills of the dramatic writer and the performer. The 'entertainer', while far from being a mere lecturer, was still not that unacceptable creature, an actor, for he remained himself, a gentleman entertaining his guests – the word 'entertaining' maintains, here,

---

[22] Quoted in Jacky Bratton, 'Fanny Kemble, Shakespearean', in Gail Marshall, ed., *Great Shakespeareans: Jameson, Cowden Clarke, Kemble and Cushman* (London: Continuum, 2011), q.v. for a longer discussion of the dramatic reading.
[23] 'Mr W. S. Woodlin's Entertainment', *Era*, 1 April 1866.

something of its other sense, of the sharing of private hospitality. The Misses Mascall, singing to accompany the 'dioramic illustrations' at the Polytechnic, were adjuncts, not equals; but the leading entertainers who took up the pictorial exhibition as backing for their own performances had a different status, and they shaped 'entertainment' to suit themselves and their special position.

Woodin and Smith, like actors in previous generations, emerged from the lower and middle ranks of the middle classes. Woodin's father was a prosperous Bond Street shopkeeper in the print and picture-framing business, while Smith was the son of a country doctor and had trained in and practised medicine himself. Both decided to build a career in the new entertainment world upon their hobbies. Woodin came into the business through amateur acting; and it is important to remember that to the mid-Victorian public 'amateur' acting was the better kind. The word 'had deep resonance in Victorian culture. It carried with it conno-tations of a gentlemanly ideal of engagement in public life or the pursuit of an interest actuated by the pleasures of "love" as opposed to the money-grubbing imperatives of professionalism.'[24] This sense clung to amateur sports for much longer, and determined who was thought fit to compete for the highest honours until the mid twentieth century. In the 1850s it was completely respectable to be an amateur actor. When a group of gentlemen, chiefly Bohemian writers, got up an 'Amateur Pantomime' at the Olympic Theatre at Easter 1855, critics like Henry Morley had rejoiced to see even the mystified professional skills of clown and Harlequin taken over and done better by gentlemen.[25] Dickens, who was by nature and genius a titan of the theatre, would never act except on an amateur basis, and deliberately booked his 'Amateur Company' into the large public or institutional spaces wherever they made their charitable tours, rather than contaminating themselves and their audiences with the much more com-fortable and appropriate theatres.[26]

Woodin, egged on by his friends' admiration, stepped over the line into professionalism, as Dickens himself was eventually to do, and he adopted

[24] Seth Koven, *Slumming: Sexual and Social Politics in Victorian London* (Princeton University Press, 2004), p. 38. Koven is discussing James Greenwood's nom de plume of 'the Amateur Casual' in a famous article about the workhouses of London; Greenwood was one of the more apocalyptic critics of the entertainments of the metropolis.

[25] Henry Morley, *The Journal of a London Playgoer from 1851 to 1866* (1866; reprinted Leicester University Press, 1974), p. 96.

[26] He used the Gallery of Illustration, and Fanny Kelly's tiny theatre sometimes in town: see Gilli Bush-Bailey, *Performing Herself: Autobiography and Fanny Kelly's* Dramatic Recollections (Manchester University Press, 2011), pp. 85–9.

the same defence against being thought theatrical: he performed alone. He began professionally in 1852 with a successful advertising gimmick, a giant carpet-bag which was trundled through the streets as an inducement to attend, which then stood on the platform. He dived into it to carry out a succession of quick changes,

singing English, French, German, Italian, Dutch, and Ethiopian songs, becoming lean, fat, short, tall, masculine, feminine, and neuter (vide the knife-grinder's apparatus), in rapid succession, dipping for faces behind a table, and coming up with a fresh one for every emergency, flinging off his own identity at will, and successively presenting himself before us as Albert Smith, M. Robin, Henry Russell, Stocqueler, Buckstone, Compton, Lablache, Charles Kean, Wright, and innumerable other personages.[27]

For a background he used diorama views of real locations such as the Lake District, which his neat little programme describes in guidebook phraseology, and some of his characters were the middle-class holiday-makers to be encountered in such places. His other main attraction was his plunging into 'magical metamorphosed seas of costume', the lightning transformations from which he emerged to take his bow, 'the gentleman in full evening costume who is to be recognised as the Mr Woodin of private life'. His first two shows were written for him by E. L. Blanchard, who got him free theatre tickets like a professional, proposed him for the Arundel Club, and generally introduced him into the Bohemian world, receiving in return friendship and hospitality in his houses at Brompton and in Soho as well as payments of about £100 in all for writing two shows plus updates on his topical songs. The entertainments were steadily successful, enabling the performer to retire comfortably in 1870, at 46. Characteristically modestly, Blanchard records as Woodin's best work two sketches in his final show written by the dramatists John Oxenford and T. W. Robertson.[28] Though his conversation was often wearisomely self-centred,[29] Woodin was accepted into the professional theatre world, but importantly for his acceptance by the core audience of the 'serious', he did not appear in the theatres. His first venue was the Adelaide Gallery off the Strand, and later he used the Polygraphic Hall (see Chapter 1). The combination of factually described, realistic dioramas of the countryside, theatrical but safe amusement in their presentation, and the reassuring polite venues with middling seat prices, guaranteed him 'the favour of a very large class'.

---

[27] *Era*, 31 October 1852.   [28] Blanchard, *Life and Reminiscences*, p. 288.
[29] According to Clement Scott; see Blanchard, *Life and Reminiscences*, p. 103 n. 2.

VICTORIAN MODERNITY: THE REAL AND ALBERT SMITH

Albert Smith, presenting his 'Mont Blanc', was a more complex character and case, and his entertainments much less traditional – indeed, they partake of an aesthetic peculiar to the 1850s and 1860s, the years following the Great Exhibition. He was a Bohemian veteran when he took to 'entertainment', having earned a living writing for the stage and for the comic press since he moved to London in 1841. He had been a founding writer for *Punch* until his blunt anti-intellectualism and rejection of cant upset Jerrold and Thackeray, who thought him a self-advertising boor, and he had then successfully taken the side of the vilified Alfred Bunn in a pamphlet war, stopping the *Punch* men from further persecution of the manager.[30] Smith was both a non-conforming dreamer and a down-to-earth businessman; a very modern man of the entertainment world. His shows, presented behind the faux oriental façade of the Egyptian Hall in Piccadilly from 1851 until his premature death in 1860, were a manifestation of an obsession with the Real, with factual truth and authenticity in art that subsumes the Puritan rejection of pretence and the utilitarian preoccupation with the material, a temper that he shared with the less articulate but highly appreciative mass of the Victorian middle classes – both rowdy and serious.

Smith's work can be seen as another manifestation of the Victorian modernity so astoundingly expressed in the Crystal Palace, that reached its extreme point in the conception and the decor of the South Kensington Museum (the V & A).[31] The museum, like the Crystal Palace and the whole concept of the 1851 Great Exhibition, was profoundly disliked by the artistic elite, to whom it was vulgar and overwhelmingly inartistic, by which they meant materialist, contrary to the manifestation of the ideal in art. John Ruskin, one of the exhibition's most vociferous critics, was similarly appalled by Albert Smith's handling of a related ideal, that of Romantic landscape. The two men were roughly of an age (Smith born 1816, Ruskin 1819), both travelled to Switzerland and saw the Alps in youth, and each of them was profoundly moved; Ruskin was in Chamonix again in the summer of 1851 when Smith returned to climb Mont Blanc. To Ruskin the fat, enthusiastic little man called Smith,

[30] For an account of Smith's career, see Raymund Fitzsimons, *The Baron of Piccadilly: The Travels and Entertainments of Albert Smith 1816–1860* (London: Geoffrey Bles, 1967).
[31] See Tim Barringer, 'Equipoise and the Object: The South Kensington Museum' in Hewitt, ed., *Age of Equipoise?*, pp. 68–83, and Armstrong, *Glassworlds*.

scrambling over the Mer de Glace and eventually drinking champagne
toasts on the summit of Mont Blanc, was a cockney vandal desecrating
Nature and the religion of Art, of which the mountains were to him a
sublime and untouchable manifestation, hallowed by a lifetime of vener-
ation, inspired by the Romantic poets and artists.[32] For Smith, to whom
the Alps had also been a vision of romance ever since he was a child, their
splendour was crowned, and also claimed for himself, by his struggle to
ascend, and that triumph was captured by the large pictures that he got
the scene painter Beverley to create for the lecture he planned to deliver on
his return. To Smith the way in which, for a generation, Romantic
travellers had glorified and idealised European journeys – along the
Rhine, to Italy, and up into the mountains – was the falsification, and
his demystifying accounts of his own journeys – of the bad inns and
predatory natives and fleas and flies and heat, as well as the breathtaking
glaciers and the glorious snow down which one could slide laughing –
were the authentic truth.

This was the Real, as described by Gillen D'Arcy Wood, in his *The
Shock of the Real: Romanticism and Visual Culture*. Wood begins his
argument for extending our understanding of visual-cultural history and
modernity back to the aesthetic arguments of the pre-Victorian period by
describing the Egyptian Hall in its early days, and examining its hugely
popular exhibitions of 'the spectacle of the "real"' as condemned by
Coleridge, the theorist of English Romanticism.[33] Smith was picking up
a powerful and by then long-developing impulse of his times, which
reached its zenith in the 1860s and was pervasively important in the
theatrical culture that created the West End. Lynda Nead, in *Victorian
Babylon*, discusses the nuances of the 1860s obsession with the Real as art
in her illuminating discussion of London's gas lighting, which enabled,
amongst other things, the theatrical exploitation of the 'realistic depiction
of London street Life' and prompted the *Illustrated Times* to review
Boucicault's *Streets of London* (Princess's 1864) as uniquely attractive
because its representation of Trafalgar Square was 'the most real scene
ever witnessed on the stage in London ... a perfect diorama'.[34] But
Smith's show had gone one better than that, and brought the distant
reality of the Alps into the grasp of London audiences. He succeeded

[32] Fitzsimons, *Baron of Piccadilly*, p. 113.
[33] Gillen D'Arcy Wood, *The Shock of the Real: Romanticism and Visual Culture, 1760–1860* (London: Palgrave, 2001), pp. 1–7.
[34] Quoted in Nead, *Victorian Babylon*, pp. 98–101, p. 99.

because his show was more real than any play, however realistically staged: it was a presentation of reality itself, authentic, non-fictional and taken possession of by an ordinary man, an entirely unmade-up, unfictionalised man, a gentleman in no way different from the paying customers; one of ourselves.

When this *Era* advertisement appeared in 1856, Smith had been presenting his journey to Mont Blanc, diversified with accounts of his travels up the Rhine and elsewhere, at the Egyptian Hall for four years, each year adding more props and scenery, all authentic, all actually real bits of wood and horn imported from Switzerland and forged into the Swiss-built chalet façade before which he stood to speak. In the show Smith also deployed the 'properties' of the modern businessman: a set of rules for audience behaviour – no ladies' hats, no chatting; on his own part, good value in constantly updated songs and stories as well as the set and Beverley's realistic painting, and his punctual appearance at 8, in evening dress, as a gentleman speaking to his equals about things that had actually happened to him. He rejected costume, and Woodin's shape-changing impersonations – the ducking-down business, as he called it.[35] He made a virtue of the fact that he was not a professional performer: he sometimes prefaced songs with apologies for the ordinariness of his singing voice. Consequently he laid claim to a different relationship with his material – it was true – and with his audience – he was their equal. The old patron–player relationship of subservience and patronage was entirely superseded. He sold a good product, and people eagerly paid for value received; his show became the first long-running success in the West End. On 10 January 1856 he reached his 1200th presentation, and on 25 March, the week before this advertisement, he gave a command performance at Windsor Castle. A record number of British tourists climbed Mont Blanc that year. Those who couldn't afford to go, even on one of Thomas Cook's new tours, bought bits of the copious spin-off merchandising Smith provided,[36] when they had seen and heard about the authentic objects he brought home.[37]

---

[35] Fitzsimons, *Baron of Piccadilly*, p. 104.

[36] See some of the pamphlets, games and trinkets still for sale at www.les-alpes-livres.com/Resources/Albert%20Smith%20NPa.pdf (visited 28.4.2010).

[37] Fitzsimons, *Baron of Piccadilly*, p. 140; he also notes (pp. 147–50) the retreat from association with Smith's vulgar pioneering footsteps made by the upper middle-class British of the Alpine Club, who made him a founder member in 1857 but subsequently dissociated themselves from the hordes of Cook's tourists to whom Smith had also opened the way to the heights.

AND FINALLY, THE LADIES

The two remaining advertisements in the 'entertainers' column are for shows by women. There were several solo performers in this and in the previous generations of actresses, after the ground had been broken by Fanny Kelly, who began her one-woman show at the Hanover Square Rooms in 1830,[38] but most have been forgotten. Emma Stanley is presently very little known. In 1856 she was doing a piece called *Seven Ages of Woman*, a monologue in the Mathews/Woodin style with quick changes, impersonations and songs, which like Woodin's first two shows was written for her by E. L. Blanchard. With it she embarked in 1853 upon a tour of America with her mother, the actress Fanny Fleming. They brought the show back to London in 1855 and went to the USA again in June 1856, commencing a worldwide journey that lasted several years. Previously Emma had been a supporting actress at the Princess's in the early 1850s, and starting in the Concert Room there had done other solo entertainments. In Dublin in 1851 she had a hit with a show about the Bloomer costume called *Three T's – Tunic! Trousers!! and Turban!!!* The *Seven Ages* was her mainstay for many years, enabling her to impersonate a series of men as well as women in what sounds like an extremely taxing evening, supported by a piano and an organ.

We know little more about her: she was still performing the show everywhere from Wootton-under-Edge to Glasgow City Hall in 1874; in 1878 her business manager T. L. Harrison, who had booked her tours for seventeen years, was advertising for a new employer. Yates tells us that she 'was singularly versatile, sympathetic, and fascinating; she sang and danced excellently, had great mobility of feature, and a chic which was rather French than English'.[39] Otherwise the most significant fact we have about Emma Stanley is that unlike such men as Smith and Woodin she was born into the profession; indeed only from the base of a professional family would a woman have launched successfully into such a career. Emma did not marry, and travelled the world with her mother until she died in 1861, at which point, apparently, at the age of about 40, Emma immediately engaged the agent Harrison, and continued alone. She did not shake off her theatrical beginnings, though she often did the show in non-theatre settings. Her disappearance from history is perhaps related to a failure to cross the line from mere respectability as a servant of the public

---

[38] See Bush-Bailey, *Performing Herself*, p. 14 n. 27.
[39] Edmund Yates, 'Bygone Shows', *Fortnightly Review* (May 1886), 633–47, 643.

to personal membership of the middle classes. Fanny Kemble's
Mr Mitchell was not Emma's man of business.

'THE VERSATILITY OF WOMEN': MRS GERMAN REED

The final advertisement in the column is also by a woman, and one who
has a claim to an important place in history, though she has not been
accorded it. The 1866 Select Committee repeatedly used her work as an
instance of the puzzling new directions taken by West End entertainment;
and both her performances and her managerial moves are central to the
argument of this book. This *Era* advertisement in April 1856 announces
'Miss P. Horton's Popular Illustrations', immediately followed by the
information that 'Mr and Mrs German Reed give their NEW ENTERTAIN-
MENT ... a variety of amusing and interesting scenes from real life ... at
the Royal Gallery of Illustration, 14, Regent-street'. As Edmund Yates
affirmed, in discussing the German Reeds' performances in an article on
monologues, the wife was really a soloist and the husband the mere stooge
or feed, though an excellent musician. While the form of the advertisement confirms her primary importance, Yates has missed the husband's
other vital contribution to their success: he juxtaposes, but does not
connect, the conspicuous fact of their married status with the statement
that 'the entertainment provided not merely revived reminiscences of old
playgoers, but was exactly suited for that large class of the public which,
while hankering after amusement, professes to abominate the theatre'.[40]
   The vital move Priscilla had made is best expressed in the diary of
Arthur Munby who, dining in July 1866, took down to supper

a pleasant elderly lady, of quiet gentle manners, ladylike, selfpossest: might have
been a Bishop's wife. And who was this nice old lady? Why, she was Mrs German
Reed – Miss P. Horton; whose legs, as Ormsby said afterwards, used to be
familiar objects, when she danced & sung at the Haymarket, years ago! Nay, she
is 'entertaining' still. Does this prove the versatility of women? or not rather their
wellkept purity in many cases where fools allow it not?[41]

Horton had been a very successful singer and actress – see her largely
cross-dressed youthful career in Chapter 4 – but as she and the century

---

[40] ibid., 645. See also his *Recollections and Experiences*, 2 vols. (London: Richard Bentley, 1884), vol. II,
    p. 43, where he generalises about the husband–wife entertainer teams that writing such things is
    usually matter of providing for one good performer – the wife – and a man who can only 'be
    intrusted as feeder to his wife'.
[41] Derek Hudson, *Munby: Man of Two Worlds. The Life and Diaries of Arthur J. Munby 1828–1910*
    (1972; London: Abacus, 1974), entry for 6 July 1866, p. 227.

matured, and as perhaps her familiar legs ceased to be more attractive than
her rich contralto voice, she moved on, marrying the theatrical musician
Thomas German Reed and, as it were, leaving the business, without
actually doing so. Instead, they made their new business out of their
make-believe retirement to private life. For twenty years they were At
Home at a grand house in Waterloo Place, and welcomed personal guests
there (see Figure 4a).

In the previous year the gallery, which was designed as the major
reception room of Nash's own house when he built Regent's Street, had
been a venue for the viewing of dioramas of the Crimean War patronised
by the highest in the land, including the Queen. The Telbin paintings
and their patrons conferred on it a legacy of fashion and high repute, and
Priscilla Horton's 'Illustrations of Real Life' were viewed in their first
season by many notabilities listed in the press, headed by the Duke and
Duchess of Wellington.[42] The name of the show invoked Telbin's 'illustrations' of the war, the overland route to India and other such topics; and
Telbin and the famous scenic artists the Grieves still provided the painted
setting for the German Reeds, but this time of a drawing room, and of
scenes viewed through its windows. Within that frame, during the first
seasons, Priscilla worked out a novel performance, 'illustrating', rather
than acting, modern people.

The critics, men of the theatre business and so familiar with the sight of
Mrs German Reed in her undress early years – costumed as a pantomime
fairy, as Ariel, as the Fool in *King Lear*, as a ballet girl or a dancing boy –
struggled at first to express her transformation into a commanding and
gracious figure in a large crinoline (the steel frame version of which was
patented that summer) welcoming them to her own drawing room. They
praised the decor, calling it 'an ensemble such as Madame Vestris would
have rejoiced in when the Olympic Theatre was under her tasteful direction'. The claim is paradoxical: it says that the highly respectable show has
a theatrical good taste last seen in the 1830s when Vestris – the most
famous legs of the century – attracted the nobility to her Wych Street
musical theatre; Madame Vestris's ultra-fashionable theatre, unblushingly
offering a highly decorative programme of sweet music and female
attractions, was got up to suggest her private boudoir. Mrs German
Reed's gallery, twenty-five years on, has all that taste, and none of its
savour: it is irreproachable, and suggests not a smart brothel in Wych
Street, but a drawing room in the wealthy suburbs. Grappling, with some

---

[42] See the list in the *Daily News* review, 19 May 1856.

(a)

(b)

Figures 4a and 4b   Mr and Mrs Reed, at the Gallery of Illustration. Two pictures from *The Illustrated London News*, February 1856, showing the opening weeks of the gallery's entertainment, emphasising the 'drawing-room entertainment' apparently in an opulent private house, and showing Thomas German Reed still in his private persona interacting with Priscilla German Reed in costume, 'illustrating' a character difficulty, with Priscilla's offering within this setting, early critics got into deep theoretical waters. Her 'personations' they said were sharply delineated, comic, and 'realistic'.

The characters are supposed to be drawn from 'real life', and from the extreme truthfulness they may be; in an extent of caricature which is a trifle more marked than we are accustomed to. It is nature, slightly exaggerated. We do not cite this as a fault, because, although it may sound like a paradox, 'character' must always be exaggerated in representation, or the public will not admit that it is 'natural'.[43]

Mrs Reed and her supporting men were aware of the critical challenge they presented in doing something so very new – bringing the latest canons of 'realistic' representation to bear upon musical imitations. They were performing modern popular songs for a polite audience. It is striking that the published song sheets of the work of Mrs German Reed in character (see Figure 5) are at first glance indistinguishable from the equally innovative new song culture whose point of origin is the music hall – the character drawing on the cover and the verses and choruses within partake of the same broadly comic representation of contemporary life. Just as the music hall comedian George Leybourne impersonated on stage the cats-meat seller or the policeman, Priscilla Horton illustrated the farm servant or the housemaid; but the different verb is significant. She might sing in the first person as the girl, but Mrs German Reed's perspective was firmly that of the girl's employer, the mistress of the house. The Reeds were members of the servant-employing classes, and they were especially aware of creating a new relationship with their similarly placed audiences: an intimate, even an interactive relationship.

   Thomas's on-stage contribution was as butt or long-suffering ordinary man – not an actor – trying in vain to get on with his work as a composer of an opera, a phantom called 'The Lady of Lucerne', which never, of course, got beyond a few bars. Here is *Lloyd's Weekly Newspaper* on their second show, that began in January 1857:

The new entertainment is new in the first part only. The second, the private agonies of Mr Reed, remains still as attractive as ever. He is so dear a friend, that his misfortunes ... are perennially pleasant; and we cordially wish him every

---

[43] *Era*, 14 December 1855; and see *Punch*, 20 June 1863, where she is described as the only actress 'with any notion of ladylike demeanour', one who 'knows how to speak plain English, as plain English ladies do' as well as being able to act the transition from a mannish old maid to 'a lisping maiden of eighteen' (p. 257).

Figure 5   Priscilla Horton (Mrs German Reed) on the cover of the song 'I never does nothing at all'. This is an image from sheet music sold for amateur singers to use, indistinguishable from similar songs taken from the music hall repertoire and bearing images of music hall stars; it illustrates the continuity of the development of the popular music business at mid-century, as well as showing another of Mrs German Reed's 'Illustrations of Character' in costume and action

want of success in proceeding with his opera. Moreover, there is another charm in it – the gratification of seeing public people in private life. And this desire has been also been sagaciously gratified in the new first part . . .

The Reeds – familiarity is most natural – Commence with a quarrel. Mr Reed has been out of town, and returns all but too late to commence the expected 'Entertainment – the Lady of Lucerne'. In the meantime Mrs Reed has concluded an engagement to go all over the uninhabited world on a professional visit. If Miss Hayes and others could go to California and Timbuctoo, why should not Mrs Reed go to the Sandwich Islands, where there is an excellent theatre at Bath-bun Bay? all arrangements are made, even to advertising for a governess for Our Ward, who is to be left behind; and Mrs Reed just steps out, probably to purchase floats, when the governesses come tumbling in like a land slip. They are all very eccentric, and calculated to frighten nervous gentlemen. Mr Reed is in despair. One lady will only superintend the instruction given by various masters; and, besides, she could not think of living in a family of professionals. Another young lady applies for her daughter, who speaks all the languages (of Great Britain) in perfection. But even these desirable accomplishments are useless – Mr Reed is so very particular. A third young lady may be described as gushing. Claudine Delacour prides herself principally on being thin, but dresses in the pyramid fashion, or tent and tent pole. She is gay and rattling, and sings 'The Travellers Lay' with a volubility which leads her to the other end of the English language in five minutes. She disappears – with all the jewellery; and after M. le Vicomte de Fanfaronade has come in search of her it becomes certain that Mr Reed has been victimised in more ways than one. But he has borne it all very well, and his decorous agony contributes no little to the general amusement. It is to be feared that he did not enjoy the various songs nearly so much as many people present did; but then he was in despair about the 'Lady of Lucerne' . . . It is our great pleasure to announce, not to exhaust these new personations; and also to impress the fact, that all the best of the former remain. That wonderful 'Farm Servants Song' will cling to the memory long after the days when policeman shall be no longer typical of love and hunger; and even to that termination of eternity when mops shall cease to be left on staircases.[44]

As the reporter says, the success of this lies in a kind of excitement generated for the audience by the appearance of intimate admission to the domestic lives of the talented, the amusing, who sing and impersonate, but also by the discovery that they are not all that unlike ourselves – they too quarrel and have problems with servants. The sense of intimacy is deliberately fostered, and of jokes – often very theatrical jokes – that the audience can feel themselves clever and sophisticated to be able to share. Left alone on stage in *Our Card Basket*, 1861, for example, a piece which

[44] *Lloyds Weekly Newspaper*, 1 February 1857.

was by now something very like a play, with a plot about a couple of social climbers called Candytuft, the additional member of the troupe, John Parry, says

I wish I had some one to whom I could mention Candytuft's absurd notion. Nothing is more annoying than to have a good thing in your mind and no one with whom to share it. [*looking at audience*] You may be a month in this House and never see a strange face from morning till night.[45]

And of course they all laughed. The illusion of sharing real life between the performers and the loyal and returning audience is fostered by all such means. As they began to employ dramatic writers to create materials for them, Brough, Brookes, Lemon and the others must have been instructed to sew in jokes about the metatheatricality of the performance, its self-referential style, its games with 'illusion' and 'reality'.

The convention in the earliest days was that Thomas maintained the fiction of real life – he spoke directly to the audience, he dressed in evening dress, and received his guests in real time, or gamely played himself in the scenarios they announced that they would 'illustrate'. The actress Priscilla not only sang but also acted, changed her costume and persona, including some male impersonations, though sometimes only in 'half-length' portraits which avoided the memory of the youthful legs (see Figure 4b). The gender politics are quite complex here; it is, as Munby says, a question of holding in mind the 'the versatility' (read, deceptiveness) 'of women' alongside their 'purity'. The audiences were won over by the clever path the Reeds trod, and the shows became ever more theatrical as they became familiar.

Their first additional performer was John Orlando Parry, himself a solo performer, son of a famous Welsh musician, who had left the stage in 1853 suffering from stage fright and turned to his other skills as draughtsman and cartoonist, and songwriter for others – he created Albert Smith's most successful songs. He returned as himself in 1860, strolling on to the stage at what was supposed to be the Reeds' holiday cottage and showing them his sketches before seating himself at the piano and delivering what we might recognise today as a solo spot in a revue. He could create a semi-burlesque, part-tragic version of the whole of Boucicault's melodrama *The Colleen Bawn* in half an hour, or render *Mrs Roseleaf's Evening Party* with

---

[45] Add. MSS 53003B: 'Part 1 of Mr and Mrs German Reed's Entertainment of popular Illustrations from Real Life for 1861 Entitled "Our Card Basket"', fo. 5. On John Orlando Parry, see Peter Sheppard-Skaerved, Frances Palmer and Janet Snowman, *John Orlando Parry and the Theatre of London* (London: Janet Snowman, 2010).

nothing else to assist the illusion than a fan, a bouquet, and a white handkerchief. Mr John Parry brings all the prominent personages of the evening vividly before us; and the hostess, full of anxious amiability; the 'gushing' girl, bursting forth with mild platitudes; and a representative of 'swelldom', with drawling lisp and mincing tone, are invested with wonderful reality. The performer, by his consummate mastery over the instrument, makes the piano imitate sounds that completely illustrate the musical peculiarities of an evening party, and he sings not merely solos, but imaginary duets, till the ear is deceived by the contrast of the voices, and the eye searches for the executant of those high notes and quavering embellishments.[46]

The reviewer continues with the information that the audience was 'of the usually fashionable and numerous kind' and indeed the company's fashionable status is confirmed in March when they are amongst those commanded to sing at St George's Chapel on the morning of the royal wedding.

Thomas German Reed developed into something of an actor himself, and when they all three became sufficiently senior and wealthy, and fully accepted as a fixture of polite society, he was able to return to his roots in theatrical music and expand the gallery's performances, engaging a small company of singers to produce '*opera di camera*', producing Balfe operettas on the perfectly accoutred pocket handkerchief stage and importing Offenbach's new music from Paris. He commissioned work from the young W. S. Gilbert and Arthur Sullivan (separately, though they probably actually met at the gallery) and his was the professional transfer of Sullivan and F. C. Burnand's *Cox and Box*, originally created from Maddison Morton's non-musical farce for the high-class amateur Moray Minstrels. The 'entertainment', in short, is an important element – far more than a niche – in the reshaping of the stage into the new West End.

THE WORRIES OF THE 1866 SELECT COMMITTEE

Having made this survey of *The Era* in 1856, and seen the buds from which the growth of the West End was breaking forth, the apparently rather oblique preoccupations of the Parliamentary Select Committee of 1866 seem more comprehensible. The committee was summoned to deal with a matter handled in 1831/2 and supposedly laid to rest in 1843,

---

[46] *Era*, 4 January 1863.

the licensing of theatres in the metropolis, which was now perceived to
be a problem once again. The theatre managers certainly thought so:
Benjamin Webster, by this date an aging and somewhat disgruntled
manager of West End theatres, averred that he was sorry to have argued
for theatrical free trade before the 1831/2 Select Committee. Now, faced
with the challenge of the music halls and other entertainments, he was
all for protectionism. The committee members had their own precon-
ceptions and objectives, which chiefly focussed, as they had in 1831,
upon the desirability of the universal availability and appreciation of
Shakespeare; additionally, they were concerned once more with the
links between theatre and sexual activity, and listening on the second
day of the inquiry to the evidence of Henry Pownall, twenty-four years
chief magistrate of Middlesex, led them to a fixation with the possibility of sexual activity in private rooms annexed to the new entertainment venues, the Alhambra or Cremorne. Their central concern,
however, was with the unexpected, unruly and incomprehensible development of this new world of entertainment, which they sought to
understand, in order to control it. Their questions therefore circled
round the music halls, on the one hand, often represented by the
Alhambra, and the many extratheatrical entertainments, epitomised
by the German Reeds.

They questioned their witnesses about how they should define a
play – how many performers did it have to include? How do you find
good acting? Did costume make it a drama? Did scenery? When were
operatic selections in a music hall an opera? They grill the often,
apparently, rather exasperated or slippery respondents from the trade
on the material facts – does the Royal Opera House have a bar from
which one might see the stage? What was the difference in effect
between the beer pumps installed at the back of the pit at the Adelphi
and the tables for drinks set out in a music hall? E. T. Smith,
proprietor of Cremorne as well as Astley's in 1866, and one-time lessee
of Drury Lane, asserted, in his own obvious interest but entirely
illogically, that to give a dramatic licence to somewhere with food
and drink on tables in the same room as the stage meant 'you bring
the drama down to a pothouse'.[47] But many of the committee thought
that not such a bad idea; even where the audience could drink and
smoke a cigar, they felt, there would be a better tone to proceedings if
they were watching a play; 'Shakespeare' was always and everywhere

[47] Minutes of the Evidence to the 1866 Select Committee, Answer 3621.

preferable, in their eyes, to 'nigger songs'. The problem was that, as their witnesses insisted, straight Shakespeare was not what the paying audience wanted. Confronted with the reality of the developing West End, reading through the *parti pris* descriptions offered by their witnesses, they saw a complex of venues and kinds of provision for amusement and refreshment, where music and prostitution, drinking and drama, were played out in uncontrollable combinations, and new forms, responding to new needs and sensibilities, were rapidly emerging.

Seen in longer perspective, the scene they were surveying is the matrix of twentieth-century commercial entertainment; and the same issues, claims about what exactly is or should be part of 'theatre' or 'drama', what is compatible with the high art of dramatic performance, preoccupied practitioners and critics at the other end of the West End's development. These are the same grounds on which avant-garde theatre artists from Brecht to Peter Brook challenged the bourgeois dramatic or 'deadly' theatre that they felt responded to, rather than challenging, audience taste.[48] In the questions of the committee in 1866, and indeed in the *Era* advertisements in 1856, one may see the same issues about manipulating audience engagement and comfort or consent that Brecht confronted, and the same distractions crowding in upon Brook's sacred empty space.

In the twenty-first century we have resolved the food and drink issue on what we think are the rational, risk-averse grounds of health and safety; but the solution went through many phases, from afternoon tea in the stalls to dinner theatre in the countryside. What remains true, and what the witnesses to the 1866 Select Committee already knew, is that the exact location of the bar, the chosen moments and the physical demands of the transition from music to drinking, spectacle to feasting, are commercially and psychologically vital to the magic of the moment; the magic that is, in this analysis, that of festival, which may contain many possible means of transcendence and joy, from tragedy and laughter to drink, dancing in the aisles and popcorn.[49]

---

[48] See Bertolt Brecht, 'The Modern Theatre is the Epic Theatre: Notes to the opera *Aufstieg und Fall der Stadt Mahagonny*', in *Brecht on Theatre: The Development of an Aesthetic*, ed. and trans. John Willett (London: Methuen, 1964), and Peter Brook, *The Empty Space: A Book About the Theatre: Deadly, Holy, Rough, Immediate* (London: MacGibbon & Kee, 1968).

[49] See Barbara Ehrenreich, *Dancing in the Streets: A History of Collective Joy* (New York: Metropolitan Books, 2007).

Theorists and practitioners in the twentieth century invoked, in opposition to this down and dirty idea, a sacred conception of drama which was intensely self-conscious on the part of the executants, putting their experience at the centre. This is perhaps the issue at the heart of debates about the value(s) of the West End: there, the audience experience is what matters most. Our disputes therefore repeatedly invoke the political as well as the artistic valences of smoking and drinking at the performance. Having settled upon an essentially consumerist notion of the good being what anyone wants it to be, we nevertheless continue to discriminate between the status of venues according to whether they are pubs with a platform for a stand-up or the Barbican Centre with a theatre whose auditorium is more or less composed of a series of separate padded cells. Whether proper drama can be appreciated by people sitting at tables with drinks before them is an aesthetic/political issue of some importance still, in terms of audience choices and self-definitions; but more important to my discussion is the understanding that all these enjoyments come together in the West End in a particular pattern, with meaning that is encoded in place itself. It is the West End as a whole that is the venue, within which we now have the twenty-first-century desideratum of apparently free choice.

Choice, and price, are also still important in the matter of the physical comfort of the audience experience. Brook's 1968 appeal for a 'rough', a dangerous, theatre is an explicit reaction against what he understood to be the deadening effects of the century-long development of comfort and safety in the entertainment offered in the West End. But one might think of the issue differently from the perspective of the 1850s and 1860s, when danger in the metropolis was a very much more pressing reality for many people, especially women. From the perspective of a large slice of Victorian society – including everyone who could afford to spend money on leisure – the West End, if it was to be an evening destination, had to work to be perceived as both exciting and sufficiently safe. A surge in the growth and the differentiation of West End venues made it possible for more people to be entertained there. Single young men with very little money could enjoy the latest music and comedy for the (inflated) price of one drink in a tavern concert room or, eventually, in the Oxford or the Empire Music Hall. Their still serious-minded mothers and sisters found they could go, without male escorts, to the Gallery of Illustration and treat themselves to sprung-seated, reserved stalls, an attended cloakroom, a neatly printed programme (the Entertainments seem to have been the first shows to offer such a booklet) and an impeccable even though funny, mildly satirical, view of their own world.[50]

As already noted, beyond the questions of safety, tastes and the consumption of food, drink and tobacco, questions of dramatic form loomed large in the Parliamentary Select Committee hearings. The witnesses were often naïve in their responses to questions about how important scenery is to a play, but with hindsight its centrality to the West End experience is indisputable. Visual spectacle and the illusion of reality presented to the eyes reach from the Crimean panoramas to *Avatar* in 3D. What the committee were trying to tease out in their questions about the uses of spectacle, music and costume was a new understanding of the performer–audience relationship and the illusions involved in that – the sense of what is special about the staged performance, and at the same time how that represents something to which the spectator can relate or aspire. Many of the new devices for working with the aspirations and dreams of the audience emerge first in the West End through the entertainments, rather than in the more conservative theatres. The relationship fostered by the German Reeds and John Parry to a loyal, returning group who feel themselves guests rather than customers is ahead of, and in a way more subtle and deeply rooted than, the flattery meted out to the stalls by the society dramas at the Prince of Wales's and the St James's theatres later in the century. The Gallery audience felt they shared the stars' private life, and they perhaps read about it in the *Ladies Newspaper* with the same fascination as someone following twenty-first century celebrities in *Hello!* magazine. Albert Smith's printed napkins and cut-out parlour games about Mont Blanc are a century ahead of the T-shirts and masks taken home from *The Phantom of the Opera*. And certainly when the superstars like Rachel, Jenny Lind and, most powerfully, Charles Dickens arrived in town their enthusiasts turned out to see and hear then with the rapture we recognise today as part of celebrity culture.

---

[50] The Gallery of Illustration audience was more female than male, according to clues in the press; in autumn 1862, for example, a robbery at the omnibus junction at Chalk Farm was reported, involving a mother and daughter attacked while they were changing buses on their way home, having been to the Gallery of Illustration. They were waiting there to meet the young men of their family, who had been visiting some other entertainment. See also *Daily News*, 5 September 1859 on the last gallery matinee of that season, at which the 'audience was chiefly composed of ladies, and the effect produced as they all rose *en masse* when Mr and Mrs German Reed came forward was extremely brilliant'.

CONCLUSION: MEN IN BLACK

Such enthusiasm could in some circles in 1856 have been bestowed upon the popular preacher, and some of the reports of, for example, the anti-slavery and the temperance lecturers who appeared at the Exeter Hall read like accounts of twentieth-century pop-star hysteria. The success of the shows I have been discussing was partly based upon a capturing and modifying of that emotional enthusiasm, and steering it into performative channels that would not scare away the serious audience, who were afraid of any uncontrolled experience which might lead them to the bad, to the evils of drink and sexuality which they associated with the theatres. For this purpose the illusion of real life was centrally important, and hence the connection, however factitious, with the lecture imparting 'true' scientific or geographical information. The sense that Thomas German Reed and Albert Smith and even Woodin, in his last moment when he appeared in evening dress, were only presenting themselves, not some sort of pretence, was a key element in this; and Charles Dickens presented his readings to 'highly respectable' audiences including people who would have considered his performance 'an improper one if Mr Dickens had worn a fancy dress'.[51]

This was the moment, the 1850s, that consummated what has been called 'the great masculine renunciation' of colour in dress, in favour of clothing that was, in all even minimally formal situations, entirely black and white. Therefore one of the ways in which the stage seemed unreal and indeed passé was in its clinging to coloured and loudly patterned male dress, so that a comedy actor appeared on stage, and, if he were not well off, also in the street, in clothes that no one with any pretensions to style would wear. The connotations of and reasons for the wearing of black, its associations with piety but also with money and power, have been discussed at length since Weber pointed out the links between Puritanism and capitalism;[52] its significance here is in the way in which the entertainer circumvented suspicion of the illusions fostered by the stage by wearing a black dress suit, like a clergyman or any other professional gentleman.

---

[51] Newspaper report on his appearance at Preston in December 1861, quoted in Malcolm Andrews, *Charles Dickens and his Performing Selves: Dickens and the Public Readings* (Oxford University Press, 2006), p. 47.

[52] See John Harvey, *Men in Black* (London: Reaktion Books, 1995), and Elizabeth Wilson, *Adorned in Dreams: Fashion and Modernity* (London: Virago, 1985).

But of course, as men renounced colour and display, women took to paler and also brighter colours, more exhibitionism, the occupation of the maximum amount of space with skirts many yards round the hem, the opposite of the utilitarian efficiency of the dark business suit.[53] *Mrs* German Reed it was, too, who moved through an exaggerated set of personae and a differentiated set of costumes, imitating a series of other people: the actress, as ever, is the pretender. She managed to carry off the trick of making herself acceptable through her husband's non-acting, his 'genuine' and 'gentlemanly' self-presentation, and even eventually made space for him to dress up and take on other roles; but the Reeds were the top of the tree, and possibly felt to be exceptional. Even the next husband and wife team in the pecking order, Mr and Mrs Howard Paul, were more vulnerable to censure. Isabella Featherstone, Mrs Howard Paul, had a career that mirrors Priscilla Horton's, moving from starring as soubrette to leading as a respectable wife in a drawing room entertainment. Within this, she made a speciality of her shockingly life-like impersonation of the tenor Sims Reeves, a careful imitation of his voice, face and hair, and impeccable male evening dress. The feat is mentioned in most of their reviews, as a remarkable – an astonishing – and, one feels, a slightly odd phenomenon; and on at least one occasion, in 1859, she felt obliged to defend herself in the press against the 'narrow prejudices' of the 'provincial towns' where disapproval had been expressed at her refusal 'to remain within the circle of the crinoline' and her unwillingness to 'sacrifice a rare natural gift (I mean the ability to sing within the tenor range) from motives of false delicacy'.[54]

The Howard Pauls toured more than they appeared in London, though they did regular short seasons at St James's Hall. It is by no means a coincidence that the entertainers in general, including the German Reeds, had a major support base in the northern industrial centres rather than just in the West End. The new form was calculated to appeal to the powerful but often difficult to seduce businessman and his family, the serious stratum of the middle classes that was only slowly returning to the world of leisure, and their power base was outside London.[55] The

---

[53] See Alison Gernsheim, *Victorian and Edwardian Fashion, a Photographic Survey* (New York: Dover Publications, 1963/1981), for detailed calendaring of the shifts in female dress, and especially the development of the huge circle of the skirt.

[54] *Glasgow Herald*, 21 September 1859.

[55] See Louise Purbrick, 'The Bourgeois Body: Civic Portraiture, Public Men and the Appearance of Class Power in Manchester, 1838–50', in *Gender, Civic Culture and Consumerism: Middle Class Identity in Britain 180–1940*, ed. Alan Kidd and David Nicholls (Manchester University Press,

entertainer in his evening dress, visibly marking an equal, and also an intimate, real, direct relationship between speaker and audience, was to evolve into a characteristic form of the West End stage, the singer and raconteur at the piano, and to enable the development of much sophisticated musical theatre. But its impetus came at least partly from beyond the entertainment centre. This was, perhaps, one of the less than obvious ways in which a British culture that originated in Manchester and Leeds imprinted itself upon the metropolis. The new entertainers were not mere stage-players: Thomas German Reed, Albert Smith, even Adolphus Francis, wanted to be recognised as their audiences' peers; Edmund Yates, perpetually aspiring to secure middle-class status, abandoned his successful career as an entertainer, unable, I would suggest, to sustain his idea of himself as a gentleman while appearing before audiences professionally.[56] The well-known image of Macready taking his longed-for farewell of the theatre in 1851, alone in the centre of the stage at Drury Lane clad from head to toe in the prim, knife-sharp evening dress of the private gentleman, makes the point too, from the other direction. Thus one might say that Arnold's serious middle classes, rather than the gay or rowdy portion whom he considered responsible for its 'contemptible' theatre, created a vital element of the new West End.

1999), pp. 81–98 for a study of the importance of the dark suit to Manchester self-presentation in this period.
[56] See his *Reminiscences*, vol. II, p. 78.

CHAPTER 3

Bohemian domesticity: the city of the mind

The mapping and guiding of Chapters 1 and 2 moved from the material –
walking the streets – towards the conceptual – a textual negotiation of the
layers of class interpellation, the spinning and gatekeeping of the press.
These two layers tended to demonstrate that the West End is as much in
the mind as on the streets of London; it is an idea about a space, the
special and elusive place that is the goal of dreams of pleasure, of
admission or exclusion, figuring both disappointment and desire. This
third topographic take on the making of West End theatre is a final step
into spatial abstraction, exploring Bohemia, the city of the mind, where
the performances were made. It seeks to understand how the stage
community, and specifically those who wrote for performance, understood their own position in the world, and how women operated and were
understood in that imaginary sphere. I have stressed the importance of a
class-based understanding of British identity, pleasure and recreation,
with in the background Walter Benjamin's conception of the Parisian
Arcades as representing in fantastic form the collective dream consciousness of pleasure, distorted by class oppression but still a necessary basis of
human change and progress,[1] and using Raymond Williams's stratifica-
tion of culture into residual, dominant and emergent strands.[2] Twenty-
first-century ideas about class, however, are inflected by concepts of
differentiation and difference that go beyond the foundational Marxist
and post-Marxist analyses, to questions including the gendering of rank
and power. I hope the female players so far noted are evidence that
women had an important role in the economy of the West End. Here
I shall explore the psychic, and consequently the historiographic, barriers
to the recognition of that importance. The walkers in Chapter 1 were a

---

[1] See Susan Buck-Morss, 'Walter Benjamin – Revolutionary Writer (1)', *New Left Review* 1:128 (July–
August 1981), 50–75. www.newleftreview.org/?view=225 (visited 16.07.2009).
[2] Raymond Williams, *Marxism and Literature* (Oxford University Press, 1977).

woman, and a journalist; here I will look at the overlap between these two categories, not simply in terms of embodiment – there were many female writers for the periodical press – but in terms of class definition and identity conflicts for the male Victorian writer.

THE LOST LEADERS

This chapter therefore concerns the writing of plays in the context of mid-Victorian middle-class society, as London's West End developed. It begins with the curious fact that no drama that survived unquestioned in the canon of English literature through the twentieth century was written and staged in London between *A School for Scandal* in 1777 and *The Importance of Being Earnest* in 1895. Of course many successful plays *were* staged during this long century. The great melodramas of the first nineteenth-century decades are now being studied in appropriate ways and placed on a footing with the other manifestations of Romanticism. As their time passed, London theatres still often produced plays that were performed hundreds, even thousands of times, like Douglas Jerrold's *Black-ey'd Susan* (Surrey 1829). It was Macready's serious ambition to discover and encourage new dramatic writers, and if he found Robert Browning's work intractable and Bulwer-Lytton's patchy, and Thomas Noon Talfourd proved a one-play wonder, still his efforts brought him, at least in his own opinion and in the estimation of his contemporaries, several highly productive collaborations with major writers. At his farewell dinner it was said[3] that he had created a renaissance of the drama, and more than fifty new plays were admiringly laid to his account; he commanded considerable audiences over decades in the plays of, for example, the Irish dramatist Sheridan Knowles, whom he discovered and brought to London, making a hit of his *Virginius* (Glasgow 1820) and eliciting from him successes such as *The Love Chase* (Haymarket 1837). Vestris's management at Covent Garden in 1840–1 also created a new hit, by buying a draft of a play from the company actor John Brougham and getting the 19-year-old Dion Boucicault to write it up with a good part for Charles Mathews.[4] *London Assurance*, a five-act comedy in the eighteenth-century form but with a contemporary setting,

---

[3] By Bulwer-Lytton, from the chair, 1 March 1851; see Charles H. Shattuck, ed., *Bulwer and Macready: A Chronicle of the Early Victorian Theatre* (Urbana: University of Illinios Press, 1958), pp. 1–3.
[4] See Clifford John Williams, *Madame Vestris – A Theatrical Biography* (London: Sidgwick & Jackson, 1973), pp. 175–6.

launched Boucicault on a career of writing highly successful plays, some of
which might perhaps be said to have entered the canon of Irish literature,
though not without much raising of eyebrows; but his playwriting contemporaries have been comprehensively forgotten outside the academy.
Why should this be? And why did the major nineteenth-century author
who might have written great plays, Charles Dickens, give up creating
texts directly for the stage after a few early efforts, and spend the rest of his
career always hiding his wide and important stage work as performer,
director and producer, and also as writer of scenarios and characters for
the stage, behind his novels and journalism? The answer is, I think,
connected with the conflicted nineteenth-century conceptualisation of
the writer, coming to an acute crisis in the special case of the writer for
the stage.

THE HERO AS MAN OF LETTERS

At the mid-century Victorian writers were in a particularly tense relation
to the new conception of the middle classes. They had to create, in print,
an understanding of the right relation between the worlds of work and the
home, and simultaneously to negotiate their own place within these
spheres as that of slightly anomalous, but very important, men of their
times. All middle-class work was under review. In Laura Fasick's terms,
at this time 'Victorian England seems to have been particularly concerned
with ideals of honorable work (and what made work honorable), responsibility, and earnestness'.[5] Creative writing as a profession was particularly
in need of justification and definition. Sitting in one's room, making
things up, might not appear to be as earnest and responsible as many
serious callings in the public services or in business, but at the same time
its products were obviously influential as well as potentially profitable: the
burgeoning realist novel was one of the major vehicles of hegemonic class
power. As Mary Poovey has demonstrated, 'one effect of the "literary" in
this period was the textual construction of an individualist psychology ...
this process was part of the legitimation and depoliticization of capitalist
market and class relations'. She added the important further observation
that 'the definition (and defense) of the English writer's social role was
intimately involved [with] stabilizing and mobilizing a particular image
of woman, the domestic sphere, and woman's work [was] critical to all

[5] Laura Fasick, *Professional Men and Domesticity in the Mid-Victorian Novel* (Lampeter: Edwin Mellen
Press, 2003), p. 10.

three'.[6] Writing fiction was important work, then; it actively contributed to the establishment and definition of the separate spheres of home and work, women and men; but there was a status, and indeed a psychic, problem for the writers, who worked not out in the world of commerce and conquest, but at home – with the result that some of them were indeed not men at all, but anomalous, potentially troubling, working women. The writer's craft therefore became a debated site of gendered self-definition, with men self-consciously asserting the naturalness and the importance of their writing. The writer was a flashpoint for what Eve Kosofsky Sedgwick calls the 'positive and negative self-definition of an anxious and conflicted bourgeoisie'.[7]

The developing debate was memorably formulated by Carlyle in the ostensibly masculine and class terms of the distinction between leadership and trade, in his lectures 'On Heroes and Hero-Worship' delivered at the Hanover Square Rooms in May 1840. He began with the premise that 'the first and chief characteristic of a Hero' is that 'he is heartily *in earnest*'.[8] Carlyle's types of masculine leadership and virtue begin with 'the God' and 'the Prophet', and then take in Shakespeare and Dante as examples of 'the Poet', before arriving at 'the Man of Letters', 'one of the main forms of Heroism for all future ages'[9] because the printing press means that his influence reaches further than ever before. To do his heroic duty, the Man of Letters must be 'inspired': 'I say *inspired*; for what we call "originality", "sincerity", "genius", the heroic quality we have no name for, signifies that.' Such inspired sincerity is all that saves writers from '[t]hat waste chaos of Authorship by trade'.[10] Professional writing, as a 'trade', is a dangerous pitfall, whose avoidance requires heroic efforts of self-discipline on the part of artists and stern judgement from the reader. We should only accept from the poet 'the *true* Beautiful; which ... differs from the *false* as Heaven does from Vauxhall'[11] – a telling reference to the meretricious theatricality of one of London's oldest pleasure grounds.

---

[6] Mary Poovey, *Uneven Developments: The Ideological Work of Gender in Mid-Victorian England* (London: Virago, 1989), p. 89. See also James Eli Adams, *Dandies and Desert Saints: Styles of Victorian Masculinity* (Ithaca, NY: Cornell University Press, 1995), which 'examines the various ways in which male Victorian writers represent intellectual vocations as affirmations of masculine identity' (p. 2) and the 'interplay between Victorian literary forms and the social logistics of masculine self-fashioning' (p. 3).

[7] Sedgwick, *Epistemology*, p. 193.

[8] Thomas Carlyle, *On Heroes, Hero-Worship and the Heroic in History* (1840; London: Chapman & Hall, 1872), p. 171.

[9] ibid., p. 143.   [10] ibid., pp. 144, 170.   [11] ibid., p. 76.

Carlyle's lectures in the Hanover Square Rooms were intended to be
nothing like such false performances: having chosen Shakespeare as one of
his two exemplary poets, he did not mention anywhere that this poet wrote
for the stage, and seems indeed uneasy with his having written in verse. He
suggests modern writers should avoid anything that could be, or seem, so
'hollow and superfluous': 'I would advise all men who *can* speak their
thought, not to sing it; to understand that, in a serious time, among serious
men, there is no vocation in them for singing it.'[12] His modern 'man of
letters' was a writer for the periodical press, and indeed the huge growth and
importance of periodicals and serial publications of all kinds was a defining
condition of mid-century writing; and within it, though unremarked in
Carlyle's lectures, the realist novel took shape and came to command the
highest rewards and respect. Author's copyright, an issue actively pursued
since the 1830s, was still a distant hope for playwrights, but by 1844 England
had an International Copyright Act that enabled novelists to make a good,
and sometimes an opulent, living from their books. The realist novel
developed by leaps and bounds, becoming one, and not the least important,
of a new network of taxonomic, philanthropic and bureaucratic cultural
underpinnings of the modern capitalist economy.

But anxieties about writing such things were fuelled, rather than
allayed, by the possibility of making an upper-middle-class income from
the pen. With gentlemanly incomes and prominent positions at stake, the
up-and-coming novelists of the day, Dickens and Thackeray, established
writers like Bulwer Lytton, and leading journalists, locked horns over how
writing was to be understood, received and rewarded in what has become
known as the 'Dignity of Literature' debate.[13] Bulwer Lytton, who was
both a successful novelist and a much performed playwright as well as
being a landed gentleman, an MP and a conspicuous society dandy, was
perhaps the leading nineteenth-century theorist of and campaigner for the
rights and dignities of the writer, including the right to a handsome profit
from successful works.

Thackeray, like Bulwer Lytton, came from a moneyed upper
middle-class background and found himself obliged to make a living by
his pen. He, however, found the self-promotion and publicity-seeking of
the older man insufferable. Bulwer's claims on behalf of literature seemed
to Thackeray to undermine the very dignity and independence they both

[12] ibid., p. 85, emphasis original.
[13] See K. J. Fielding, 'Thackeray and the "Dignity of Literarture"' parts I and II, *TLS*, 19 September
1958, p. 536 and 26 September 1958, p. 552.

craved. He fiercely wanted to believe that 'the literary profession is not held in disrepute; nobody wants to disparage it; no man loses his social rank, whatever it may be, by practising it'. But, as K. J. Fielding has observed, a few weeks after he wrote these words in the *Morning Chronicle*, Thackeray received a sharp personal reminder of the social unacceptability of writing satirically for the press, when he was blackballed at the Athenaeum.[14] Radical contemporaries of Bulwer Lytton, such as Douglas Jerrold and younger men from less securely middle-class backgrounds such as Dickens and Edmund Yates his protégé, who became embroiled in these stand-offs in the 1860s, were more concerned with the welfare of neglected writers, whatever their social origins, and with their own need for secure professional status derived from their work. Theirs was an essentially middle-class impulse in tune with many newly organising and self-conscious professional groups at the time, such as lawyers and surgeons.

The running battle between these touchy individuals is relevant to the development of the West End stage in several different ways. The protagonists were men of letters whose own work included plays, and one of their immediate objects of charity, Sheridan Knowles, was in an indigent state despite huge success as a dramatist because of the absence of copyright protection for his work. Dickens galvanised support for the poor writer by the characteristically energetic and high-profile means of amateur dramatics. He got Bulwer Lytton to write (and Bulwer Lytton got Macready, the professional master of the stage on the brink of retirement, to critique and improve)[15] a brand new, and pertinently themed, comedy, *Not So Bad As We Seem*, about the life and times of an eighteenth-century pen-pusher. Dickens himself swaggered in the role of the rakish but good-hearted Lord Wilmot. The first performance took place in May 1851 in a specially constructed theatre within the saloon of Devonshire House, the private Piccadilly residence of the Duke of Devonshire, with the Queen and Prince Albert in the royal box on the first night. Dickens then added a farce to the bill, in which he played, opposite the dramatist Mark Lemon, 'what is called a "personation" part', – dressing in quick succession as a hydropathic doctor, an old lady and a deaf sexton.[16] The whole performance, complete with its fit-up stage, then decamped on 28 June to the Hanover Square Rooms, and their success was such that on 1 August they were still advertising 'positively the last performances'.

---

[14] Fielding, *TLS*, 19 September.
[15] See letters and a sheet of corrections reproduced in Shattuck, ed., *Bulwer and Macready*, pp. 242–4.
[16] *Times*, 28 May 1851.

On 14 May, speaking on behalf of the authors at the annual dinner of the old Royal Literary Fund at the Freemason's Tavern, Thackeray pointedly detached himself from such proceedings. He 'repudiated on the part of his brethren that pity which so many people, taking their cue from the degraded literary hacks of the days of George II, were so very much disposed to bestow upon them. "The Patron and the Jail" had alike ceased to be words of fear in the ears of the literary men of England.'[17] He made sure that everyone knew his position by elaborating on the theme in his lectures on *The English Humorists*, this time at Willis's Rooms, in May and June 1851, in which he voiced his contempt for such literary hacks as Swift, and discussed the unfortunate poverty of the 'author by profession' Oliver Goldsmith, winding up with a fierce repudiation of any such state of affairs in his own time: he proclaimed that to anyone who claimed that the man of letters is not held in high esteem today 'I say with all my might – no – no – no'.[18]

REAL MEN DON'T WRITE PLAYS

But that esteemed hero, the man of letters, could not be a writer for the stage. Thackeray emphatically did not write for the stage, and his representations of its denizens, in *Pendennis*, for example, and in the much more openly sneering picture of a stage diva and her personal relationships in the novella *The Ravenswing*, put clear blue water between himself and such low people. Dickens, on the other side of the debate, still could not come out as a man of the theatre. There is a brutally simple, but inadequate, reason one might give for this, in terms of money: Dickens did not commit himself to the stage until, with the readings from his own work, he worked out a way to make as much money by that means as he could from writing novels. But given that he did actually involve himself in the professional theatre, through the dramatisations of his work that he encouraged and sometimes directed (see below, Chapter 6), and that he also spent untold hours upon his Amateur Company, his phenomenal levels of energy and productivity would surely have allowed him to become a fully-fledged dramatist and theatre manager, had he chosen to do so, and still to have written his novels and edited journals. Many people who worked with him attested not only to his great power as an actor, but also to the demanding, meticulous nature of his stage direction, which set standards that we might well call a rigorous new

[17] *Times*, 15 May 1851.   [18] Quoted in Fielding, *TLS*, 26 September.

professionalism. But there was something in the roles of actor, director and writer for the stage that prevented him from seeing himself, or wanting others to see him, in that way, once he was successful; and that deep reluctance casts light upon other tensions and consequent occlusions in the history of the West End.

John Glavin suggests that 'Nicholas Nickleby, and his creator, refuse the refuge of the theatre' because, until the ending of the patent monopoly, only shame and humiliation could be found there. Citing Kristina Straub, Glavin notes that 'the actor's body ... entered the nineteenth-century marked as "the site of struggle among competing definitions of masculine sexual identity"' and that this was enough to deny men such as Macready the cherished status of respectability, of professionalism in an increasingly professionalised masculine social sphere. Glavin asserts that 'of course, after the monopoly's 1843 repeal, the social and psychic standing of actors changed rapidly. By the 1861 census, acting had become an official profession'[19] and could rapidly shed the stigma of sexual suspicion. There seem to me, however, to be elements in the 'exaltation and repression' of the theatrical profession in its relation to masculinity that were still important after 1843. Moreover, writers of any kind in the mid-Victorian period had to confront issues of male identity – 'manliness' – that made working on or for the stage doubly difficult. So Dickens's working involvement with actors and actresses meant that he had to present himself with great care for the boundaries of class and status, even before his separation from his wife and his commitment to a lifelong, entirely clandestine extramarital relationship with an actress.[20] The end of his marriage, and his immediate entry into the homosocial world of his young men friends, such as Sala and Wilkie Collins, in Paris and London, and then the relationship with Ellen Ternan, no doubt influenced his decision to become a reader, a stage professional, at least as much as did the 1843 Theatres Act; both the public and the private dimensions of theatrical life are relevant to the occlusion and abjection of writing for the stage in the mid century. To explore that idea further we may follow Dickens's friends and colleagues into the peculiarly mid-century world of Bohemia, where many writers, and all the people of the stage, were at home.

---

[19] Glavin, *After Dickens*, pp. 116, 87.
[20] See the brilliantly assembled story told by Claire Tomalin in *The Invisible Woman: The Story of Nelly Ternan and Charles Dickens* (Harmondsworth: Penguin, 1991).

BOHEMIA: SELLING THE CITY OF THE MIND

I dwelt in a city enchanted
And lonely, indeed, was my lot;
Two guineas a week, all I wanted,
Was certainly all that I got.
Well, somehow I found it was plenty;
Perhaps you may find it the same
If – *If* you are just five-and-twenty,
With industry, hope and an aim:
Though the latitude's rather uncertain,
And the longitude also is vague
The persons I pity who know not the city
The beautiful City of Prague!

How we laughed and we laboured together!
How well I remember, today,
Our 'outings' in midsummer weather,
Our winter delights at the play!
We were not over-nice in our dinners,
Our 'rooms' were up rickety stairs;
But if hope be the wealth of beginners,
By Jove we were all millionaires!
Our incomes were very uncertain,
Our prospects were equally vague,
But the persons I pity who know not the city
The beautiful City of Prague!
William Jeffrey Prowse[21]

The notion of a Bohemian lifestyle developed in Paris through the 1830s
and 1840s; something like it developed in London in the second of those
decades. From the beginning, 'Bohemia' was more of a notion than a new
reality, a way of presenting themselves that was created by the writers for
the newly powerful periodical press and the stage; it was a reaction to the
pressures of self-definition from which Dickens and other middle-class
men suffered. In 1845–6 the Parisian hack writer Henry Murger wrote a
series of articles about his own group of artist and writer friends for a
small periodical, the *Corsaire-Satan*. These became a volume, *Scenes from
Bohemian Life*, in 1851, but before that, in 1849, their image was spread
much more widely when Murger collaborated with a young vaudeville

[21] *Nicholas's Notes and Sporting Prophesies, with some miscellaneous poems, serious and humorous*, ed.
Tom Hood (London: Routledge, [1870]). Prowse, b. 1836, was the son of Marianne Jeffrey,
published poet and friend of John Keats. Aged only 15 he began writing for the ladies' annuals,
then the sporting and comic press in London, but died in 1870 of a lung disease.

writer, Théodore Barrière, to create a huge success at the Varieties Theatre, *The Bohemian Life*. According to Jerrold Seigel, French Bohemianism was a marker of a change in the way of life of the artist which is 'as easily summarized as it is often noticed: patronage gave way to the market'. 'The decline of aristocratic social relations meant the liberation of some who had been oppressed by them, and the emergence of a society that encouraged all who could to develop their talents.' He stresses that Bohemia was

not a realm outside bourgeois life but the expression of a conflict that arose at its very heart ... Bohemia grew up where the borders of bourgeois existence were murky and ambiguous. It was a space within which newly liberated energies were continually thrown up against the barriers being erected to contain them, where social margins were probed and tested.[22]

London's Bohemia differed from the French model. It had no clearly demarcated locations within the city as Paris had in Montparnasse and the Left Bank; the British insisted that 'the beautiful city' was a city of the mind, and their descriptions tend to invoke Shakespeare (of course) to demonstrate this, since in *A Winter's Tale* he had imagined Bohemia as having a sea coast, which the real country did not. An important function of that desubstantiation of the concept was to stave off its more bodily implications: because, for the English, the tension between Bohemia and the conventional bourgeoisie concerned gender and sexuality as much as art and freedom.

Parisian Bohemia included the notion of middle-class young men gaining sexual maturity by keeping house with 'grisettes', young women workers in the city whose pre-marital sexual openness reflected an ancient peasant morality rather than that demanded by and for the bourgeoisie. Moreover, some high-profile French writers living in this world were themselves female – George Sand, for example, achieved wide success as a journalist and novelist, living cross-dressed as a man in publicised sexual relationships with male artists. In depicting London's Bohemia (first named in print by Thackeray in *Vanity Fair*, 1847)[23] writers could make no acceptable excuse for a link between artistic freedom and sexual

---

[22] Jerrold Seigel, *Bohemian Paris: Culture, Politics and the Boundaries of Bourgeois Life, 1830–1930* (Baltimore, MD: Johns Hopkins University Press, 1986), pp. 13–15, 10–11.

[23] The popular stage had seized upon the word well before, in 1843, when many London theatres ran translations of Eugene Sue's *Les Mystères de Paris* under titles such as *The Bohemians, or The Rogues of Paris* (Stirling's Adelphi version), but this Newgate sensation drama had nothing to do with artistic middle-class rebels.

experimentation, and therefore strove to conceal or deny it completely. As discussed above, for middle-class Englishmen who wanted to be writers, class definitions were complicated by acute tensions over gender. In addition to the problem of the doubtful masculinity of the domesticated occupation of writing, they had to contend with a further class paradox around the definition of masculinity itself. Herbert Sussman asserts that 'for the early Victorians the problematization of sexuality and of manliness were conjoined' and 'manliness as *control* validated the hegemony of the bourgeoisie over what was seen through middle-class eyes as the libertinism and idleness of the gentry and the irregularity and sexual license of the working class'.[24] They described their Bohemia, therefore, as if it were a homosocial space, involving no women, whose presence would connote either the loss of respectable sexual control, or the sharing of a workspace with females who could also do this job.

There was a further gender-related issue, the question of domesticity, involved in this second prescription. While manliness meant success in competition with other men in the world of work and public endeavour, it was also felt that bourgeois masculinity included a particular relation to the domestic sphere, as the breadwinner for a home, wife and children. The concept and practice of British Bohemianism had to deal with these cross-currents. In the tricky negotiation of a place for the creative writer, therefore, I would suggest that writing for the stage became the abjected form of composition, partly at least because it was too inextricably and visibly involved with working women outside the domestic sphere. The Bohemian life, as described by the writers themselves, was a site for these conflicts of manliness, sexuality and domesticity; as such it needed to be represented as homosocial, and its vital links to the sexualised world of the theatre and self-supporting women were concealed.

British Bohemia was created in print, partly at least so that the writers could reclaim control of it and determine how their involvement there was to be read. Thackeray in his late novel *Philip* (1862) famously and sentimentally evokes the

land of chambers, billiard-rooms, supper-rooms, oysters; a land of song; a land where soda-water flows freely in the morning; a land of tin-dish covers from taverns, and frothing porter; a land of lotos-eating (with lots of cayenne pepper), of pulls on the river, of delicious reading of novels, and saunterings in many

---

[24] Herbert Sussman, *Victorian Masculinities: Manhood and Masculine Poetics in Early Victorian Literature and Art* (Cambridge University Press, 1995), p. 10 (emphasis added).

studios; a land where men call each other by their Christian names; where most are poor, and almost all are young.[25]

Young and idle, he suggests, though Jeff Prowse, the much less prominent Bohemian quoted above, insists that they 'laughed and laboured' together, sustained by 'industry, hope and an aim'. Prowse is nostalgic and sentimental too, and intent upon aligning the Bohemian life with an acceptable masculine work ethic; a harsher view is that of Robert Brough, whose barely fictionalised autobiographical novel *Marston Lynch* was the first serial in the Bohemian-run periodical *The Train*, edited by Edmund Yates.

Brough, who came to London from Manchester very young to seek his fortune as a satirical writer and had several theatrical successes, collaborating with his brother William, tells in this novel a sorry tale of his hero's early lionisation followed a sudden drop out of fashion and into illness and near starvation; the author himself died before the serial was complete. Sala, introducing the unfinished novel in volume form in 1860, hastens to excuse the managers of the theatres from any blame in Brough's own fall – he 'never received anything but kind and generous treatment' from the likes of Buckstone and the Keeleys, Sala asserts, and the only problem was that they could not be for ever producing new pieces, nor poor Brough writing them. But Marston Lynch's Bohemia is a place of conflict and self-loathing:

The inhabitants of Bohemia may be characterised generally as men with high artistic or literary aspirations who cannot succeed in life. The causes of their non-success may be infinite. The Bohemian may be indolent, or vicious, or ignorant, or simply incapable ... He may be a high-art dramatist, believing in his powers to resuscitate the Elizabethan drama (the Bohemian has generally faith in his own powers for achieving something or other that is not wanted) – which is as dead as Queen Elizabeth herself, and no one wishes to be startled by the apparition of its ghost – and unable to devote his mind to the supply of any real literary want of the day, such as novel, essay, or leading article ...

The Bohemian may simply be an ambitious ass, willing to turn his hand to any thing, but capable of accomplishing nothing satisfactorily; or an unfortunate waif or stray, thrown by accident on to the uncongenial soil, without strength and skill to wrest from it even such bitter and scanty fruits as it is capable of producing; or he may be a man of genius, with a tendency to fly off at a tangent from his existing engagements in pursuit of some new experiment of living – or, simply, to get drunk and forget them.

[25] Collected edition, 2 vols. (London: Smith, Elder, 1879), vol. 1, p. 158.

There is another phase of Bohemianism, an exceptional one, it is true, which is, perhaps, the most deplorable of all – the literary Bohemian endowed with great and available general powers (what the French so happily characterised by the simple word *facilité*), who has sold himself into slavery, who writes in violation of his conscience and instincts, for the sake of a little ready money. His extrication from the gulf is far more hopeless than that of his needier and less capable brethren, who have still some sustaining principle and have not forfeited all hope of self-respect. Respectable people, shaking their heads, will deplore that such a man, with his vast talents and abundant earnings, should lead the life he does – namely, one of utter improvidence and dissipation. But respectable people – perfectly satisfied with the propriety of their own pursuits, whatever they may be – do not know that this man's intellectual perceptions of what is right and wrong make him regard his exercise of those talents, for which they envy and admire him, with loathing, and the money it brings him as the wages of sin . . . He is at war with society, and usually dies with his weapons in his hands.[26]

This remarkable denunciation of the Bohemian life circles round the central paradox about the relation between art and commerce: the man of letters is either inevitably poverty-stricken, because he creates things no one wants to buy, or, worse still, he is feted and well paid for what he makes, but that proves to him that he is misusing his gifts. Genius must be unrecognised. Good Bohemians are never successful. Brough seems to say that the ambition to write five-act verse dramas is rightly a failure because it does not accommodate itself to the market; but, if an artist knows what will sell and does make money, then he has mere facility and is prostituted and self-betrayed. The relationship of money and art is an embarrassment. One of the problems for theatrical creativity at this period is that putting on shows costs money: by the 1850s, as the scenic stage developed, a great deal of money. The playwright could not simply rise above base considerations of cash; and the actor, who generally accepts that his success can be measured by how much people are prepared to pay for his work, still struggled for middle-class respectability and dignity. It is striking that when Edmund Yates undertook the editing-down of Anne Mathews's four-volume biography of her husband Charles, he cut the many extracts from Mathews's letters in which he had reported to his wife upon his earnings while on tour.[27] To the previous generation a good house meant a good reception and this was made tangible in a

[26] Robert Brough, *Marston Lynch: His Life and Times, his Friends and Enemies, his Victories and Defeats, his Kicks and Halfpence*, with a Memoir by G. A. Sala (London: Ward and Lock, 1860), pp. 315–18.
[27] See Anne Mathews, *The Life and Correspondence of Charles Mathews, the Elder, Comedian, by Mrs. Mathews*, a new edition, abridged and condensed by Edmund Yates (London, 1860).

very welcome fat fee; the Bohemian writer would rather represent it as an artistic triumph alone.

Writing for the stage was certainly ill paid.[28] Yates betrays at least one of his reasons for chafing as a tradesman of the stage early in his *Recollections and Experiences* when he contrasts the amount a writer could earn for a play in the 1850s, with what was being paid as he wrote, in 1884. At mid century, he says, even a leading playwright like Buckstone received only '£70 for a three-act drama, and £10 for the provincial rights for twelve months'. By contrast, in 1884 a friend confides that he has so far grossed 'within £150 of a total of *ten thousand pounds*' for a play, with royalties still rolling in 'at the rate of £100 a week!'[29] There is an interesting ambiguity in Yates's exclamatory naming of the very high modern figures, as if they too strike him as somehow not quite right. Had he known about it, he might have found food for further thought in the information that Dickens had received an advance of £6,000, eventually netting £10,000, for a novel, *Our Mutual Friend*, in 1865.[30]

At the humble, Bohemian end of the scale, E. L. Blanchard lived by his pen at the starvation rate of around £130 a year in the 1840s and 1850s. He started writing for performance as a teenager at the rate of 10s an act for a melodrama,[31] but by the time he was 20 expected £1 for a song – though he often had to wait for it, or chase the purchaser – and eventually could make up to £30 for a whole one-man show, as he did from the very successful Woodin. For years he wrote all the dramatic criticism for *The Era* for a few shillings a week, rising to as much as 15s for the long 'Easter Entertainments' column. One day in 1853 he met C. L. Barnett, the Adelphi stock playwright, who said he could 'scarcely get bread. Writing plays is all very well, but I only wish a widow with a little money would turn up. I'd marry her and open a shop, and sell cooked pork.' His enthusiastic description of the utility and longevity of pork, in all its forms from hot and cold slices through sausages and faggots down to the condemned dry remains ground up for a seasoning, has something of Dickens's whimsical but seriously disapproving characterisation of Crummles in *Nicholas Nickleby*. Crummles too paid the writer in

---

[28] See John Russell Stephens, *The Profession of the Playwright: British Theatre 1800–1900* (Cambridge University Press, 1992), which suggests (pp. 48–9) a direct correlation between the impoverishment of dramatic literature and the low prices paid for stage writing at mid-century – as if it were self-evident that the dramatist had (and has) a right to live from his pen alone.

[29] Yates, *Recollections and Experiences*, vol. 1, p. 34 (emphasis original).

[30] John Sutherland, *Victorian Novelists and Publishers* (London: Athlone Press, 1976), p. 42.

[31] Blanchard, *Life*, vol. 1, pp. 27–8.

shillings, and deployed the resulting entertainments as a commodity, packaged and repackaged to abuse the taste of a gullible public. No widow or little shop materialised for Barnett, who ended his days in the workhouse.[32]

Since the Bohemian lived in such a conflicted relationship to money, it would seem that he would be bound to fail at the other middle-class test, that of being a provider for domesticity. But Brough's denunciation prefaces an incident in the novel which takes a quite different line in attempting to tackle that problem, flipping from bitter self-reproach to saccharin sentiment, wish-fulfilment and self-justification. After his initial theatrical successes, Marston and his young wife Lucy are living in Cecil Street, off the Strand. He has been editing and writing a satirical journal and has consequently antagonised all the literary world. Lucy has a baby; the journal ceases publication. Marston 'finished his five-act comedy in a hurry' but finds that the theatre manager whose favourite actress he has criticised in his journal leads the rest of them in rejecting his work. He falls seriously ill. Lucy is alone in London, cut off from her family, and cannot appeal to Marston's friends because she is afraid of them, their drunkenness, oaths, incessant smoking, and their unorthodox views about politics and the Church; but four of them turn up. Dr Nusscracker the foreign-language teacher and 'red republican' ministers to Marston's brain fever, while Markworth, an educated 'young man of good family' whose father lost his fortune by speculation and shot himself, and who therefore scratches a bare living by his talents as a writer – a vocation he cannot abide – immediately sits down and fulfils all Marston's commissions for translations and journalism. Mr Walrus '(the distinguished dramatist, poet, essayist, caricaturist, and, in his opinion, vocalist and actor)' bleeds his rich uncle for money until the publishers pay up, and the drunken 23-year-old painter Clough is 'called, from the easel and brushes he loathed, to run errands, make beds, wash invalids, and nurse babies; and he was supremely happy'. '"What an excellent family man you would make, Mr Clough"' Lucy exclaims, as he miraculously quiets the baby by walking him in and out of all the pubs in the Strand.[33]

The most striking aspect of these fictional Bohemians, then, when they are actually personified rather than theorised about, is their compassion – their affectionate fellow-feeling. This is expressed through their gender-challenging, all-embracing domesticity: like men, they bring in food, invoke rich relations and settle down to work and provide income, and

---

[32] ibid., pp. 108–9.   [33] Brough, *Marston Lynch*, pp. 321–2, 327, 326.

like women they nurse the sick and look after the weak – both the baby and the helpless wife Lucy. Brough has Lucy become 'an absolute little queen of Bohemia, without knowing it' her plight having called up all the latent 'tenderness and pity'[34] of the rough male group. The reader is invited to condescend and to know better than her as she puzzles over what is going on. The conventional blindness of her judgement of the Bohemians – she remains horrified by their manners – is never allowed to be modified by her experience of their actions. The patronising infantilisation to which the author subjects her is one of the ways in which the Bohemian writers cope with their own feminisation, their abject position as impoverished writers within their homosocial world. As Adams has it, their type of Victorian masculinity has to cope with 'social and economic stresses' that lead them to lay a powerful emphasis upon 'the domination of women'.[35]

Bohemian men are made to enact both sides of the domestic couple in many more of these novels – one might cite David Copperfield exercising his storytelling powers to woo and placate the hyper-masculine Steerforth, Thackeray's aspiring and silly young Pendennis kept afloat by the gruffly cynical writer Warrington, or Lewes's poetic Percy Ranthorpe writing his play while living under the wing of bluff, handsome medic Harry Cavendish who frequents the Cyder Cellars but has 'sensibility' which makes him beat a costermonger who is cruel to a donkey.[36] All these odd couples and communities of friends find the domestic ideal is too strong to reject: British Bohemian authors do not wish to construct the life they describe as one of unredeemed squalor, nor be seen to rely upon prostitutes and grisettes, as their Parisian counterparts are allowed to do. So they take on and share out the feminine attributes amongst themselves, recreating domesticity, depriving any women in their sphere of even that degree of agency.

ROLLING LOGS AND STARING OUT OF WINDOWS: WEST END CLUBS

The Bohemian appropriation of the domestic sphere is not only fictional. It can also be discovered in the accounts Victorian writers give of their real-life associations, especially in clubs. Theatrical clubs, a simple

[34] ibid., p. 329.   [35] Adams, *Dandies and Desert Saints*, p. 3.
[36] G. H. Lewes, *Ranthorpe*, 1847; Thackeray, *Pendennis*, 1848–50; Dickens, *David Copperfield*, 1849–50.

necessity to a profession which needs to conduct its personal and social life after the playhouses close, which in the eighteenth and nineteenth centuries could mean the small hours of the morning, have been in existence time out of mind. But the mid nineteenth century was a high point in the creation of co-operative social clubs for the middle-class man. The new clubs went beyond the occasional meetings of the old dining clubs, to providing a social space and daily facilities which enabled the participants to enjoy service, food and accommodation more cheaply than they as individuals could possibly have afforded: a kind of 'experiment in applying co-operative principles to upper middle class life'.[37] Christopher Kent, the historian of the phenomenon, suggests[38] that they came into existence in London because the city lacked Paris's café culture for leisure and meeting with friends; the significant difference is, of course, the British assertion of the propriety of such places by the exclusion of women. Through the club, therefore, men appropriated domesticity, creating a home from home that was often felt to be more comfortable than the female-dominated space of the private drawing room; a simple table and a social fireside where they could make the rules to suit themselves. A man sought to mix with his own kind in such an institution; and the Bohemian writer or artist separated himself from the bourgeois, not least in the degree of informality, cosiness and at-home familiarity – domestication – he liked in his clubs.

Bohemian clubs picked up the late-night theatrical clients, and also came to cater for journalists who required a place to gather and, importantly, to work late in the evening for the next day's paper. Even the famously exclusive and solemn Athenaeum was founded with the intention of serving 'as a rendezvous for literary men and artists',[39] but the list of Bohemian clubs is normally headed by the Garrick, founded in 1831 with the express intention of mixing theatrical and musical artists with gentlemen, in a suite of upstairs rooms in King Street, Covent Garden. Like the Athenaeum, it took the usual trajectory of the successful gentleman's club, steadily up-market, especially after it moved to its present much grander premises. The Savage Club was founded in 1857 by 'a little band of authors' wishing to escape the 'chilling splendour of the modern club', and it was Robert Brough, author of Marston Lynch, who named it

[37] Kent, 'Whittington Club', 32.
[38] 'British Bohemia and the Victorian Journalist', Australasian Victorian Studies Journal 6 (2000), 25–35, 30.
[39] Christopher Kent, 'The Idea of Bohemia in Mid-Victorian England', Queen's Quarterly 80 1973, 360–9, 363.

after the frequently drunken and destitute eighteenth-century writer.[40] Older, humbler institutions survived alongside these new foundations. Evans's song and supper rooms was only a couple of doors away from the first premises of the Garrick, and was not even a club, having no membership fee, but according to Clement Scott 'no club room' was ever warmer or more comfortable 'after the play of a winter's night' than the 'bright fireside in the picture room at Evans's' where 'you could sit up chatting and smoking until three or four o'clock in the morning' and, he says, expect to meet everyone from Bob Keeley to Dickens and Thackeray.[41] Yates says that before his own time there was a Cyder Cellar Club, held in that pub off the Strand, which was followed up in 1852 by the Fielding Club, founded 'in consequence of the impossibility of getting supper at the Garrick, or, indeed, of infusing anything like liveliness into that temple, after midnight'.[42] It took over the premises of an old tavern called Offley's in Henrietta Street, Covent Garden.

There were other old and unpretentious theatre taverns in the district. E. L. Blanchard's unhappy married life and desperate hand-to-mouth career as a writer for and about the stage meant he frequented the Bohemian clubs more or less daily. He describes the Wrekin, a tavern in Broad Court which links Drury Lane and Bow Street. There in an earlier time the 'Catamerans', who included Sheridan, the Kembles, Mathews, Morton, Monk Lewis and all the rest of the Covent Garden and Drury Lane elite, had assembled. Subsequent theatrical and literary generations also held their clubs at the Wrekin. Douglas Jerrold belonged to one called the Mulberry which required members to write a paper about Shakespeare to be admitted. Miss Huddart, Phelps's business partner in the lease of Sadler's Wells who was briefly a West End manager herself (see Chapter 5) had a husband called Warner who was licensee of the Wrekin, where his business partner, 'a blythesome widow, bearing the unromantic name of Browne', established 'the Rationals' club to which most of the actors at Covent Garden and Drury Lane belonged. Hemmings of the Haymarket took it over and kept the place going as a house of call for the press and the stage. He died in 1849 and the leading Bohemians migrated to the Bedford Head in Maiden Lane – a short walk away across Covent Garden Piazza – and became the Bedford Club, which quarrelled with itself (in what might be called a rather emotional,

[40] Andrew Halliday, ed., *The Savage Club Papers* (London: Tinsley Brothers, 1867), pp. ix–x.
[41] Scott, *Drama of Yesterday and Today*, vol. 1, p. 340.
[42] Yates, *Recollections*, vol. 1, pp. 235–6.

indeed feminised, fashion) and then reformed, calling itself the Re-Union, which met three nights a week.[43] In 1859 Re-Union members – or by another account Savage Club members who found some of the 'ultra-Bohemian' members there objectionable – formed the Arundel, in 'two or three rooms' of a building on Arundel Street off the Strand. They moved to Salisbury Street, Strand in 1861, to a riverside mansion where their billiard room/dining room was on the ground floor and above was a beautiful old room with views along the Thames that accommodated smoking, grog-making on the fire, good conversation and drunken teasing, by such as Edward Murray 'the witty brother' of two minor London actors, 'who pretended to be Eve, in the corner of the room, whilst [an elderly solicitor called] Horsley grovelled on his stomach across the dirty floor in the character of the Serpent tempting Eve'. It was a night haunt, both for work – the writing of reviews – and pleasure – the gossip and 'shop' that was talked there; and Clement Scott waxes lyrical about 'exquisite day dawns on the river', the 'first pure bursts of light that found the grand old room of the Arundel still occupied'. The rule was that the last man to leave put out the gas and locked the doors.[44]

All this convivial activity was, of course, more than that, and more than a substitute for staying at home with the wife. The club or tavern was the workshop and office of some writing members, and the matrix of the working practice for them all. The nightly talk included the concocting of ideas for periodicals and pantomimes, the exchange of information about what writing work was available, the passing on of commissions when a member had work and wanted leisure, or was too ill to do it; they invented journals and farces, and helped each other out with loans or introductions to powerful editors and managers. Here is a hands-on, indeed hand-to-mouth version of the social practice that underpinned Victorian business as described by Davidoff and Hall.[45] They see the public sphere working through homosocial clubland as one of the reasons that active involvement in work and the creation of wealth was impossible for ladies, who could not go where the deals were struck, and had no

[43] Information is drawn from Blanchard's 'Licensed Victuallers, their Manners, and their Parlours' in *The Town*, 20 April 1839, quoted at length in Scott, *Drama of Yesterday and Today*, vol. 1, pp. 312–17, and his own commentary pp. 307–12.

[44] Scott, *Drama of Yesterday and Today*, vol. 1, pp. 332–6; a circumstantial but partly contradictory account of the Savages, supplied to him by Lionel Brough, appears in the footnotes of Scott's edition of Blanchard's *Life*, vol. 1, pp. 182–3.

[45] Leonore Davidoff and Catherine Hall, *Family Fortunes: Men and Women of the English Middle Class 1780–1850* (London: Hutchinson, 1987), p. 428 and passim.

access to the groups who raised capital. But in the theatre, capital was cultural and corporeal and women were partially its possessors for that reason. The writers justifying the Bohemian life leave them out; but they must have been there, in some way or other, if only as objects of transaction. I think they were in fact very much more than that. Female agency has been obscured by the urgent demands of masculine identity formation in the accounts I have so far cited; but the theatrical/Bohemian public sphere differed, I would argue, from the closed all-male world of bourgeois business, precisely in its responsiveness to female importance – even where that response is to seek to appropriate or deny the power to which it is reacting.

BOHEMIAN GIRLS?[46]

W. M. Thackeray, a leading Bohemian in his younger days, paints a somewhat class- and gender-hostile picture of the women who were involved in the performance world, and who were to be met with in the theatres, taverns and concert-rooms. His picture of them is as helpless pawns in the hands of lower-middle-class men who use them for their own profit. La Fotheringay, with whom Pendennis falls in love, but who is actually dense and vulgar, and manipulated by the raffish Costigan, is the best-known example, but he tells the same story at much greater length in the short novel *Ravenswing*, which tells of Miss Crump, whose antecedents are a flunkey who has retired to keep a public house and Morgiana Budge, 'so well known to the admirers of the festive dance on the other side of the water as Miss Delancy' who still has the entrée to all the theatres and ambition for her daughter as a singer:

the dear girl sang with very considerable skill, too, for she had a fine loud voice, which, if not always in tune, made up for that defect by its great energy and activity; and Morgiana was not content with singing the mere tune, but gave every one of the roulades, flourishes, and ornaments as she heard them at the theatres by Mrs Humby, Mrs Waylett, or Madame Vestris. The girl had a fine black eye like her mamma, a grand enthusiasm for the stage, as every actor's child will have, and, if the truth must be known, had appeared many and many a time at the theatre in Catherine Street.[47]

[46] Balfe's *The Bohemian Girl* was one of Bunn's successes at Drury Lane in 1843, and the Adelphi borrowed the name for a play. The opera has a gypsy central character and an exotic setting.
[47] W. M. Thackeray, 'Men's Wives: The Ravenswing', in *Ballads and Tales* (London: Smith, Elder, 1869), pp. 239, 240.

For Thackeray the physical talents and attractions descending from mother to daughter are distasteful, even dangerous, especially to the men ensnared by them in the louche and vulgar world of the stage. As Auerbach has it, 'a fear of female energy coursed through right-thinking Victorians'.[48] Thackeray makes their alluring world full of upstart trades-men, despicable and idle half-gentlemen, mercenary managers and lying pressmen, all living in the half-light of gambling clubs and back-street public houses and circling the questionable talents of women like the Ravenswing, who may be personally innocent but whose influence is destructive, if they are young, and their power malign when they are older.

   Brough's Lucy Lynch is not shown with this barbed hostility, but she has no power, is not an actress or a writer herself, and she entirely fails to understand the creative world into which she is thrown by her husband; the part she plays for the Bohemians is confined to that of mascot, a cherished talisman of domestic values beyond their grasp – despite their demonstrated domesticity. The writers who depict the Bohemian world in fiction and in memoirs have an investment in suppressing the presence of women, both to fend off bourgeois suspicion of their respectability and to bolster the essential masculinity of themselves as writers. Professional skill must be claimed as masculine. Moreover they habitually, in the works of fiction they produce, write weakness and incapacity into women by their gallant and patronising representations of them. One of the most extreme instances of this is the work of Mark Lemon, whose farces and journalism frequently include very weak, silly women whom we are expected chival-rously to laugh at and to love. An instance is his farce *The Ladies' Club* (Olympic 1841), where they assert themselves by instituting a club, because their menfolk are always out at their clubs, and vote for various measures, including the promotion of the rights of women, by means of coloured balls of cotton placed in a reticule. It was a successful play, quite often revived, exciting much mirth, especially when the leading role was taken by the 25-year-old Mrs Stirling, who was to become a famous after-dinner speaker at annual meetings of the Theatrical Fund, always answering the toast on behalf of 'the Ladies'. Lemon was lucky in his writing career, largely because he was in on the beginnings of *Punch*, but he was also supported by the professional successes of the women in his family. He married a sister of Emma Romer, one of the leading sopranos of her day in English Opera. His wife's cousins Annie and Elizabeth Romer married the brothers Brough; they too were successful stage

---

[48] Nina Auerbach, *Ellen Terry, Player in her Time* (London: J. M. Dent, 1987), p. 105.

singers. None of this female competence and high earning power is apparent in Lemon's writing, nor in Robert Brough's.[49]

UPPER BOHEMIA – THE MID-VICTORIAN SALON

London's Bohemian fiction writers, I have suggested, were very disinclined to reveal that women were a presence, even an important force, in their artistic/domestic world. There are more references to influential women in accounts of the real-life drawing room meetings of ladies who were able to spend their own or their husbands' money on regularly entertaining an artistic circle of guests; but these tend to be disapproving. Lady Blessington presided over such a meeting at Gore House in Kensington in the 1830s, and the cream of literary society was to be met with there: besides a variety of titled gentlemen – without their wives – Dickens, Lytton, Thackeray and Macready are all recorded amongst the guests. This was 'upper Bohemia' – Lady Blessington was not visited by respectable ladies, and the money for her entertaining eventually proved to be nothing but a mountain of debt; such doings smacked of idleness and luxury, the kind of association with self-interested patronage and sexual favours in which the middle-class writers did not wish to be implicated. It was particularly important, however, to the money-hungry theatre world, and had existed there long before the notion of Bohemia took hold. The culture of patronage made the theatres, the opera house and especially the green-rooms the haunts of titled idleness; it continued long after the mid century and was later institutionalised and sentimentalised in the Gaiety Girl and the notion of the 'Naughty Nineties'. The writers of the 1850s do not record the connection between theatre and salon as central to Bohemia. Dickens was greatly displeased when Sala wrote a piece for *Household Words* about these people which slipped into the journal while Dickens was away in Paris.[50]

But such patronesses and the gatherings they facilitated were still important in the artistic world, after the patronage culture had ostensibly given way to market relations, and it is in accounts of the salon that theatrical women can most easily be seen. Eliza Lynn Linton moved to London aged 23 in 1845, made an early success with two novels and

[49] Both Sala and Yates conflate Lemon's wife with her sister Emma, but obituaries in *The Era*, 19 April 1868 for Robert Romer, and 12 April 1874 for Emma Almond, make clear the web of relationships.
[50] P. D. Edwards, *Dickens's 'Young Men': George Augustus Sala, Edmund Yates and the World of Victorian Journalism* (Aldershot: Ashgate, 1997), p. 16.

became the first woman to hold a salaried position on the *Morning Chronicle*, before quarrelling with the editor in 1848 – a typical trajectory of the Bohemian writer, despite her gender. She recorded such a salon patroness in her disguised autobiography *The Adventures of Christopher Kirkland* published in 1875. Mrs Hulme was a composite, she claimed, of women she had known in London in the 1840s and 1850s.

The people who crowded Mrs Hulme's unaired and undecorated drawing-room were, to say the least of it, oddly mixed. Among good, steady, high-nosed folk, with whom conventional propriety was as sacred as the Decalogue and the religion of white kid gloves that for which they had the most practical respect, were to be found seedy foreigners who had no investments outside their sharpened wits; obscure artists whom the Academy rejected and the picture-dealers would not endorse; shabby literati, said to be capable of great things but achieving only small ones, and living by methods unknown to men of letters in the mass; handsome women, with invisible husbands and curiously constant male friends; unengaged actresses, whose jewels, fine dresses and pretty little broughams did not suffer from their enforced want of work; and every shade and kind of Bohemianism extant ...
    Her evenings were singularly pleasant. There was always good music by professionals, for whom this was a kind of unpaid and unfruitful advertisement. Sometimes there was an impromptu charade; or a pretty aspirant gave the walking scene of Lady Macbeth, or Juliet on the balcony, as a proof of her powers – if only that stout sleek impresario in the huge white waist-coat and heavy golden chain would make her the leading lady at so much the week. Or a clever imitator reproduced Buckstone, or O. Smith, Paul Bedford or Webster, Wright or Liston, Farren, 'Little Munden', or Robson, to the life, and the stock catch-words 'brought down the house' as at the real thing ... And always there was plenty of wit and laughter, with a subtle suspicion of garlic and tobacco, and an ever-present sense of hunger and impecuniosity.

Here is the group Brough simplifies and fictionalises, but without his excision of theatrical women. The actresses are at work here, networking: they are seen to be somewhat vainly but nevertheless actively in pursuit of jobs, connections, notice. It is striking that Linton recalls the 'high-nosed folk' as willing to be present, and amused by the social expression of the talents of the theatricals, despite the obvious transgressions of the actresses and indeed the hostess. It amuses the by then conservative author, looking back in 1875, to contemplate the hypocrisy of the 1840s, which comforted itself that Mrs Hulme

had lived a great deal abroad, where it was supposed she had adopted her loose ways and put off more than her English stays. And the pernicious influence of all that bad foreign example to which she had been subjected was her excuse with those who could not approve yet would not renounce. Thus, nothing worse was said of her, by even the strictest of the Pharisees who consorted with her, than: 'What a pity it is that Mrs Hulme knows such very odd people! She is really too kind-hearted and indiscriminate!'[51]

There were several prominent upper Bohemian salons: Little Holland House, for example, in Holland Park in the heart on London, presided over by Sara, Mrs Princep, sheltered the Pre-Raphaelite painters and the beautiful Louisa Herbert. Ellen Terry was brought there at 16, as bride and model for the elderly artist G.H. Watts; she fled three years later, back to her work on stage.[52] Edmund Yates records the less rarefied atmosphere of Mrs Milner Gibson's house, where she 'presided over the miscellaneous company' in the 1850s that extended from Louis Blanc and Mazzini to leading theatre families like the Keans, the Wigans, even Mrs Dickens and Mrs Proctor, as well as a gaggle of Radical MPs and hungry foreign exiles.[53]

(BOHEMIAN) FAMILIES (OF CHOICE)

In 1899 Clement Scott, writing, of course, from the nostalgic, masculine point of view, gives us a more mundane sociability in the lives of Bohemian theatricals of both genders, and makes their working society seem more normal, less transgressive of bourgeois family values. Writing about the moment of his own entry into this world, around 1860, he speaks of

The great acting families, the Mathews, the Keeleys, the Farrens, the Vinings, [who] formed a little colony of their own down Brompton way ... where they lived unpretentious, unostentatious and hardworking lives, keeping themselves to themselves as humble citizens when off the stage, like sensible people as they were ... they had their clubs of course, and the leading lights of the profession belonged to the Garrick, where they might be found sometimes in the afternoon, or, with their coats off, playing bowls at Kilpatrick's, in Covent Garden; but domesticity was very dear to one and all of them.[54]

The 1851 census shows that this is factually true, insofar as these well-known theatricals did indeed live in Brompton. Their dear domesticity was, however, by no means as rosy as Scott implies. Charles James Mathews and his wife Eliza Vestris kept house at Green Lawn in

[51] Eliza Lynn Linton, *The Autobiography of Christopher Kirkland* (1885), transcribed, encoded and proofed by W. Charles Morrow, ed. Perry Willett for the Victorian Women Writers Project Library, Library Electronic Text Resource Service (LETRS), Indiana University, Bloomington, pp. 38–42.
[52] See Auerbach, *Ellen Terry*, pp. 78–131.   [53] Yates, *Recollections*, vol. I, pp. 252–3.
[54] Scott, *Drama of Yesterday and Today*, vol. I, pp. 428–9.

Brompton Road for an extended family of teenagers belonging to her sister Louisa, whose husband James Anderson was a malicious and self-seeking witness against the Mathewses in 1843 when they were declared bankrupt. Only a few doors away lived Benjamin Webster and his long-time, but unofficial, partner Celeste Elliot, whose relation to the Head of Household is entered as 'widow'; in Brompton Square live the Keeleys, an orthodox family unit of parents and two daughters, but a few doors away are William Farren and his *soi-disant* wife, whose preference for Farren over her actual husband Faucit traumatised the childhood of her impeccably respectable daughter Helen, actress and later personal friend of Queen Victoria: in the 1840s Helen was living with them in Brompton when Sala's mother taught her French for free, presumably out of compassion.[55]

These miscellaneous instances of the real complexity of family and social relations are not perhaps as significant as the personal myth pro-mulgated in Clement Scott's account of a social group to which he belonged as a young man in 1860, just setting out on a career in theatrical journalism. He is seeking, in this book of his old age, to pass on his understanding of the way in which he and his generation changed theatre for the better. The example he offers shows that he felt the Bohemian combination of domesticity and professionalism generated theatrical art; the family of choice, and the generosity and mutual support of a talented circle, with its unquestioning if often tacit inclusion of women as equal partners, provides him with an ideal. He begins with the assertion that his office colleague Tom Hood, hard-working journalist and civil servant, not a playwright nor even much of a playgoer, should be given some of the credit for the creation of the marvel that was the Prince of Wales's under the Bancrofts. Hood was young and poor in the early 1860s, but he conceived of a 'very humble literary salon' held, with the aid of 'his good-natured and enthusiastic wife', every Friday, 'with a plain old-fashioned supper of cold roast beef, salad, bread and cheese, potatoes in their jackets, and whatever we wanted to smoke or drink within reason'. Here the 'staunch determined "pals"' met, away from 'the alluring cafés of the Haymarket' and the casinos and dancing rooms, to 'discuss the books we had read, or the plays we had seen, to hear good music, to crack jokes, to tell good stories and to plan out papers and periodicals' for which they had no capital. They were the archetype of the Bohemian family circle, and, in Scott's phrase, they 'rolled logs' for each other. 'When

---

[55] *Life and Adventures of George Augustus Sala*, 2 vols., 2nd edn (London: Cassell, 1895) vol. 1, p. 58.

Tom Robertson could not do his "Theatrical Lounger", in the dear old *Illustrated Times*, he handed it over to [W. S.] Gilbert; when Gilbert was too busy he passed it on to me; when I wanted a holiday, the *Sunday Times* ... was the perquisite of Gilbert.'[56] What he does not say here, but his wife reveals in her memoir after his death, is that she too was part of this circle, and when Scott became dramatic critic to the *Daily Telegraph* in 1871 she stepped into his place and wrote a regular column for the magazine *Truth*.[57]

But Scott does quite ungrudgingly reveal the leading part played by a woman of the theatre, Marie Wilton, in the theatrical renaissance he felt was set rolling by groups like the Hoods' dinner companions. Their regular meetings, which read like an extension of college life, included a Pembroke friend of Hood's called Fletcher, who was married to Marie Wilton's sister. So they were all excited when Marie Wilton and H. J. Byron took on the old Queen's Theatre, to replicate the programmes they had been involved in as leading player and writer at the Strand theatre. He describes Wilton's 'diplomatic' and skilful company management, collecting the best of the Strand actresses and adding provincial hopefuls, including Squire Bancroft, destined 'to be the right hand of Marie Wilton, as her husband, in her projected stage reforms' and 'by his own merit and modesty' and 'tact, far-sightedness and equable temper' to rise with her to the top of the tree. The writer Byron dropped out, so the 'plucky little woman was virtually stranded' and chose first to marry Bancroft, who loved her from his boyhood (nothing is said of whether she loved him) and was 'a first-class man of business'. Then she turned to Tom Hood's salon, and plucked out her winning card – the dramatist Robertson.

Seldom were two artistic minds so admirably brought into sympathy. Robertson had a profound belief in the genius of the actress; Marie Bancroft not only was enthusiastic about Robertson's talents, but had the great gift of being able to draw out, and encourage, the best points of his sensitive and affectionate temperament, ever alive to work, but deadened a little with the rough treatment of the world which had not dealt too kindly with him. These two were bound to work well together.[58]

Scott makes it quite clear that the Hoods' guests were a family of choice, and that the journalist/theatrical group meshed with their families by blood and marriage, as well as the college friends like Fletcher, across any

[56] Scott, *Drama of Yesterday and Today*, vol. 1, pp. 479–82.
[57] Mrs Clement Scott, *Old Days in Bohemian London* (London: Hutchinson & Co., n.d.), p. 27.
[58] Scott, *Drama of Yesterday and Today*, vol. 1, pp. 482–8.

possible gender boundaries; his assertion about the working partnership between Marie Wilton/Bancroft and Tom Robertson is notably
even-handed in its acknowledgement of the woman's power, even though
he wishes to stress that her managerial gifts are of a feminine kind – the
ability to bring out the best in a man.

When one begins to look, other powerful theatrical women can be
seen, either clearly or between the lines, in other Bohemian accounts of
their own working lives. George Augustus Sala is not ashamed of his
origins as grandson of an opera impresario, godson of one of Dora
Jordan's daughters, Lady Fitzclarence. He is proud of his mother as a
working woman of the theatre – she sang Countess Almaviva to Vestris's
Susannah at Covent Garden in 1827. Thrown on her own resources by her
husband's death, she raised her sons by teaching singing in the Italian
manner to the daughters of the nobility, and drawing room behaviour to
young officers of the Household Guards at her London salon. 'In the days
of her early matronhood,' Sala says, 'I can only, of course, remember her
as something majestic, and to me at times positively awful.'[59]

Reporting upon the Bohemian world of London became something of
a specialism for Sala, between his wild adventures to report upon more
far-flung exotic places, and he never distanced himself from it, as did the
more typically embarrassed witness, Edmund Yates. Yates begins his
Memoirs with the people he remembers from his childhood in the 1830s
as coming to his parents' home, when they were managing the Adelphi, to
'that queer little private house over the theatre'. Dramatists including
Miss Mitford and Miss Pardoe came to offer plays with good parts in
them for his mother; she was the main drawing card of the Adelphi and
presided there over a dinner table that included the elder Mathews and
most other leading players of the day. He recounts a story in which she
put down the aggressive wit and practical joker Theodore Hook by a swift
and crushing response to a snobbish remark from him to a neighbour at
the table about the temperature of her claret.

Edmund's childhood memories also include finding visiting giants and
contortionists in the drawing room, and seeing Braham, Miss Romer, Mrs
Honey, Mrs Waylett, Mrs Keeley trying over their songs for the piece in
rehearsal at his mother's little piano. The prompter, the scene painters in
their working clothes would come up for a hurried consultation; Sam
Lover would bring in a ballad for Mrs Fitzwilliam or Mrs Fortescue,
Maria B. Hawes the oratorio singer who lived opposite came calling, and

---

[59] Sala, *Life*, vol. I, p. 25.

Mrs S. C. Hall, who lived in Brompton, would come by actually to see little Edmund and bring him a copy of her children's annual.[60] This is, in short, an idealised picture of the middle-class family still living over the shop, with all that implies of the continued involvement of the centrally important woman head of the household in the family business; but despite his writing up his childhood as a time of wonder and pleasure, Yates is unable to see the working women he describes in the role of equal partners in the creative world. Writing in 1884, he is determined that no one shall see his mother as déclassé by her theatrical origins and work, and so he says that she had always detested the theatre, as her actor father had before her, and moved away to a suburban house on Fred Yates's death in 1842; he has to concede that she continued to star at the Adelphi under the management of Madame Celeste for a further six years.[61]

Edmund Yates is in some ways the typical – typically extraordinary – mid-Victorian Bohemian writer. He produced many, many columns of journalism, edited a disparate array of journals, wrote nine plays in collaboration with others, wrote in his own name – though possibly with the unacknowledged help of a woman writer, Frances Cashel Hoey – nineteen novels, plus innumerable poems and some published song lyrics; he created a successful one-man show, collected his journalism into several volumes, wrote his own autobiography and edited others, was a protégé of Dickens and furiously denounced by both Thackeray and Trollope. He gossiped maliciously in print to the extent that he was sacked from the Garrick club in his youth and actually imprisoned for libel in his middle years; he became a successful touring lecturer in America and a bankrupt, the unfaithful husband to an heiress and the father of four sons, a civil servant in the Post Office for twenty-five years, and the first British writer to sign himself a flâneur.[62] The vigour, the prolific, if conflicted and self-deceiving, creativity that Bohemia contributed to the creation of London's West End and its culture is evident in his work. And that input derives at least in part from the women in his life, from the mother whose excellence as an actress he discounted and denied and the loyal wife he married very young and frequently betrayed, to Frances Hoey, the woman whose novels he is said to have published under his own name.

[60] Yates, *Recollections*, vol. I, pp. 22–7. [61] Ibid., pp. 299–301, vol. II, p. 78.
[62] This summary is derived chiefly from *DNB*.

PART II

Making

CHAPTER 4

Performing the crisis

This book has so far attempted to bring into focus the phenomenon of West End entertainment as it came into being in the middle of the nineteenth century, seeing it as a topographical and conceptual novelty much wider than the study of the Drama has previously allowed. The second part of this book will examine the ways in which the theatre, specifically, contributed to that phenomenon, and seek to make good my assertion that women played a much greater part in the foundation of West End theatre than has previously been allowed. It will not, on the whole, treat the generation-long period on which it focusses, from 1831 to 1866, chronologically or developmentally, but this chapter will tend to concentrate upon the earlier part of the period, the rapid social evolution which saw the rise of the female players who in their maturity became the moving spirits considered in the succeeding chapters.

Asserting the rising importance of women in the theatre business in the 1830s and 1840s begs the question of why women should have moved into a powerful position there just at the point normally associated with the separation of home and workplace, leading to the binary gendering of the social and public spheres. The mapping of the domain of entertainment in the first half of this book suggests that this paradox might be thought of in terms of the anxieties associated with catering for, and participating in, the new leisure culture, fraught as it was with psychological difficulties for the expanding and various Victorian middle classes. This was a moment, one might say, of aporia: a doubtful place, a weakness in the rhetorical construction of the world. Through such stressed-out openings we may sometimes see the eruption of that which is normally held in check, or indeed that which is actively being suppressed: in this case, the freedom and power of women. Chapters 2 and 3 suggest this possibility, in that they pinpoint the ways in which gender definition became of central importance, influencing the status of the writer, the acceptability of the actor, and the self-consciousness and willingness to participate of every audience member. This chapter will seek to show how women came forward, in those circumstances, to play a leading part in the transformation of the culture of performance. It will explore their presence upon the debatable, liminal ground. Women on stage came to occupy the exposed positions that men found it difficult any longer to hold: as gentlemen became black-suited and valorised the Real, and so stiffened into postures that repudiated the play of feeling and the assumption of roles, women stepped up as ubiquitous players on the stages of the capital. They took upon themselves not only the feeling and colour assigned to their own sex, with its unashamed emotional extroversion, but also the playful roles and the brilliant costumes that men had set aside, weeping and dancing and strutting the stage in jewelled doublets and feathered hats as well as silken breeches.

CATEGORY PANIC IN THE 1840s

It is commonplace, a truism, to speak as the preceding chapters have done of the 1830s and 1840s as a period of transition and change. Commentators at the time were acutely aware of far-reaching cultural shifts. They remarked and explored them in the booming genres of journalism and the realist novel, as well as in a taxonomical and legislative drive to describe, classify and prescribe how classes and individuals were to be conceptualised and expected to relate to each other in modern society. What has been less remarked is the way in which the stage took part in this discourse. A false impression that because the Drama was not at the leading edge of literary sensibility all performance was left behind by the main energies of the culture has obscured important synergies between the changing times and theatrical change and innovation in the 1830s and 1840s.

One way of understanding how the structure of feeling in the early nineteenth century is acutely realised in the life of the stage is to think in terms of what Marjorie Garber has called 'category panic'.[1] Such panic is, according to her account, continually present, and sometimes reaches crisis, in modern society. Displaced, metaphoric ways of dealing with it have accordingly developed. By her definition a 'category crisis' is the experience of 'social, cultural or aesthetic dissonances' where a 'failure of definitional distinction' occurs and fixed borderlines become permeable, permitting border crossings and, indeed, she argues, demanding them.

[1] Garber, *Vested Interests.*

The 1830s and 1840s witnessed category crisis of remarkable intensity, to which the development of so many measures for counting, classifying and controlling the people were the rational, scientific response. But, as Garber suggests, where 'an irresolvable conflict or epistemological crux that destabilizes comfortable binarity' occurs, and is too difficult or too occluded to be faced directly, then it is likely that the destabilised binaries (which may be between any such categories – 'black/white, Jew/Christian, noble/bourgeois, master/servant, master/slave') may be represented by, displaced on to, the male/female binary. That division, she argues, is then 'put under erasure in transvestism, and a transvestite figure, or transvestite mode, will always function as a sign of overdetermination – a mechanism of displacement from one blurred boundary to another'. Garber looks at how this displacement worked in Renaissance Europe, when 'transvestism was the specter that rose up – both in the theater and on the streets – to mark and overdetermine this crisis of social and economic change'.[2] I would suggest that major features of the early nineteenth-century stage are similarly a response to category crisis, and new and often transvestite performances came into being to help to negotiate as well as to represent social change.

In the performance of everyday life, the transvestite phenomenon in the first half of the nineteenth century can be seen in the craze for public dancing in masquerade, which was, as often as not, *en travesti*. The stately, only covertly transgressive public masquerade or *bal masque* had an important place in eighteenth-century high culture, but it had ceased to be important, according to the definitive study by Terry Castle, before the turn of the century. As she points out, eighteenth-century critics were always disturbed by the 'antitaxonomic energy' of the practice, and by the end of the century the modern world-view 'characterized everywhere by a fear of ontological promiscuity and a desire for firm conceptual boundaries' had asserted itself to suppress the masquerade.[3] But it had an afterlife in the later 1830s and the 1840s in a much wider and wilder craze, with dances from low entertainment venues, the taverns, ballrooms and pleasure gardens, crossing over to the major theatres and opera houses of London and Paris, where by the late 1840s concerts 'à la Musard'– named after the early organiser-conductor in both cities – became a byword for the vulgar extremes of popular music and the intoxicated excesses of

[2] ibid., pp. 16–17.
[3] Terry Castle, *Masquerade and Civilization: The Carnivalesque in Eighteenth-century English Culture and Fiction* (London: Methuen, 1986), p. 102.

participatory dance and display. Promenade concerts held in theatres as
well as in music saloons and ballrooms invited social dancing, and the
complex evolutions of earlier court styles simplified into energetic quadrilles and polkas. In this exuberantly corporeal pleasure it was feared that
the elaborate quasi-historical and 'exotic' costumes favoured by the
dancers blurred all distinction of rank and gender, so that fashion and
fakes, self-indulgence and crime mingled.[4] In 1835 *Figaro in London*,[5]
smarting about the Lord Chamberlain's closure of the Strand Theatre
for lack of a licence, calls the masquerades at the Opera House 'exhibitions of licentiousness and immorality' where deluded genteel people pay
a guinea to walk about in a theatre with 'depraved and abandoned
wretches'. By 1846 *The Satirist*[6] is complaining of this 'at best un-English
amusement' at Covent Garden, where the costumes are stupid or
indecent: 'a strip of pink leg, a novel Order of the Garter, frequently
making its appearance between the stockings and shorts of the lady
cavaliers, during "*un moment de gaiéte*"'.

That the great and small theatres had come to offer such entertainments was one more in the list of outrages over which such reactionary
critics, the champions of the Drama, fulminated in vain. Their main
concern, however, was the loss of ontological certainty and boundary-
keeping between the various entertainments of the stage itself. They were
outraged by the category crisis and boundary erasure manifest in the
decline in the primacy of the tragic drama, and the rise of new performance genres – not only the maligned mongrel form of melodrama, but
also Grand Opera and the Romantic ballet. Grand Opera is reckoned to
have begun with Auber's *Masaniello; ou La muette de Portici* at the Paris
Théâtre de l'Académie Royale de Musique in 1828, from a Scribe libretto
which culminates in Fenella the mute heroine throwing herself into an
erupting Vesuvius. The piece, dealing with revolutionary Neapolitan
politics, was credited with actually triggering revolution in Belgium in
1830. Grand Opera was, however, the voice of bourgeois rather than
popular self-assertion, and came overwhelmingly to be managed and
produced by an international body of commercial entrepreneurs – a word
imported into English in 1825, by one of them, John Ebers.[7] In

---

[4] '[I]t was the very fluidity of carnival – the way it subverted the dualities of male and female, animal
and human, dark and light, life and death – that made it so inimical to the new "anatomizing"
sensibility that heralded the development of modern bourgeois society' (ibid., p. 103); and see Mark
Edward Perugini, *The Omnibus Box* (London: Jarrolds, 1946), pp. 223–52.
[5] 7 March 1835.   [6] 29 March 1846.
[7] John Ebers, *Seven Years of the King's Theatre* (London: Ainsworth, 1828), p. 115.

consequence opera came to be dominated in performance by the star singers, predominantly women, who were lavishly paid by the highest bidders to sing the new music across the borders of the western world. Many of these divas were regularly singing old and new transvestite roles.[8]

The entrepreneurs' consumerist appropriation of a previously exclusive art, which expanded to cover the western world and breached the boundary between aristocratic and middle-class elites, was followed up by a similar flowering of stage as well as social dance. The interpenetration of opera and dance is institutionalised in the pairing of the two in the opera houses of Europe, where, as mentioned above, social dancing in the form of opera balls became an increasing part of the offering of the providers. Operas such as *Masaniello* were regularly rearranged into music for *bals masques* – indeed Auber's critics said his musical and especially his rhythmic freedom in composition was limited by this expectation – and music lovers would be familiar with an image of Fenella and her brother, dancing a quadrille, on the cover of the sheet music.[9] Stage dance, meanwhile, evolved a new level of expertise and a new pleasure. Here the signifying move is conventionally regarded as Marie Taglioni's fairy performance in *La Sylphide* at the Paris Opéra in 1832. The Romantic ballet, making the crossing as opera did from aristocratic sexualised consumption to bourgeois artistic appreciation, became overwhelmingly concerned with the borders between humanity and the supernatural and animal kingdoms, and it became an art that tested the bounds of gender. Taglioni's dancing embodied moral superiority in her literal elevation on to pointe, an apparent escape from the weight of the body, so that ballerinas following her floated free of the confines of the earth into an ethereal femininity which was more acceptable as an aesthetic image than the sexualised scopic luxury previously embodied by the female dancer. At this point men faded in significance as leading dancers – with the consequent 'transvestite effect' of women such as Fanny Ellsler dancing many male roles.

---

[8] And some sang male roles clearly not written for them: see for example the evening Bunn arranged at Drury Lane on 3 July 1833, which combined the penultimate English appearance that epoch-making season of the ballerina Taglioni in *La Sylphide* with Wilhelmine Schröder-Devrient singing not only her signature cross-dressed role of Beethoven's Fidelio, but also the hero in the climactic act of Rossini's *Otello*, with Malibran as her Desdemona. For critical discussion of operatic cross-playing, see Corrine E. Blackmer, ed., *En Travesti: Women, Gender and Subversion* (New York: Columbia University Press, 1995).

[9] See Maribeth Clark, 'The Quadrille as Embodied Musical Experience in 19th-century Paris', *Journal of Musicology* 19:3 (summer 2002), pp. 503–26, 519–25.

These border transgressions reverberated through London entertainment, where the decade between the acts – the Dramatic Authors Act of 1833 that followed the Parliamentary Committee's enquiries in 1831–2, and the Theatres Act of 1843 – was a battleground in the theatre: see the Introduction above. Bunn the entrepreneur of opera and dance and Macready the champion of the Drama contended in vain to make the ancient, bloated and now blighted patent houses work for either of their visions. The most artistically successful patent house manager between the acts was Eliza Vestris, and even she could not make money. But Vestris, I would argue, was clearly the beneficiary, and her success the sign, of theatrical category crisis.

ELIZA VESTRIS: A CAREER ON THE CROSSWAYS

In 1840, when she became artistic director of Covent Garden, Vestris was already a successful opera singer, star actress and theatrical manager; during the 1830s she had taken a pioneering position in the nascent West End. Eliza Vestris's career is well known, by comparison with many of her female contemporaries, but it is worth beginning with a consideration of her trajectory because it so clearly exemplifies the negotiation of successive category crises. Born in 1797 and brought up a professional in the elite European performance tradition, which valued virtuoso talent and training and understood how to please a fashionable audience, she probably learnt French, Italian and music at home in London from her mother, who was a concert pianist and the daughter of a French dancing master. Her singing coach was Domenico Corri of the King's Theatre. She married Armand Vestris, third generation in a family of leading Italian dancers, and in 1815 made her operatic début at the King's on his benefit night. They went to Paris together in 1816, after she had successfully sung Susanna in *Le nozze di Figaro*.

She returned to London, without her husband, in 1819. But she did not go back to the opera house, where greater singers were at work; instead she made her first boundary crossing, moving to appear in the London theatres. She embarked upon a decade of personal success as a scandalous beauty, exploiting the stage as well as acquiring a string of wealthy lovers to build her own popular but also fashionable profile. This began with the transvestite effect: the *succès de scandale* of her famous breeches performance, the lead role in the operatic burlesque *Giovanni in London* at Drury Lane in May 1820, which made her beautiful and visibly accessible legs a legend. She was the toast of the town. One of her lovers, the Radical MP

Thomas Duncombe, sat on the Parliamentary Select Committee on the Drama in 1831. No women were committee members, of course, and nor were any representatives of the many female theatre workers called to give evidence. If any of them was actually consulted, then we may assume it was Eliza Vestris. She was now 33; and she was, it seems, aware of journalistic and critical reaction against elite culture as culpably luxurious and wanton, and of the struggle that managers like Robert Elliston were having to fit the old style of dramatic entertainment to the patronage of the new general public. So at this point of crisis, she had made her second transgressive move: in December 1830 she took on, in her own name, the lease of the Olympic, only a few steps from Drury Lane.

There were other women involved prominently in the upsurge of new theatres at this moment, even named as managing stage ventures – Harriet Waylett, for example, appears on many bills around 1830 as being in charge of the stages leased by her various male associates – but Vestris stood out alone on her own stage and proclaimed herself

> A warrior woman – that in strife embarks,
> The first of all dramatic Joan of Arcs,
> Cheer on the enterprise thus dared by me!
> The first that ever led a company.[10]

At the Olympic she then proceeded to pioneer the theatrical changes which the select committee was subsequently set up to implement. The refurbished little theatre[11] was well decorated, intimate, and tasteful, like a fashionable drawing room; a modern place, unencumbered with the expensive traditional baggage of the patents. There Vestris emerged as the ultimate transvestite performer, not only 'Joan of Arc' but notably in the gorgeously costumed roles of exotic kings and classical gods, in metatheatrical fantasies invented for her by J. R. Planché, a writer with a particularly keen nose for what was clever, pretty and fashionably titillating without being too undeniably risqué. Besides these sumptuous Olympic extravaganzas, Vestris offered light musical pieces and farces, well mounted, often changed, merry and undemanding, and made a point of finishing by 11 p.m. These apparently simple changes to common practice made her theatre newly fashionable, the quintessential expression of the late Georgian age. It attracted the *beau monde*, who amused

---

[10] Quoted from her opening address in Charles E. Pierce, *Madame Vestris and her Times* (London: Stanley Paul & Co., n.d.), p.168.

[11] Leased to Vestris by John Scott, who had bought it after selling on the Sans Pareil/Adelphi, which he had built twenty-five years before to house the successful dramatic ventures of his daughter Jane.

themselves there before moving on to their night pursuits, and also brought in aspiring City men and their families, who came to see and to be part of fashionable company while getting home early enough to be in the office the next morning. She brought the pleasures of the patronage of opera and ballet within reach of middle-class aspiration, without challenging its musical appreciation or its self-definition as perfectly sober and moral. Her sensational transvestite appearances in clever classical and fairy-tale burlesques exploited and at the same time minimised, excused and made acceptable sexual appeal, turning her licentious reputation into an asset that connoted good taste and an acceptable luxury for the consumer rather than a threat from a woman exploiting weak men and participating in aristocratic power.

In 1838 a further shift became necessary: about to make what she hoped would be a profitable tour of the USA (a growing feature of theatrical life much accelerated by the first Atlantic passenger steamships in that year) Vestris was advised that to have a hope of pleasing moralistic American audiences she needed to be married to the consort whom she took with her, Charles James Mathews. They were wedded accordingly, and though they did not succeed on their tour they came back ready for the next step up the theatrical ladder in London. The management of Covent Garden, however, did not work out well financially, and the Mathewses had to make a further step forward, crossing another boundary into intelligent modern comedy at the Lyceum in October 1847, leaving behind the diamonds and cross-dressing to create a more intellectual bridgehead for the critical tastes of the likes of George Henry Lewes and John Oxenford, dramatist and drama critic of *The Times*. They were to become one of the married couple managements that will be considered in Chapter 5.

At Covent Garden in 1840 Vestris was as always working on the leading edge, making an extraordinarily bold step for a woman in taking on the patent. The reverberations of her effrontery can be felt in Macready's vitriolic attacks upon her in his diaries, and in other writings which were published nearer to her own day. She employed the young George Vandenhoff, aspirant son of a more famous actor, who in 1860 wrote about his experiences under her management twenty years before with a blend of cheap malice and forced admiration that indicates, by the deep unease of his tone, the profound gender challenge represented by Vestris's success. Beginning his comments with misogynist sneers about her age when he met her – at 43, he says, she was 'already in the "sere", with a good deal of the "yellow leaf" visible;

that is, when the blanc and rouge were off', he concludes them by patronising 'Poor Eliza Lucy' as a kind of 'burlesque semi-royalty, the royalty of the theatre'. He is forced to admit that she managed the huge theatre well, with not only a decently conducted green-room serving tea and coffee, but fair contracts for her staff and a perfect stage, whose *mis en scène* other managements would have done well to copy.[12] However, he sums up her career thus:

She had latterly, for many years, been a standing favourite in the English theatres, in characters requiring a certain *espiéglerie*, nearly allied to effrontery, together with fair musical capabilities – the soubrette chantante, in fine. Her speciality had been what are technically called breeches parts, from their requiring a lady to invest herself in mannish integuments. Peg Woffington, a century before, had been great in these assumptions, and her Sir Harry Wildair turned the heads of the beaux, by its easy abandon, and graceful *etouderie*, to say nothing of the display of her *tournure*, which completed the witchery.

Now, Vestris was admirably gifted, cut out, and framed to shine *en petit maître*; she was remarkable for the symmetry of her limbs, especially of those principally call on to fill these parts; she had a fearless off-hand manner, and a fine mezzo soprano voice, the full contralto notes of which did her good service in 'Don Giovanni' (a sort of burlesque on the opera), Captain Macheath, Carlos in 'The Duenna', Apollo in 'Midas', and other epicenes. For purity of intonation and simple truth of expression, her singing of 'Had I a heart for falsehood framed' in 'The Duenna' and 'In infancy our hopes and fears' in 'Artaxerxes', have seldom, if ever, been surpassed. She was the best soubrette chantante of her day; self-possession, archness, grace, coquéterie, seemed natural to her; these with her charming voice, excellent taste in music, fine eyes and exquisite form made her the most fascinating and (joined to her *esprit d'intrigue*) the most dangerous actress of her time. Believe it, reader, no actress that we have now can give you an idea of the attractions, the fascinations, the witcheries of Madame Vestris in the hey-day of her charms.

That day, with its triumphs, its intrigues, its conquests, its 'Handsome Jacks', its 'Lord Edwards', and 'Honourable Horatios' was nearly past ... her last throw of the dice was Covent Garden Theatre, with a husband to bear the liabilities.[13]

This is a passage notable for its swings and reversals of tone, its grudging and undercut admiration, its lasciviousness, malice and unease. Vandenhoff finds Vestris – who gave him his first acting job – outrageous, and makes haste quite slowly to box her power up and set it aside, while working to assert his own superiority both to her and to the latter-day

[12] George Vandenhoff, *Dramatic Reminiscences; or, Actors and Actresses in England and America*, ed. Henry Seymour Carlton (London: Thomas Cooper & Co., 1860), pp. 3, 14, 12, 50.
[13] ibid., pp. 4–5.

reader who has missed her. This is partly achieved through the repeated crossing over to the French language, which is less a matter of disguising meaning than of reinforcing it without being obliged to spell out the sexual responses he invokes. He expects his reader to take his innuendos all the more obscenely for their association with the French, a whole nation regarded by the British as being chiefly a sign for sexual transgression. He suggests that Vestris, like Woffington and all legendary actresses, embodies *Frenchness*, meaning not only availability but, more shockingly, female sexual appetite. Not only mischief and assurance but the very turn of the thigh are expressed in that labile language. Moreover the sexuality invoked is not straightforwardly gendered: Vestris shines in 'epicenes', boy roles and gay uniforms and brigands like Macheath, a speciality expressed, again in French, as *en petit maître*. The men, the little masters, that she portrays are effeminate, in the Victorian as well as the modern sense: they are creatures who are made less manly, less admirable, not by their attraction to other men but by their narcissism, their elaborately self-conscious dress and their attention to women, to sexual pleasure. The transvestite representation Vestris flaunts, with her middle-range voice and her free movement and her self-possession, is neither man nor woman – certainly neither gentleman nor lady. And it is very dangerously attractive.

'ESPIÉGLERIE' AND THE FASHIONABLE AUDIENCE

Vestris's heyday in such representation was over by 1840, as Vandenhoff enjoys pointing out, and he suggests that the racy late-Georgian culture of which she was a leading figure, along with the 'Handsome Jacks' she bedded, is itself a thing of the past. Enjoyment of exotic sexual transgression was, however, still possible in Victoria's reign by crossing the national boundary and John Mitchell, who managed many new entertainment ventures in the mid century, had a great success in that line in the season of French performances that he staged at the fashionable St James's Theatre in the summer of 1842 – see Chapter 1. He brought to London the long-standing star of the Paris Palais Royale theatre, Virginie Déjazet. She was actually only a year younger than Vestris, and similarly ambitious in management – eventually she managed the Folies Theatre in Paris with her son, and renamed it after herself, under which name it is still open in the twenty-first century. In 1842 she was, according to the *Morning Chronicle*, 'a person *sui generis*' with a style 'a mixture of lightness, flippancy, *espiéglerie*, point, and apparent exuberant animal spirits' which made her 'a prodigious favourite'.[14] Fanny Kemble Butler saw her at the St James's, and was amazed

> by a woman, who moves with more complete *disinvoltura* in her men's clothes than most men do … my eyes and mouth opened wider and wider, not so much at the French actress, as at the well-born, well-bred English audience, who, women as well as men, were in a perfect ecstasy of amusement and admiration. I certainly never saw more admirable acting, but neither did I ever see such uncompromising personal exposure and such perfect effrontery of demeanour. I do not think even ballet-dancers more indecent than Mademoiselle Déjazet, for the revelations of their limbs and shapes are partial and momentary, while hers were abiding and entire through the whole of her performance, which she acted in tight-fitting knee-breeches and silk stockings; nor did I ever see such an unflinching representation of unmitigated audacity of carriage, look, and manner, in any male or female, on or off the stage.[15]

All the newspapers agree on Déjazet's storming popularity with the elite, named in the *Morning Chronicle* in a long list that begins with the Marchioness of Aylesbury; these ladies apparently found the French language (which was very colloquial and difficult to follow, in this instance) and the high prices they paid for seats a sufficient guarantee against any suspicion that they were in fact applauding a very shocking performance. Fanny Kemble remarks that half the 'assembly of fine ladies' cannot have not understood the performance, but 'it must have been "nuts" to the clever, cynical, witty, impudent Frenchwoman, to see these *dames trois fois respectables* swallow her performances *sans sourcilliez*'.[16] Identifying, it seems to me, with Virginie's professional sangfroid, Fanny uses French here to claim equality with the other actress and to show a kind of appreciation of her assumption of power, in a way exactly opposite to Vandenhoff's objectification and repudiation of Vestris.

Vestris made her lifelong boundary-pushing central to the development of theatre in the 1830s and 1840s, while Déjazet was able to operate freely there by being an outsider, a special case; between them, however, they set an agenda of actresses playing in male dress that was pursued by the mainstream of comic and musical performances in the nascent West End. I have written elsewhere about this phenomenon in general,[17] and will only summarise here the way in which the transvestite effect is to be met

---

[14] 12 May 1842. [15] Butler, *Records of Later Life*, vol. III, pp. 21–3. [16] ibid., vol. II, p. 224.
[17] See Jacky Bratton, 'Mirroring Men: The Actress in Drag', in Maggie Gale and John Stokes, eds., *The Cambridge Companion to the Actress* (Cambridge University Press, 2007), pp. 253–71.

with at every turn in the little theatres of the time, and was a dominant performance style adopted at some point by virtually every actress, and indeed by some of the actors, who were to become the leading players of their generation.

As Vandenhoff's invocation of Woffington's famous Harry Wildair demonstrates, the display of the actress in male dress simply because it is close-fitting and bifurcated, revealing the body and allowing her (dancing) legs to be seen and enjoyed, goes back in Britain to the seventeenth century, when women first appeared on the public stage. It continued unabated into this period, and onwards until changing codes of gender in dress rendered it obsolete in the twentieth century. This was clearly the point being made when the painter Maclise wrote to Charles Dickens in 1841 about Julia Fortescue's representation of the character of Barnaby Rudge. He enthuses about 'the small waist – the neatly turned leg – and the woman bust – the tunic exactly reaching where we wish it' to show 'the wild attractions of her legs'.[18] Fortescue's personal history illustrates exactly the position of such a performer, as it had been for generations: she was a famous beauty, kept by Alan Hyde (second Baron) Gardner; they had three sons, in 1842, 1843 and 1846, and then married in 1856. Before her marriage she appeared in a series of Dickens's plays, and was employed by him in his Amateur Company – where the actresses were professionals. One of the illegitimate sons was granted a title in his own right, for services to the nation. One of her great-grandsons is the theatre critic Benedict Nightingale.[19] A parallel tale could be told of Louisa (formerly Sarah) Fairbrother, who played roles such as Aladdin in *The Forty Thieves* at the Lyceum in 1844, the opening spectacle of the Keeleys' management (see Chapter 6). She is pictured in the role sporting a painted beard and pencil moustache, with diaphanous harem trousers looped up to show her thigh. She too was a mother at the time: she bore three sons to Prince George the Second Duke of Cambridge, and married him morganatically in 1847, just before the third. These are Vestris's heiresses; of course the well-married few represent the tip of an iceberg,

---

[18] Madeline House and Graham Storey, eds., *The Letters of Charles Dickens 1840–1841*, vol. II, p. 331, from a letter from Maclise to Dickens, 16 July 1841.
[19] See a letter from him to *The Times*, 13 December 2003.

comprised of the hundreds of working women for whom the wearing of quasi-masculine dress was a professional advertisement, with heterosexual consumption, whether in palace or brothel, never far from sight; they are the embodiment of the trope of the actress/whore over several centuries.

Neither was there anything new on the early nineteenth-century stage about the interchangeability of girls and boys under a certain age. It had always been the case; and if the bias is towards girls playing boys, this is probably because début roles for children tended to be masculine – the obvious cases are the little princes in *Richard III* and Arthur in *King John*. The casting of rather older girls to play these very little boys is also a practical way of securing better behaviour.[20] The peculiarly nineteenth-century extension of the practice was the proliferation of such roles in early melodrama, where the young, even non-speaking child was a powerful token of innocence, in parts that could require considerable pantomime skills from the little performer.[21] The appeal of the pathos of such representations survived beyond the high Romantic phase of melodrama, and provided starring roles for many young, and even not so young actresses who had a sufficiently small stature and fragile appeal. There are hundreds of examples: roles like Dickens's child heroes (Smike, Oliver Twist, Little Nell, Paul in *Dombey and Son*, Jo in *Bleak House*) lead on to innumerable suffering and dying infants of both genders or, effectively, of none.

The transvestite effect possibly begins to assert itself in the marked preference of the 1830s and 1840s for girls in these pathetic roles – very few little boys got to play Oliver Twist, and when it did occur reviews tend to be dismissive. The *London Dispatch* of 25 November 1838, for example, preferred Mrs Keeley's 'painfully true' representation of Smike at the Adelphi to 'Master Owen' giving a 'modest, quiet, gentle' performance of Oliver Twist at the Surrey, which 'of course' failed to interest anyone. The *Examiner* is equally underwhelmed by Master Owen, preferring the comic performance of a 'clever half-boy half-man actor in the person of a lanky youth called Master Young' who played Noah Claypole, in full leathers.[22] It would seem that pathos was becoming difficult to feel in association with the masculine: suffering is passive, pathos is therefore feminine in essence. Many subsequently powerful and successful women

---

[20] See the discussion of Fanny Kelly's infant professionalism in Bush-Bailey, *Performing Herself*.
[21] See Peter Brooks, *The Melodramatic Imagination: Balzac, Henry James, Melodrama, and the Mode of Excess* (New York: Columbia University Press, 1985), pp. 33–4.
[22] 25 November 1838.

began their careers in these sad child roles: Marie Wilton, for example, born in 1839, was playing a Lilliputian emperor by the time she was 6, followed by Fleance in *Macbeth* and Prince Arthur in *King John*, but made her first important mark as little Henri, the son of Charles Dillon's Belphegor the showman in a storming and lachrymose metatheatrical melodrama of the 1850s.

I would suggest this phenomenon is part of an overall shift whereby, as gender definition began to tighten, roles began to be created and assigned for stage exposition in ways which reinforced certain secondary character-istics and ruled out others as part of the modern construction of man and woman. Some actresses, however, found ways of confronting the trend, broadening the new stereotypes within gender boundaries, and play-wrights, whether consciously or not, created many roles that offered scope for exploration, and for loosening up the assumptions of the audience. The obvious examples are the star roles of Louisa Nisbett (b. 1812), a leading actress and creator of roles in the 1830s and 1840s, who had two particular signature parts that achieved this: Constance in Sheridan Knowles's *The Love Chase* (Haymarket 1835) and Lady Gay Spanker in Boucicault's *London Assurance* (1841, at Covent Garden under Vestris). Both are comic roles that explore love and marriage by pushing at the division of masculine and feminine behaviours: Constance and her neigh-bour Wildrake have known and teased each other since they were chil-dren, and it takes the whole of the play, and several scenes in which he flinches as she mocks and mimics his sportsman's hyper-masculinity and he attempts to learn to dance and to walk like a town gentleman, for her to come to a recognition of him as her lover. Lady Gay Spanker is the same breezy, domineering girl grown up and married, and moved back to the country, where she organises other people's duels and love affairs as well as her own dogs and horses and her passive husband Dolly. And there were many minor farces and comediettas that made similar explorations of the gender boundaries – but always ended by tightening and confirm-ing them. Their quasi-realistic comic plots are predictable, though no doubt performances sometimes rendered them irresistible; but it is more interesting to look to the rather more displaced boundary-challenging elsewhere on stage, and conjecture what might have been happening when the gendering of emotions and behaviours led to uneasy transvestite theatrical manifestations.

As youth and pathos became preferably feminine, age and self-assertion became ever more ugly in a woman, so that men played comic dame roles and even, strikingly, such roles as Lady Macbeth and Medea, with which the burlesque actor Frederick Robson alternately amused and chilled audiences at the Olympic in the 1850s – see Chapter 6. Fanny Kemble found cause to complain that actresses increasingly refused to put their best efforts into, or even to accept, tragic roles in which they could not be charming, docile and ladylike. She also remarks that the only Romeo with whom she ever acted who really 'looked the part' was Ellen Tree, who was 'broad-shouldered as well as tall, and her long limbs had the fine proportions of the huntress Diana'.[23] Tree was also a success in the classical verse tragedy *Ion* in 1836, playing a philosophically trained boy who becomes a king, and kills himself in order to bring about republican rule – not, presumably, intending this Radical expedient as a suggestion to the Princess Victoria, about to ascend the throne. Actresses finding the narrowing confines of female roles irksome occasionally rebelled by attempting a Shakespearean hero such as Hamlet or Richard III when they had a chance, as for instance on a benefit night; but Romeo was so frequently and perseveringly played by women that it is a different case. It was even composed as a mezzo-soprano role in Bellini's *I Capuleti e i Montecchi* (Venice 1830). Romeo therefore becomes in this period worth listing as a transvestite role, because the masculinity it embodies – passionate, petulant, impetuous, Latin – is outside the straitening definitions of British manliness. Its most famous female exponent was the American star Charlotte Cushman. Joseph Leach in his biography of Cushman picks up the apposite Victorian judgement: in Romeo she was 'just *man* enough to be a *boy!*'[24]

The transvestite effect, then, as well as being a displaced expression for crises of category definition at large, was fed by the narrowing of definitions of true masculinity and femininity, that left much ground outside, unaccounted for, which became the territory of a particular kind of theatrical experiment and display. Conventions created and explored at this moment flowed through theatrical discourse for the rest of the

---

[23] Frances Ann Kemble, *Records of a Girlhood* (New York: Henry Holt, 1883), p. 200.
[24] *Bright Particular Star*, Yale, 1970, quoted in James Loehlin, ed., *Romeo and Juliet*, Shakespeare in Production series (Cambridge University Press, 2002), p. 29. Leach is quoting a Victorian response to Cushman in these words. Loehlin agrees that 'The character of Romeo, as understood in the nineteenth century, was incompatible with Victorian notions of masculinity' (p. 31). The oddest female Romeo I have found occurs in a review of Avonia Jones, a rather short-lived British star of the 1850s, whom *The Era* of 1 March 1857 reports as having played Juliet in America, at Richmond, VA, 'to her mother's Romeo'.

century, at the centre of commercial theatre-making independently of, indeed in defiance of, the slow emergence of realism in the intellectual avant-garde of drama.

Its most recognisable expression is the pantomime. Marjorie Garber argues that J. M. Barrie's *Peter Pan*, not written until 1904, 'is in a way a theoretical deconstruction of Panto, an exposure of its underlying fable' and that fable is, she claims, 'a contest between a boyish woman hero and a feminized male villain, both of whom are crossover figures, repeatedly twinned in the text: Peter Pan and Captain Hook, a dream and a nightmare of transvestism'. Peter, the boy who refuses to grow up, was always to be played by a woman, 'because', Garber says, 'a woman will never grow up to be a man'; while Hook, 'the logical extension of the pantomime Dame',[25] is a dandified, piratical quasi-cross-dresser in the curly wig and frogged velvets of a cavalier of Charles II's time – an extreme type of effeminate masculinity (still cropping up, incidentally, in for example Johnny Depp in *Pirates of the Caribbean*). Both boy and cavalier were guises assumed over and over again by the actresses of the 1830s and 1840s, in a teeming variety of extravaganzas, burlesques, musical farces, holiday spectacles, sketches and interludes that was eventually narrowed down into the Victorian pantomime.

Examples are everywhere, in the transpontine and City theatres as well as the early West End: Mrs Honner (b. 1808 as Marcia Macarthy), a small woman with a big voice, specialised in energetic boys or women disguised as them in the predominantly working-class theatres of London, where in 1838 she jointly managed Sadler's Wells with her husband. Fanny Fitzwilliam, on a single bill, 23–4 November 1836, for the transpontine house recently renamed the Victoria, played Harry Harley in *The Middy Ashore* followed by a comic interlude in which she took two roles: the heroine Rosalie Bouquet, and then Achille de Entrechats, Maître de Dance and Serjeant of the Guarde Nationale. It is striking that most of the powerful West End actress-managers of the 1850s and 1860s played these transvestite roles in youth. Marie Wilton, who became Mrs Bancroft, is the obvious example, already mentioned, who claimed – strategically – that she went into management to get away from being constantly cast as a comedy boy. The generation immediately before her included Ellen Tree, born 1805, who was to become a Shakespearean director as Mrs Charles Kean; Mary Anne Hehl, born 1813, who as Fanny Stirling was the spokeswoman of the

[25] Garber, *Vested Interests*, pp. 176–85.

profession for many years; Priscilla Horton, born 1818, who created an entirely new form of serious entertainment as Mrs German Reed; and the inimitable Mrs Keeley, Queen Victoria's favourite player, born Mary Ann Goward in 1813. They were usually trained as professional singers, and their early stage roles included singing chambermaids and the like, but they rose to fame for their transvestite specialities. Tree, as already mentioned, played important male roles including Romeo in her young days. Fanny Stirling was one of the many slender girls who looked killing in fancy stage versions of the already-elaborate military fashions of the day: disguised as a pocket-sized officer, '*en petit maître*', she and others like her were able to flirt outrageously with heroines and comment pertly upon overdressed fashionable fellows, playing with the border between the sexes in dress and behaviour.[26]

Mary Ann Goward figures largely with her husband Bob Keeley in Chapter 5, and her integration of boy roles, and of his impersonation of elderly women and of oppressed, stupid, subordinated masculine types who are also a kind of 'boy', into their management strategies will be explored there. But here it is worth noting the considerable work Mrs Keeley did in such roles before she reached that distinction. Her most famous role – for her biographer Walter Goodman[27] a lifelong memory – was as the boy anti-hero Jack Sheppard in the Adelphi adaptation of Ainsworth's novel of eighteenth-century crime. As Jack she appeared framed in a lovingly recreated Old London, first in full shirtsleeves and apron as a carpenter's apprentice, where she really planed real planks of wood and stood on the counter to carve her name on the beams of the shop, then, donning the picturesque long coat and waistcoat that echoed the highwayman Macheath, she daringly bluffed and climbed her way out of confinement in Newgate Jail (see Figure 6). She undertook this charming figure of transgression during the same season, 1839–40, that she played Smike in *Nicholas Nickleby*, and the reviews were full of her versatility in playing two such different boys. Reviewing Jack, one critic said

Mrs Keeley was (the assertion sounds rather strangely) the *hero* of the piece. In taking upon herself the delineation of the character, she has – in all the consciousness of high genius – dared only less than she did in consenting to perform Smike; and if, in the character under our present notice, she did not reach the same height as in 'Nicholas Nickleby', it is only because the *description*

---

[26] See Bratton, 'Mirroring Men', pp. 240–1.
[27] Walter Goodman, *The Keeleys, on the Stage and at Home* (London: Richard Bentley, 1895), pp. 1–13.

MRS. KEELEY AS JACK SHEPPARD.
Printed & Sold by A.PARK. 47 Leonard St! Tabernacle Walk.

Figure 6   Mary Ann Keeley as Jack Sheppard

of the part did not call for those high powers of pathos, the exhibition of which made her the reality rather than the copy of the ill-treated boy.[28]

---

[28] *The Odd Fellow*, 2 November 1839.

The conservative press, however, found the glorification of such Newgate heroes as Jack so dangerous, especially as embodied by the irresistible Mrs Keeley, that subsequent revivals were condemned and censored.

Priscilla Horton, who had a rich contralto voice and a gift of mimicry, played both serious and comic transvestism before she became Mrs German Reed. She moved into adult performance in 1834, playing Romeo round the minor theatres in the summer[29] before taking on the Fool in *King Lear*, when Macready reintroduced the part for the first time since the Restoration. Her range in for example 1843 at Drury Lane included the shepherd hero (a tenor role that had to be transposed for her) in Handel's *Acis and Galetea* and Ariel in *The Tempest*. From 1843 to 1850 she made a yearly or twice yearly appearance in the Planché or Brough extravaganzas that Vestris and Mathews staged at the Haymarket, under the management of Benjamin Webster. She played the hero: the minstrel Graceful in *The Fair One with the Golden Locks* in 1843, Percinet the Fairy Prince in *Graciosa and Percinet* in 1844, Jason in *Jason in Colchis* in 1845, Jupiter and the nightingale in *The Birds of Aristophanes* at Easter 1846. That Christmas Mark Lemon did the holiday piece, *The Young Pretender*, and she played Mary Armadale, who disguises herself as the Young Chevalier 'in a grand costume'. In December 1848 Planché's work returned at Christmas and she played a prince who is 'a loose gentleman at large' in *Camaralzama and Badoura*, and in March 1849 she returned to the cavalier costume as Sir Charles Rivers in *The Trumpeter's Wedding*. The next month it was back to classical tunics in *The Sphinx* as Prince Oedipus, a Corinthian prince who organises political agitation as a means of winning himself the princess. In December 1849 the brothers Brough wrote her a second version of the rebellious 'fast' young prince, called The Rapid, who gets into debt and mischief in a piece called *The Ninth Statue*. By 1850 she was 32, probably getting rather too large or mature for these parts, and began to play the heroines instead.[30]

The tone of these topical extravaganzas can be gathered from the *Era* review of 30 March 1845, when Horton was playing Jason to Vestris's Medea and Charles Mathews was a one-man Chorus. After a great deal of classically educated point scoring, the reviewer politely suggests Vestris has rejuvenated herself by a dip in Medea's cauldron, and praises

---

[29] She appears in that role for 'the 6th time' on a Victoria bill for Miss Allison's benefit on 18 July 1834.
[30] Information and tag lines drawn from press advertisements for the season.

Miss Horton 'equally at home' 'as the love-sick insinuating suitor, or the lack-a-daisical, inconstant, supercilious husband', singing 'some difficult music' with 'great sweetness and taste'. Mathews, as 'the consolidated chorus', dressed somewhere between the most modern tailoring and ancient Greek robes,

was as epicene as the half-man half-fish of Horace; was as wonderful in his actions as a male Mermaid, and as seductive as a he Syren; his moralling on love was as revolutionary as the air to which it was aptly adapted, 'the Fall of Paris'; and who can forget, after Jason has been informed that Medea is whipping his children, and his impassioned appeal to the consolidated chorus of 'Where?' Charles Mathews's outstretched arms, and indicating finger, and mock-solemn – 'Behind!'

What is important in such work is the freedom, sanctioned in burlesque by the conflation of class-biased educated play and topical allusion, to disrupt the assumptions of its audience – in an unthreatening, even a flattering, way. Priscilla Horton can make neglectful young husbands ludicrous, puncturing self-regard; Mathews can be seductively epicene, sing revolutionary anti-love songs and point at her backside. Both invoke chaos but allay panic with their sexy insouciance.

'HER ASTONISHING AND PECULIAR TALENT':[31]
THE CASE OF CELINE CELESTE

A culmination of these gender experiments as the foundation of substantial female success can be seen in the transvestite career of one actress: the hugely successful, widely admired and strangely undermemorialised Celine Celeste. Madame Celeste seems to me to encapsulate all the paradoxes and unexpectedness of the female performer in the early West End, but to have been recorded in theatre history more or less in passing, without any substantive appreciation of what she did, or of what her career tells us of the period. Even her date of birth is unclear, given variously as 1811 or 1814 or even 1816. She was always called Madame (or earlier Mademoiselle) Celeste, and thought of as the essence of Frenchness, but her names and origins seem fabricated, by comparison with Madame Vestris: the *Englishwoman's Domestic Magazine* for 1 July 1869 weaves a deliberately starry myth of transnational origins when it says

---

[31] *Bell's Life in London*, 26 February 1832.

Celeste Anastasie Elliott, neé Keppler, was born at Paris on the 6th of August, 1816. She is of good birth and parentage, of German origin on the paternal side, her father being a descendant of the German astronomer and friend of Schiller, John Christopher Keppler. Her mother was the granddaughter of the Chevalier de Rouzell, equerry to his majesty the unfortunate Louis XVI. He was one of the prisoners of the Bastille . . .

— on reaching the Bastille the reader may clearly feel the presence of melodrama and romance, confirmed when the paragraph concludes with details about the papers to the family estates having been 'concealed in his belt' when he was there and never found again. The magazine goes on to the more probable fact that she was educated for the musical stage in Paris, but it then has her running away to seek her fortune aboard the American ship *Queen Mab*, laughing as 'the American flag was hoisted' in defiance of the gendarmes in pursuit. She certainly did seek her fortune in an American engagement, with her sister Constance, in 1827. She married an American named Elliott in 1828 (which seems to suggest that she was born before 1816) and had a daughter before she and her family returned to Europe. She and Constance danced in Dublin, under Bunn's management, in October 1830, before they made their way to London. On 9 March 1831 they were noticed at the Queen's, one of many struggling minor theatres, dancing competitive pirouettes; by the 11th reporters had grasped Celeste's name. Her victory, if this was a competition, was soon clear: by the beginning of April she was appearing in plays, and Constance is mentioned no more.

Celeste rose rapidly to fame in the maelstrom of London minor theatre. A puff that appeared in the *Morning Chronicle* for 10 January 1833 claimed

Mademoiselle Celeste has performed in one year, the *French Spy* 200 times; the *Wizard Skiff* 150 times; the *Dumb Brigand* 100 times; and acted in fifteen other pieces, all written expressly for her! She has danced in them this year 600 dances; fought 626 combats; changed her dress 1,504 times; has performed at eight different theatres in London, on several occasions two on the same evening; has had thirty benefits, all good; performed at twenty-eight theatres in England, three in Ireland, and three in Scotland; and for the year 1832 received 3,120l. for her services. During her late engagements in Liverpool upwards of 3,000 persons were unable to gain admittance to the theatre.

The penchant for precise but large numbers suggests her young American husband had a hand in circulating this para. to the newspapers; but it is a true representation of her instant commercial success. Her celebrity was the more striking since she spoke no word of English, so when she began to act as well as dance all roles had to be mute; hence the pieces expressly written to showcase 'her astonishing and peculiar talent'.

We may judge what this talent was by these roles, and the strange plays that had to be constructed to display them. They begin with *The French Spy* by J. T. Haines,[32] in which she plays a French young lady who has disguised herself as a military volunteer in order to follow her fiancé, a colonel, to the Siege of Constantina; there she woos the daughter of a sergeant, to further the comic plot, before saving her beloved (who has not penetrated her disguise) from a murderous captive, which causes him to decide to dress her as a possessed Arab boy and send her into the city as a spy (see Figure 7). In the second act she does this, with a set piece of exotic dance and mime in which, having been taken for a prophetic madman, she is able to extract a plan of the forthcoming attack upon the French from the Bey; but before she can get this news out to the camp on a flaming arrow her fiancé is captured, and she has to fight for his life in torchlight upon the battlements. The climax comes when she is discovered to be a woman, and carried off to be dressed in eastern female garb; she is fighting off the advances of the Bey with his own scimitar when the French break in and blow up the city.

The Wizard Skiff, also by Haines,[33] has an even more curious and exotic political background, being set on a coast by a 'Russian military village' and involving a villain who seems to be a Russian count and also a Muslim, who has, in the back story, exterminated a Greek Archon and his family all except for a baby girl named Alexa whose tongue was cut out, as well as other nameless pollutions being perpetrated upon her. This of course is Celeste's character, but she appears in most of the play as her male avatar Alexis, coming ashore with his mates from the wizard skiff – so called to veil their vengeful operations against the dominant powers by means of superstition. They do a scene of chanting and moving in unison before concealing themselves in their secret cave on an upper level of the set. Celeste slides down a rope of sashes to woo and later to rescue the heroine, and to fight with the Count and with Wolfo the henchman who cut out her tongue. There is a central episode in

---

[32] John Thomas Haines, *The French Spy; or, The Siege of Constantina*, Dicks plays no. 680, n.d. These plays cannot with any certainty be assigned a first place and date of performance: Celeste seems to have been dashing from one minor venue to another all over London in the mid 1830s, taking the plays with her.

[33] In BL Add. MSS 59888, a (collapsing) bound volume of fair copies of Haines's plays, in which he is identified as 'the author of The Wizard Skiff'. The place and date of first performance in this case are probably Christmas 1831 at the Coburg.

Figure 7   Madame Celeste as the Arab Boy

which she masquerades as a Zingaro boy and dances a Greek wedding
dance, before the finale, which is a series of fights and flights through
dungeons and underground passages before all is once more blown up –
this time she is killed in the explosion herself, lying in the final tableau
with her hands grasping the throat of her violator. The implication may
be that she must die because of the initial 'pollution', or it may be that
she is beyond redemption in her gender transgression, for taking bloody
vengeance in a very unfeminine way.

I have not been able to track down a copy of *The Dumb Brigand*,
but her roles in it were apparently all male: Alp the brigand chief,
Henrico Rotzi a Genoese gondolier and Manuel Stanislaus an Istrian
chief (in another advertisement 'a Greek sailor'). The performance seems
likely to have been close to the other plays, involving multiple and
exhilarating transgressions of gender, race and sexuality, lots of athleticism
and some stunning exotic dances and costumes. The preposterous plots
carry quite profound implications: they allow a free-ranging fantasy that
centres upon a woman doing astounding deeds of heroism and sexual
play, distanced and also thrown into sharp relief by her silence, her
eloquent movement and her extraordinary physical capacities. One is
reminded of nothing so much as the late twentieth-century action figure
of Lara Croft, battling heroine celebrated in video games, animations, a
film and a range of clothes.[34]

By 1833 the confused effects of the 1831 committee and the consequent
Dramatic Authors Act were being felt in London: the publishers were
claiming the copyright payments that the writers thought they had been
awarded; the highly respectable player Russell had been closed down at
the Strand for lack of a licence; the Coburg, renamed the Victoria, was
staging *Hamlet*; and Alfred Bunn took leases on both the patent houses.
Such a bold venture required striking productions, and he hired Celeste
among other up-to-date attractions from the minor theatres, pairing her
with the Surreyside nautical favourite T. P. Cooke in an unsuccessful
panto called *Prince Le Boo* at Drury Lane before getting in the stud of
horses from Astley's to put on the more successful spectacle *George and the
Dragon*. He moved Celeste over the road to appear at Covent Garden as
the leader of the grotesque dance of 'folies' in the final act of an Auber
opera, *Gustavus the Third*.

---

[34] The Wikipedia entry on Lara Croft is currently (12.12.2010) enormous and scholarly: 56.73kb long,
with 161 footnotes.

Gustavus was part of what Terry Castle calls the 'vestigial life in opera' of the masquerade tradition.[35] Like many another opera of these decades, it was apparently written with the conversion of its music into quadrilles for social occasions already in mind (see above in connection with *Masaniello*), but more importantly it included a spectacular masquerade on stage: the last act depicted the masked ball at the Stockholm Opera House in 1792, at which Gustavus was assassinated. Hundreds of performers in fancy dress appeared in a vast set that mirrored the auditorium. Celeste did her breath-taking pirouettes. This worked the trick for Bunn: young Princess Victoria came to see *Gustavus* and it ran for many nights in that season and the next. Queen Adelaide commanded a performance of the next spectacle in which Celeste had a similar role, *The Revolt of the Harem*. Both pieces were imported from Paris, and both struck the British press as vulgar in the extreme, though this did not prevent audiences from flocking to see the second piece too, to ogle the evolutions of hundreds of ballet girls first taking a bath and then going though military manoeuvres as a female army.[36]

But these supporting appearances in her earlier role of spectacular dancer were by no means the best direction of Celeste's developing career, and she soon dropped out of Bunn's rackety edifice to star elsewhere. She was developing more plays, and would in time acquire enough English to speak on stage; meanwhile the writing of vehicles continued, and the plays themselves were worked over and refined. A notable example is another play, not listed above by her publicist, that began in 1831 and survived in Celeste's repertoire much longer than her early knock-down, drag-out brigand busters. *The Wept of Wish-ton-Wish* was derived from Fennimore Cooper's novel published in England in 1829 with the main title *The Borderers*. This was turned into a showcase for the actress in her round of the minors, and even appropriated by Bunn under the misleading new title of *The Indian Girl* in 1837. Before that she appeared in it at the Adelphi and the Coburg in November 1831, and possibly at the Pavilion before either of these, though it was licensed for the Adelphi. It is dramatised by William Bayle Bernard, one of the more accomplished of the bohemian dramatic hacks. It exists in two very different forms. In the licensed copy,[37] and on the bills at the Adelphi, it begins with a scene prescient of the twentieth-century musical, set on the shores of New England in 1660, with a ship worked across the backdrop, approaching

[35] Castle, *Masquerade*, p. 339.   [36] See *Age*, 9 February 1834, for example.
[37] BL Add. MSS 42913(5), fos. 188–226, licensed for the Adelphi 12 November 1831.

the haven, where a chorus of comical Puritan settlers sing and dance in welcome. They are less pleased when the vessel arrives and from it leaps a Colonel Marsden at the head of a set of bloodthirsty and libidinous cavaliers, bringing the news of King Charles II's return to power in England and, therefore, over the colony. He is in search of two 'regicides', including a Major Gough, and has with him a swashing young cavalier supposed to be the Major's son, brought up in the opposite camp and now eager to dance and drink and subdue the settlers, when the troops are loosed upon the colony's womenfolk. This is of course Celeste, playing Gough's dumbstruck daughter, Hope, who has smuggled herself home to America by pretending to be a cavalier youth. After a scene in which she tears off her hat and cloak and tramples upon them to make her father recognise her, and still finds herself 'rejected on all sides' and gives way to 'a gush of grief', she is reunited with her father and sister Faith and helps him to escape from the Colonel in her cavalier costume. Back home at Wish-ton-Wish there is a confrontation between the settlers and the Narragansetts, whose leader Connuchett instantly falls in love with Hope and carries her off with him when the blockhouse is burnt. Act 2 opens with a second folksy musical scene, in which the Narragansetts sing and dance and mime their piscatorial daily occupations, and we learn that time has passed and they are about once more to attack in an attempt to regain Wish-ton-Wish, their ancestral home. Hope Gough is now Connuchett's wife Narramatta, and she is soon leaping to his defence. The settlers capture him, and she wields a sword and captures a settler's gun, but she is subdued into trailing along behind when they seize her baby and hold it up between themselves and her fire. She spends the rest of the play shrieking with horror and running between her old and new families, miming complex action and reaction as she is torn between her husband and child and revived memories of her father and mother, ending on a tableau in which she dies of grief in Connuchett's arms, under the red oak tree of his fathers, after he is executed by the Mohican leader who sides with the settlers.

Later Celeste cut out the opening episodes in which she dressed as a cavalier and substituted a short opening which tells a back story more like Cooper's novel, in which Hope Gough is carried off by the Narragansetts as a little child, and brought up with them, thus giving a more plausible reason for her inability to speak English. The second version is a more coherent play, cutting out the transvestite effect in the strutting *petit maître* to focus on cross-racial familial conflict, as in a striking exchange at the end of Act 2, scene 2, when she has been returned to the settlement but has lost her wits at the shock. She is sitting dumbly unresponsive to her grieving father when Conanchet (as he is now spelt) is heard off, as a captive, calling her name. She looks up:

GOUGH: She hears his voice when she is deaf to mine.
FAITH: He is her husband!
GOUGH: Her destroyer!
CONAN: (*nearer*) Narramattah!
MUSIC
Narramattah shrieks and springs through window – scene closes rapidly.[38]

The melodramatic intensity of Celeste's physical performances carried the audience through the desperate emotional tangle that Bernard had derived from Cooper's meditation on the American 'borderers', a book which had sought to understand the transgressive and tragic amalgamations created by European immigration.[39] The added comic subplot is very important in the play, moderating its intensity, absorbing any nervous laughter that might undermine Celeste's tragic impact: throughout the final scenes the degradation and death of the heroic chief and his suffering wife and child is parodied, in rapid alternation of scenes, by the reunion of the clown Skunk, who has been masquerading as a native American tribesman of the Mud Turtles, with his wife and fifteen children – not all his. The religious and racial clashes that made up the new culture of America in 1660 are sufficiently distanced from the English context of the 1830s, perhaps, to make Celeste's frenzied suffering of internal division, forced transgression and inevitable loss seem a fantasy comfortably removed from their own liminal concerns; though she was in fact even more successful in her American tours with these transvestite, transracial and transgendered exhibitions. The play needed to be altered, and the cross-gendered element was dropped, as the category panic of the 1830s passed by, but Celeste remained an exceptional and a very successful performer, and her subsequent long-remembered acting successes, such as the Indian huntress Miami in Buckstone's *The Green Bushes*, which she first performed in her first year of management at the Adelphi, in 1845 (see Chapter 6), were founded upon these first unspeaking but eloquent transvestite performances.

---

[38] French's edition, no. cliv, anon., n.d., n.p., Act 2, scene 2.
[39] For a discussion of the early nineteenth-century term 'amalgamation' for cross-racial breeding and Cooper's attitude to the story he tells, see James D. Wallace, 'Race and Captivity in Cooper's *The Wept of Wish-ton-Wish*', *American Literary History* 7 (1995), 189–209, esp. 203–7.

CONCLUSION

Celeste's rise to fame was followed by decades of evergreen success as the partner of Benjamin Webster; Chapters 5 and 6 will follow her into that highly successful career. Her early years were an outstanding and extreme, but by no means unique, example of the extraordinary experience of the actresses who stood in the breach/breeches of category panic in the 1830s and 1840s. Her 'peculiar talent' could not have been more transgressive, crossing the boundaries between British and French, European and Native American, language and muteness, dance and acting, as well as male and female. Perhaps the collected examples here, in the work of the likes of Mary Keeley as Jack Sheppard and Virginie Déjazet as a precocious princeling as well as Madame Celeste as heroic brigand or possessed dervish, point to an even deeper area of cultural border negotiation: the difference between right and wrong. The narrowing redefinition of gender boundaries, which offered an appropriate and powerful way of showing this story on stage, was only part of a new substantiation of social role definition that touched every aspect of middle-class life. That was, in global terms, a new sense of what one could and could not do – what was right, proper, responsible, behaviour for the class in power; what was hegemonic. In the performances of Keeley as the thieving artisan Jack Sheppard and Celeste as a dumb cavalier kissing the Puritan wives, the law-abiding, anxious general public could enjoy and also rule out many kinds of aberrant behaviour, and come to a safer grasp of its own place. That this process was part of the founding of the West End – the place where there would be forever licence and holiday, bright lights and naughtiness – seems to me both appropriate and important.

CHAPTER 5

The shaping of West End management

The story of the Victorian entertainment world has not so far been told with women in an important managerial or empowered capacity at its centre. Kerry Powell's intention in his *Women and the Victorian Theatre*[1] was to argue that 'Victorian theatre conspired in producing repressive codes of gender even as it provided women with a rare opportunity to experience independence and power', taking as his evidence for this the rhetoric of social control through masculine assertions of gender superiority that he found pervasively present in late Victorian theatrical writing. He is entirely justified, from that perspective, in his assertion that women's theatrical power is 'a forgotten tradition' buried by the defensiveness of men and their 'pervasive rhetoric' of the impossibility of women writing plays or managing playhouses. But his interest is chiefly in correcting the record of playwriting, at the end of the century, rather than in exploring the decades of female management and stage power that preceded it, and caused the 'masculine panic' that wrote them out of the record. In this chapter I intend to step back beyond the point at which the formation of that united male front blocked our view of the successful theatre women of the mid century.

I have already indicated the received history, which is that the theatrical managements of Macready, Charles Kean, Samuel Phelps, Benjamin Webster and Squire Bancroft are to be understood as the foundations of London's theatre in the 1840s, 1850s and 1860s – the piers of the bridge by which the gulf between the Romantic stage, on the one hand, and Ibsen and Henry Irving on the shores of Modernism, on the other, may be negotiated. That is the late-Victorian perception, readily accepted by subsequent writers and still influential in Powell's book, since he came to the issue via work on Oscar Wilde and the late Victorian popular stage, where misogyny is entrenched. But a fresh look at even the male

[1] Cambridge University Press, 1997, pp. xi, xii, 13–63.

145

commentators in the mid and early Victorian periods suggests a less
embattled, more even-handed appreciation of the managerial achievements of women; and it is not difficult to tell another story, even about
Bancroft, Kean, Webster and the other dominating male figures of the
time, by reference to the copious evidence of the contemporary press. We
need to remember that these dominant men were not by any means alone,
and to attend to the wives and partners who worked with them; and,
looking a little further, to discern that there were many more working
managers, some of whom were female, making up the rest of the mid-
century landscape. Numerically, and no doubt in terms of the wealth and
publicity they generated, there were more men than women in charge of
Arnold's 'contemptible' theatre (see Chapter 2) – more, but actually not
overwhelmingly more. The appearance of female absence is misleading.
Many successful women, managing, directing and organising as well as
acting, have been discounted – their stories deliberately suppressed,
according to Powell's account; and an examination of their contributions,
rather than a focus upon the rhetoric of their suppression, might go some
way towards a better account of the origins of the West End as it has
developed.

I therefore intend to approach these neglected creators by addressing
the striking and widely ignored fact enunciated by Tracy Davis: 'in
nineteenth-century Britain, theatre is the only branch of industry or
commerce where women, in significant numbers, were up-front business
executives'.[2] Davis points out that 'during the 1850s and 60s at least fifty
women managed theatres in Britain',[3] and exemplifies the public impact
of the managements of Eliza Vestris and Marie Wilton. She suggests that
the 'wo-manager' presented a challenge to 'gentlemanly capitalism', a
challenge which was controlled, but not by any means dismissed, by
masculine dominance of the sources of investment capital. During this
period banks, and the less formal marts for the circulation of money,
would not treat women as equals or as potential business partners, at least
in part because their status in law rendered them not responsible as
debtors. Therefore they had great difficulty starting businesses. But it
was possible (though very risky) to start up a theatrical venture even in
London with quite a small financial investment. The prominent Drury
Lane entrepreneur E. L. Chatterton, for example, had almost nothing of
his own at the outset, and no credit or wealthy friends, but nevertheless,
when he was inspired to turn theatre professional by Mrs Warner's

[2] Davis, *Economics of the British Stage*, p. 273.   [3] ibid., p. 300.

management at the Marylebone, he was able to plunge into management at the Lyceum with a fellow actor, staking that major undertaking by appeal to his father and mother.[4] Women could and did do the same, and some had besides other means of eliciting funds in the private sphere.

To see how the presence of women in management worked, it is therefore necessary to consider first the personal relationships within which the wo-managers operated. Davis suggests that in order to understand how women participated in the public sphere of theatre business it is necessary to regard them as 'a category unique among performers and possibly among the categories of people typically excluded from full and uncontested public participation'.[5] In the examples she takes, Vestris and Wilton, she demonstrates that by entering into their management of theatres well before they recruited husbands to join them in the business, they can be said to 'suggest new ways of conveying the conjunction of the intimate sphere with business, allowing women strength and mastery but making them conjoined marital partners as a distinct subaltern category'.[6] Their work was read by their contemporaries entirely within the frame of their femininity. In other words, if we are to understand the place and contribution of women in this unique sphere of Victorian business, we have to take into account that they brought with them into their public life the relationships of the private and the intimate sphere. By understanding how this worked for a range of such women, what their personal, that is familial and marital, relationships were and how these were imbricated with their working lives in the theatre, we may understand the contributions they made to the formation of the West End and its style.

THE THEATRICAL FAMILY

In *New Readings* I offered a genealogical model for the understanding of women as holding power, posited upon their strength within theatre families.[7] Almost all the women who succeeded in theatre management in the West End did so from a base within a theatrical family, even where that was only one generation deep – a father and mother who had taken to the stage, and allowed or encouraged their children to follow them. Blood families like the Vinings, for example, who were a dominant clan within

---

[4] See John Coleman, *Players and Playwrights I have Known*, 2 vols. (London: Chatto & Windus, 1888), vol. II, pp. 334–7.
[5] Davis, *Economics of the British Stage*, p. 290.   [6] ibid.   [7] Bratton, *New Readings*, pp. 171–99.

the Brompton colony of 'great acting families' whom Clement Scott speaks of as standing above the melting pot of Bohemian London (see Chapter 3), included successful actors and sometimes managers of both sexes, and at the end of the period of formation of the West End they threw up one of its major women managers, Mathilda Vining. Family links are often hidden by other names, and Mathilda always used the name Mrs John Wood, though her actor husband had been dead three years when she took over the licence of the St James's theatre in 1869, backed, it would appear, by her own savings and perhaps her family's money. She had already managed a theatre in San Francisco, and at the St James's was a highly successful and 'brisk innovator'[8] over the next eight years, as well as a 'comedienne with a broad sense of fun' and an 'almost masculine style of droll urbanity'.[9] According to the *Era* report of her return to the British stage, this manner was that of the currently celebrated 'Yankee gals'.[10] She continued to star on both sides of the Atlantic; and later was equally successful in management at the Court Theatre in Sloane Square.

The West End was a new world, however, and there were opportunities within it for women who lacked the advantages of the Vinings. Deep theatrical roots provided a kind of aristocracy of theatrical rather than landed property within which women could take a leading place, if their talents so enabled them; but a new kind of success story, in some ways peculiar to the rapid changes of fortune amongst the entrepreneurial middle classes of the first half of the century, is exemplified first by Jane Scott, and in the next generation by the Swanborough family. Jane Scott, born 1779, was the daughter of a successful tradesman in the Strand, John Scott, an inventor of new colouring agents who also imported and developed optical devices and toys – the forerunners of photographic projection. Jane was talented and persuasive, and her father had sufficient faith in her to buy up twelve adjoining tenements beside his shop and build for her use a theatre, the Sans Pareil, which was to become the Adelphi. She began with solo turns and performances by her singing pupils, but in 1807, profiting from the current Lord Chamberlain's desire to reform the old patent monopoly by allowing the beginnings of West End performance, the Scotts acquired an annual burletta licence. This led to a successful series of seasons during which Jane Scott wrote and starred

[8] Barry Duncan, *The St James's Theatre, its Strange and Complete History 1835–1957* (London: Barrie & Rockliff, 1964), pp. 142 et seq.
[9] ibid., p.147.   [10] *Era*, 18 November 1866.

in her own melodramas and comedies, and hired a strong supporting company of actors, singers and dancers. She retired, having made a substantial fortune for herself and her father, in 1818, and only then took to herself a husband – a young half-pay officer whose naval career had ended with the cessation of hostilities. They retired to Surrey with her fortune and his social credentials, and set up as gentlefolk.[11]

The Swanboroughs were similarly theatrical nobodies (their name was not even originally the romantic-sounding Swanborough, but simply Smith) who emerged from the London commercial class, and in one generation took a leading place both in the West End and in provincial legitimate theatre. Henry Valentine Smith, born 1803, and his wife Mary, born 1806, lived in Golden Square Soho, where he was an actuary and accountant, and where their five children were born. They prospered sufficiently to buy a house in Beaufort Street, Chelsea and fit out a lumber room for their hobby of amateur theatricals,[12] with the probably unforeseen result that their children all became stage professionals.

First the eldest son William, born 1832, went off to the north of England and, calling himself 'Sheridan Smith', took up with the touring theatricals; in 1851 he was managing a travelling Italian opera troupe visiting the industrial towns. In August 1852 he attempted a bold, not to say foolhardy, stroke, a return to town in grand style: he rented and opened the languishing Drury Lane, charging cheap prices, billing an unknown American tragedian as his leading attraction. The astonished press were under the impression he was a US entrepreneur with £10,000 in his pocket.[13] He closed within the week, unable to pay his company. Back in the north, he attempted to run the ancient and collapsing York circuit; his wife (Kate, a sailor's daughter) became proprietor of the Theatre Royal Leeds, wooing in vain an impoverished working-class audience.[14] Cutting and running once more for home, William reappeared in London, now acting under the name of Swanborough, in January 1856. He was being dunned for debts to the York bill printers, and became officially insolvent in March. In January 1857 he set up as a 'polyphonic entertainer' – a one-man show – and went on tour again. The next year he worked his way back to London, acting at the Lyceum before he made another plunge, taking the aged and tottering Strand

---

[11] *DNB.*   [12] 'A chat with Edward Swanborough', *Era*, 1 July 1893.
[13] See *Preston Guardian*, 18 October 1851; *Reynolds's Newspaper*, 25 July 1852; *Era* 8 August 1852.
[14] *Hull Packet*, 4 August 1854; *Era*, 1 July 1855.

Theatre and announcing on 14 March 1858 that it was closed for refurbishment, but would open at Easter – under the direction of Miss Swanborough.[15]

This was his sister Louisa Smith, born 1834, who had made her début as Miss Swanborough early in 1854 in Miss Glyn's company, supporting the serious drama in Liverpool. In January 1855 she made her London début at the Theatre Royal Haymarket playing Juliet to Charlotte Cushman's Romeo.[16] Her success was immediate: by January 1856 she had played Viola in a Haymarket *Twelfth Night*, moved to the Olympic and the Lyceum and appeared before the Queen in St George's Hall. Her brother, on returning to London, took her stage name; now he stepped back, retreating to provincial management in Birmingham, allowing her much steadier hand to set up the beginnings of a family business that continued unbroken for twenty-seven years, 1858 to 1885, at the small and previously precarious theatre in the Strand.

Having laid the foundations of the Strand's success (see Chapter 6) Louisa decisively married out, aged 27, in the spring of 1861. He was a Major William Lyon, Marylebone vestryman, opera-goer, a public-spirited Liberal concerned with various good causes, and a man of considerable wealth. She retired permanently from the stage; her father, the accountant, became the manager at the Strand. By this date all his other children were in the business, though the boys were not on the boards. Arthur began as treasurer at the Prince of Wales's Birmingham, which was another venture of his elder brother. Arthur married Eleanor Bufton, a leading performer at the Strand, in the spring of 1860, and subsequently became acting manager there – what would now be called front-of-house manager. Edward, the next boy, born 1841, also combined the parental gift for figures with his siblings' stage proclivities and became the Strand's treasurer for many years. They both went on to manage large music halls – Arthur the Royal Holborn, and Edward the London Pavilion. Ada, the youngest Smith/Swanborough, born in 1845, made her début in burlesque at the Strand in 1861, and had a long and successful acting career thereafter; she was the only one of the family to make it into the *Dictionary of National Biography*.

The elder Mr Smith/Swanborough had been deaf since 1847, and perhaps found the demands of running a West End theatre rather too

[15] *Liverpool Mercury*, 26 March 1856; *Hull Packet*, 28 March 1856; *Era*, 11 January 1857; *Era*, 14 March 1857.
[16] *Era*, 19 February 1854 and 28 January 1855.

much; at any rate, in 1863 he cut his throat.[17] Mary his wife stepped in –
perhaps the histrionic tastes had been hers? – and was the lessee of the
Strand in its most prosperous days in the 1860s, when it was the talk of
the town with its company that included not only their own Ada and
Arthur's wife Eleanor Bufton, but also Marie Wilton, Lydia Thompson
and Frederick Robson – see Chapter 6. Like the cockney paint-maker
John Scott, who fifty years before had created a setting for the enterprise
of his theatrical daughter Jane and so found himself an incongruous
theatre manager, old Mrs Swanborough was the butt of many jokes in
the profession. H. J. Byron, who wrote their most successful burlesques,
dined out on his stories of her for decades; but there is no denying the
success of the theatre under her long management. An essential element of
West End style originated in this little family theatre; its nature is
discussed in the next chapter.

THE 'DEMI-MONDE'

Perhaps the oldest way in which private and public life were connected for
the woman in theatre was, as in the case of the Byzantine Empress
Theodora (*c.* 500–48), for an actress of beauty and charisma to form a
relationship with a wealthy and high-ranking man. The most usual result
was that the woman left the stage to live with him, sometimes to marry, as
in the case of Louisa Swanborough mentioned above. There are countless
examples of such liaisons before and during the nineteenth century, but
also significant variations upon the pattern. One of its most obvious
potential stresses was the tension between the wealthy or high-ranking
lover and the greater personal attraction of another man, often a colleague
in the theatre; this was the cause of many scandals, like that which dogged
the diva Mary Paton, who first married Lord William Pitt Lennox then
divorced him and chose the tenor Joseph Wood instead. Paton could
reasonably have argued that Lennox failed to keep his side of the bargain,
since he was a profligate who expected her to keep on working, taking her
high earnings for his own use. Their *demi-mondaine* Regency world
included many theatrical ventures in which gentlemen of birth and
sometimes fortune involved themselves actively in theatrical management
as well as forming liaisons with actresses, and these women – Harriet
Waylett is an example – often appear, normally quite fleetingly, as

[17] *Daily News,* 28 May 1863.

'managers' of theatre seasons financed by their lovers. How much artistic control or agency they had is rarely clear.

Such a moment in the managerial spotlight came to several women in the years of upheaval round 1830, when Vestris's success at the Olympic made 'wo-managers' popular. These were not all rags-to-riches tales: an interestingly complicated example is Louisa Nisbett, née Macnamara, whose upper middle-class family and personal life resulted in a chequered stage career. Her high-ranking family had failed to stop her grandfather squandering three fortunes or her father quitting the army and taking to the stage, where Louisa joined him before she was 10 years old. Her early success in leading theatres was boosted by the strenuous patronage of her aunt Lady Cranstoun; in 1831 she left the stage to marry 'John Alexander Nisbett of Brettenham Hall, Suffolk, a captain in the first Life Guards, whom she described as "never a husband, always a lover". He was killed on 2 October of that year falling from his horse.'[18] She returned to the stage a tragic heroine playing comedy roles, and in 1834 was billed as the manager of the theatre later to become the Prince of Wales's under Marie Wilton; it drew a very fashionable audience. She soon left off managing such minor ventures, however, to return to create important roles under Webster's management at the Haymarket and for Vestris at Covent Garden before retiring once more in 1844 to marry an elderly baronet who died within two years, leaving her to return to the stage again as Lady Boothby.

A more typically *demi-mondaine* example in the next generation would be Louisa Herbert, whose theatrical successes, from an unnoticed first London début at the Lyceum under the Mathews's in 1847, culminated in the management of the St James's, 1864–8. Her fame was entirely founded upon her fashionable, pre-Raphaelite-style beauty. In 1855 she married a stockbroker and returned to the London stage at the Strand, where Rossetti sketched her as his 'No. 1 stunner'; when she had a baby, the stockbroker seduced the maid and then left for India, leaving the beautiful Miss Herbert the talk of the town, to become its leading courtesan. Her successive houses (off Eaton Square, and then a mansion in the Boltons) and her next child were given to her by one highly placed lover, John Rochfort, a wealthy amateur artist, while the third child, and the lease of the St James's Theatre, were set down to his officer friend Fred 'the Rip' Milbank. She enjoyed the society of Little Holland House, the leading salon of upper Bohemia; on stage she worked with the Wigans, moving

[18] *DNB.*

with them from the Olympic to the St James's, and her major acting successes were in plays from the novels of Mary Elizabeth Braddon, especially as Lady Audley. Her managerial claims to fame, however, were that she commissioned a Christmas piece from Tom Robertson who passed the work on to W. S. Gilbert, causing him to write his one and only pantomime; and that when Charles Reade spotted Henry Irving acting in Manchester, Miss Herbert brought him to London and gave him a successful début. She retired from the stage as her beauty faded, and in 1868 Mrs John Wood took over at the St James's.[19]

THE INDEPENDENT WOMAN

As the century progressed women with an ambition and a talent to manage their own careers and indeed their own theatres were able to modify such old-established patterns of personal life as these to make their way into more genuinely powerful positions, at the head of enterprises for which admirers provided some support or finance. Gradually the flow of benefit in such situations – from the professional mentor/exploiter or the moneyed gentleman amateur to the actress, or from actress to the aspiring writer or impoverished gentleman – becomes more obviously two-way. There also begins to be a discernable pattern: such women most often begin their careers by marrying a man who supports them in some way in their stage aspirations, and/or himself benefits by association with a rising star, and then quite quickly move away from a failed, exploitative or unequal alliance and forge a successful career for themselves. Eliza Bartolozzi is the obvious example of this scenario, keeping his name but leaving Armand Vestris behind her, managing her own life, business associates and lovers, and eventually choosing the young Charles James Mathews as a suitably gentlemanly and minor-talented consort and figurehead for management (see Chapter 4). But there are many other instances.

Celine Celeste married a rich American businessman called Elliott in the first surge of her success, but separated from him and lived in England, continuing her rapid rise to fame (see Chapter 4). After his premature death she did not choose to remarry, because her major relationship was with Benjamin Webster, who was himself already

---

[19] All information drawn from her great-granddaughter Virginia Surtees's *The Actress and the Brewer's Wife: Two Victorian Vignettes* (Wilby, Norwich: Michael Russell, 1997); Louisa Herbert did not find her way into the *Dictionary of National Biography*.

married and remained so.²⁰ Their liaison was publicly known, and was expressed in performance and theatre management. They first worked together under his management at the Haymarket in 1838, and formed an alliance that one might dub a new, almost respectable, Victorian version of an old icon: the gay couple.²¹ Fashionable and exciting celebrities of the stage, they played sparkling comedies together and were leaders in the latest craze – they danced the polka. Their friends and rivals in this, in the early 1840s, were John Buckstone and Fanny Fitzwilliam, another couple with obstacles to their marriage but not to their obvious togetherness; all four appear on a striking series of exuberant bills, performing in modern theatres up and down the country, and coming together in the West End.²² The artistic impact is discussed in Chapter 6.

In 1843, following the act freeing the theatres (for which he had originally been an advocate and campaigner), Webster brought his attention back to the serious drama. He recruited a strong acting company and sprang into spirited year-round production of major plays at the Haymarket, now that he was no longer confined to a summer season, making it 'the constant home of the drama'²³ for three years without a closed period. In 1844, however, he extended his options beyond the legitimate by also leasing the Adelphi, for more popular productions. There Celeste, with whom he had shared the management of the Theatre Royal Liverpool for a year already, was in charge. For the next nine years she was its star performer and its directress both on the bills and as a real responsibility. Her contribution there to the developing art of the West End is also discussed in the next chapter. When they fell out in 1859 she became lessee at the Lyceum for two seasons (1859–61) before touring the world alone, and returning once more to appear for Webster at benefit nights, in his declining years.²⁴

Independent Victorian actresses less historicised than Vestris or even Celeste are easy to find, once one begins to look amongst the ex-married, or unmarried, theatre women. Mrs Warner, for example, born Mary

²⁰ To his third wife, Sophie, who had their first child four months after the wedding, lived twenty-four years more, but is never mentioned in the family records again. See Webster, *Same only Different*, p. 39.
²¹ See John Harrington Smith, *The Gay Couple in Restoration Comedy* (Cambridge, MA: Harvard University Press, 1948), which identifies in this way the pair of stage lovers whose charming demeanour outweighs or justifies, for the audience, the impropriety of their apparent relationship.
²² See Webster, *Same only Different*, p. 62 and bills for London and provincial theatres collected at British Library shelf marks 182, 378 and 475, which include many instances of such appearances by Buckstone and Mrs Fitz, Mrs Mowett and Mr Davenport, etc.
²³ Webster, *Same only Different*, p. 65.   ²⁴ *DNB*.

Amelia Huddart in 1804, acted with her father from the age of 15 and rose to London leading roles including working with Macready under the influence of 'a strong mutual attraction' which came to nothing because he was married and principled. At 33 she chose the recently bankrupt theatre tavern keeper Robert Warner as her husband, booking agent and factotum.[25] In 1843 she ventured on her first management in partnership with T. L. Greenwood and Samuel Phelps, at Sadler's Wells, and then in 1847–8 managed the Marylebone Theatre on her own; 'She was to direct the policy and the licence of the theatre was to be transferred to her husband.'[26] The venture was financed by Walter Watts, the mysterious patron who poured money into the theatres at this point; since he was eventually revealed to have embezzled it all, he was presumably more impressed by Mrs Warner's Shakespearean credentials and presence than concerned about the long-term financial viability of the enterprise. She presented the classic repertoire, and imported even Macready to perform in it at a high fee.[27] The critics felt her season was an artistic and managerial success,[28] but *The Era* doubted the readiness of the Edgware Road district – only very marginally in the West End – for the legitimate drama, while the *DNB* implies that Mrs Warner moved into directing her own company because she wanted to play the younger parts, and that this vanity cost her the success of her management and £5,000 – which, presumably, was Watts's stolen cash.

Mary Anne Hehl, known as Fanny Stirling, lasted much longer in the business. Like Louisa Nisbett, she was the daughter of an improvident Guards officer. She went on the stage as a girl, around 1832, to support herself and her family. She married at 19 the actor-dramatist Edward Stirling; they appeared together, and he wrote roles for her, but they separated within five years. As a leading West End comedy actress she maintained herself and a daughter (born three years after the separation) until Stirling died in 1894. She was then 81 years old, and had only a few months to enjoy her immediate marriage to 'an old friend'.[29] Sir Charles Gregory was, however, an engineer, not an entrepreneur, and so Fanny Stirling never became known as a manager; though the biographer of the

[25] *DNB*.
[26] Malcolm Morley, *The Old Marylebone Theatre* (London: St Marylebone Society, 1960), p. 21.
[27] ibid., p. 22.
[28] And a benchmark: see for e.g. *Musical World*, 9 September 1848, 586: 'The example afforded by Mrs Warner has not been lost sight of by the present management. There is no theatre in the metropolis better conducted in every respect than the Marylebone.'
[29] *DNB*.

novelist and dramatist Charles Reade claims that Reade's first play was produced under her management.[30] She also, according to the same source, 'spent a week with him at Oxford before being driven away, it was said, by his mother'.[31]

Reade was more tenacious in his relationship with another comedy actress and manager, Mrs Seymour, with whom he shared a London ménage and who did her best to bring his somewhat wayward dramas to the stage successfully. This effort included a spell in the management of the St James's in 1854. This was a mysterious relationship, an example to set alongside Henry Lewes and George Eliot of the extraordinary way in which unorthodox Victorians managed their public image to outface implacable codes. Mrs Seymour was Laura Allison, another actress who had been the breadwinner of her family from childhood, and was married by them to an elderly admirer who turned out not to have the money they expected.[32] According to John Coleman, Reade was captivated by her performances in Webster's Haymarket company in 1837 and got himself an introduction, to read her his play.[33] She was living with her husband 'and his Pylades' a Captain Curling, and invited Reade to join the household. By another account,[34] they did not share quarters until Seymour and Curling were dead, and then formed two of a group of friends living together; the only objective evidence about the household arrangements is the 1871 census in which they form a unit without any other members above stairs, and where indeed even she is recorded as his housekeeper. They are presented by all who write about them as partners but not lovers:

She herself once said to Mr John Coleman: 'As for our positions his and mine – we are partners, nothing more. He has his bank-account, and I have mine. He is master of his fellowship and his rooms at Oxford, and I am mistress of this house, but not his mistress! Oh, dear, no!'

At another time, long after Mr Seymour's death, she said to an intimate friend:

'I hope Mr Reade will never ask me to marry him, for I should certainly refuse the offer.'[35]

Nevertheless Reade was broken-hearted at her death, and fulsomely memorialised her on her tombstone as 'a brilliant artist, a humble

[30] W. Burns, *Charles Reade: A Study in Victorian Authorship* (1961), pp. 38–9, quoted in *DNB*. I have not found verification of this claim: she certainly appeared in the play (*The Ladies' Battle*) at the Olympic in 1851, but the manager was Farren.
[31] ibid.   [32] Coleman, *Players*, vol. II, p. 28.   [33] ibid., pp. 9–10.
[34] Lyndon Orr, *Famous Affinities of History* (New York: Harper, n.d. [1912]), n. p.   [35] ibid.

Christian, a charitable woman, a loving daughter, sister, and friend, who lived for others from her childhood'.[36]

Henrietta Hodson, on the other hand, daughter and granddaughter of music hall singers and on the stage from the age of 6, was unabashed about her passionate cohabitation with Henry Labouchere, necessary because she had not managed to free herself of a solicitor husband named Pigeon, a youthful mistake who had already attempted to take over her earnings when she managed a company at the Royalty in the 1850s. Labouchere was co-owner of the new Queen's Theatre in 1867, and Henrietta appeared at its opening and became his partner in all senses, managing the theatre and writing herself into the census as his concubine. Later she was able to marry him, but moved on to have a son with Haydn Coffin, reportedly because she tired of Labouchere's anti-religious views.[37]

What these disparate examples demonstrate, beyond a greater variety of relationships than is allowed for in the normative understanding of the Victorian middle classes, is that actresses, uniquely in their period, could not only support themselves but could potentially succeed on their own in the business, and that this capacity gave them more choices, more independence, than their contemporaries. The ways in which that female power might be said to have shaped the West End will be the business of the next chapter. I have described only women with West End management credentials, and others might have been included, for example a list of women at the Strand before the Swanboroughs: Mrs H. P. Grattan, Mrs Hooper, Rebecca Isaacs. Fanny Kelly was a more important figure, a much-loved comedy actress with a slightly mysterious private life that included a 'god-daughter' as well as suitors ranging from potential husband Charles Lamb and would-be keeper the Earl of Essex to at least one homicidal maniac. She rejected them all, and built the theatre that became the Royalty, in Dean Street Soho, with her lifetime savings from a successful career, intending it for her own use as a dramatic school.[38] Her theatre was often subsequently managed by women: Harriet and Meta Pelham, 1864–7; Pattie Oliver (a burlesque actress from the Strand), 1867–70; Henrietta Hodson, 1872–6; and Kate Santley, 1877–8 and 1881–1905, in whose hands it was a pioneering venue for the modern drama. The St James's had a similarly persistent attraction for female managers,

---

[36] Coleman, *Players*, vol. II, p. 91.
[37] www.labouchere.co.uk/linkpages/labbyanddora.htm (Labouchere genealogy site) (visited 07.06.2009).
[38] See Bush-Bailey, *Performing Herself*.

from Jenny Vertpre in the 1830s to Mrs John Wood in the 1870s. What most of these various theatres have in common, perhaps, is small size – all the new West End theatres were relatively small, compared with the old patent houses, but Miss Kelly's was tiny, even after its rebuilding in 1861, and the Strand and the Marylebone not much larger. The St James's seated almost a thousand,[39] but it had the benefit of an audience more or less guaranteed to be polite. There as well as at the little venues, however, the female style of management and performance can be argued to have had a formative impact which will be discussed in the next chapter.

My final category of women managers, however, the most outstanding and successful group, did not feel constrained to aim for modest targets; they worked out a means of going for the West End's top prizes, as Celeste and Vestris had done. They achieved this not by egregious independence, but by finding ways – by selecting husbands – to make the normative married state suit their personal and business purposes.

MARRIAGE AND MANAGEMENT

Tracy Davis has told the story of Madame Vestris's canny progress from her initial bold venture at the Olympic in 1831 through managements at the Lyceum and Covent Garden, facilitated by her late marriage to Charles James Mathews, and it need not be repeated. Similarly, I have already outlined in Chapters 2 and 4 the climbing career trajectory of Priscilla Horton from gypsy girl at the Surrey, through Romeo and Ariel at the major houses to fashionable extravaganza princes and then to the eminent respectability of Mrs German Reed, with her own public drawing room in Regent Street. Whatever their private virtues (or, in the case of Mathews, vices), these husbands were very good career moves for two outstanding women. German Reed was a respected professional musician, which gave him standing both in the theatre and outside it, and enabled the partnership to take their new, crypto-theatrical path into the favour of the serious classes. Vestris, moving on from her period of aristocratic extravagance, chose as her husband a minor but very presentable and well-educated young actor with a good theatre name, already well loved by the public. Very similar life choices can be discerned in the triumphant careers of Ellen Tree/Kean, Louisa Pincott/Wigan, Mary-Ann Goward/Keeley and Marie Wilton/Bancroft; each of their stories can be revisited to demonstrate that these leading women actor-directors shaped their lives to

[39] Duncan, *St James's*, p. 4.

enable them to carry out their theatrical aspirations, and that what they achieved shaped the West End.

The most obviously hidden influence on the development of the West End is that of Ellen Tree (1805–80), a successful actress whose fame was – quite deliberately – entirely subsumed into her choice of the role and title of Mrs Charles Kean. It seems certain (certainly this was the story she herself told, and told herself) that her marriage with the son of the great Edmund Kean was a love-match.[40] But it was also a shrewd career move, made as the new West End was formed. One of a fashionable trio of acting sisters, Ellen first saw Charles Kean when she was 22 and he was 16, on 1 October 1827; an entirely untrained beginner, he was making his début at Drury Lane, in defiance of his declining and furious father. She was acting with the boy before the end of the next year, and played Desdemona in the performance of *Othello* in 1833 at which the elder Kean, playing the lead, collapsed in the arms of his son playing Iago. They were already in love, but her responsibilities as breadwinner for her mother and aunt prevented them marrying for ten years, until 1842.[41] By that time she had had a highly successful solo career, creating roles for the leading dramatists including a notable performance as the boy-king Ion. She was physically suited to young male roles like Ion and Romeo, being tall and athletic with a strong, serious face. As she moved on to mature roles her 'beaky face', and her sense of the propriety of maintaining a plethora of petticoats or a wide crinoline hoop, however inappropriate to the role, did not interfere with her possession of the 'personality and force to chain the attention and indelibly imprint her rendering of a part on the imagination'.[42] She was also a brilliant teacher of other performers, and what in modern terms is called a director. In marrying Kean she secured her next move, effectively into high-class management under his name. They became a celebrated and successful couple, though they never quite achieved what she most desired, the ultimate step into respectability: she would have liked him to be knighted, and so to become herself the first

[40] J. M. D. Hardwick, ed., *Emigrant in Motley: Unpublished Letters of Charles and Ellen Kean* (London: Rockliff, 1954), pp. 10–11.
[41] Letter from Ellen Kean to Mary Kean, 19/20 February 1864, in Hardwick, *Emigrant*, p. 132 – she is raging about the irresponsibility of her nieces and nephews, who are not making a home for her sister, nor showing any gratitude to Ellen herself for the expensive education she has given them.
[42] Ellen Terry, *The Story of my Life* (London: Hutchinson, 1908), p. 14.

Lady of the stage to acquire a title through professional merit. The only point in their joint career when she stepped out of Charles's shadow in public was the moment in 1856 when she sought an interview with Lady Palmerston, and then wrote directly to Queen Victoria, to try to secure a knighthood for Charles, for his patriotic services to national education. She felt they had earned that ultimate social seal of approval in their expensive and dazzling series of historicised Shakespearean productions at the Princess's Theatre.[43]

The young Charles Kean had arrived in the theatre with very little but the publicity value of his patronymic to recommend him as an actor, having been deliberately schooled at Eton to be a gentleman rather than a player. It was from Ellen Tree that he learnt to move and speak effectively on stage. In marrying him she linked herself not only to a mate whom she continued to adore, but an effective leading man for their joint enterprise of creating a Shakespearean theatre for the Victorian age. Ellen Terry records: 'What he owed to Mrs Kean, he would have been the first to confess. In many ways she was the leading spirit in the theatre; at the least, a joint ruler, not a queen-consort.'[44] Their productions at the Princess's from 1851 to 1859, conceived by Charles as prodigies of antiquarian authenticity replete with extensive written annotation and gorgeous with visual spectacle, were put on the stage by the two of them together. She acted magnificently, and she taught him to act, to modulate his melodramatic emphasis and growing force in the direction of realism and restraint.[45] Their stand-by modern production was Lovell's *The Wife's Secret* (Haymarket 1848), in which their interdependence as performers and as a couple was used to present what their audiences hoped for in a modern marriage. Her Lady Amyot, 'struggling under an imputation the most abhorrent to her pure mind' was a picture of 'such exquisite fidelity, such passionate tenderness, and such intense power' that it developed 'all the phases of the feminine character' with 'so much spontaneity' that this reviewer could not resist the conviction that he was 'witnessing a drama of real life'. He hastens to add that Charles's part was essential too, and that he 'identified himself completely with the feelings of a man whose affection for his beloved wife not even the deep wrong he believes she has inflicted on him can destroy'.[46]

Their greatest triumphs, enshrined in the received history of the period, were of course the productions of Shakespeare, financed by interspersing

[43] See Schoch, *Shakespeare's Victorian Stage*, pp. 60–2.   [44] Terry, *Story*, p. 11.   [45] *DNB*.
[46] *Caledonian Mercury*, 7 February 1848.

spectacular modern melodrama, that they staged at the Princess's. Charles conceived of the historicised Shakespeare, but Ellen brought it to dramatic life: at rehearsals he sat in the stalls ringing a dinner bell when he saw something amiss, and she sat at a desk on stage and sprang into action to regroup, instruct, direct. At a more advanced point, witnesses report, she would watch the run-through from every part of the theatre to make sure of the effect for all patrons.[47] Actors recalled her work: Ellen Terry 'admired and loved and feared her' and thought herself rarely privileged to have been trained by such an accomplished director.[48] It is only the deliberate subordination of Ellen's contribution, her readily accepted self-presentation as a mere wifely adjunct to Charles, that diminishes historical recognition of her leading role in the formation of the West End. She was the theatrical partner in what was otherwise an academic enterprise at the Princess's, whereby the stage was rehabilitated as an unimpeachable tool of education and national culture.

THE WIGANS

Another partnership in which the distinct contributions of husband and wife, making up a successful whole, is quite clear is in the story of Leonora Pincott and Alfred Wigan. Leonora was a Wallack, daughter of Elizabeth, granddaughter of William and Mary (née Johannot) – a deep-rooted, wide-ranging and talented theatre and circus clan. She was born in 1805, and soon afterwards her mother remarried the clown Dickie Usher; thereafter the little Leonora appeared professionally in the ring, rope-dancing with her Usher half-sister,[49] and made her London début in a skin part, as a chimpanzee in a pantomime at the Lyceum in 1818.[50] Her uncle James, stage-managing (i.e. directing) at Drury Lane from 1826 to 1828, took her into the company there to learn the theatrical basics, and by 1831 she was ready to be a leading member of Vestris's first company at the Olympic, a substantial young woman with black hair and flashing eyes. She married Alfred Wigan in 1839, when she was 34; he was 25. He was an 'affable gentleman'[51] having some difficulty in finding his metier – he had taught in a school, acted as clerk to his father, cut loose and became a wandering musician, then played small parts at several West End start-up theatres in the 1830s – the Queen's under Louisa Nisbett, the St James's

---

[47] See Scott, *Drama of Yesterday*, vol. 1, p. 262.   [48] Terry, *Story*, p. 11.
[49] At the New Theatre, Prescot: *Liverpool Mercury*, 31 December 1819.   [50] *DNB*.
[51] Blanchard, *Life*, vol. 1, p. 23.

under Braham, and at the other extreme with E. L. Blanchard in a very dodgy unlicensed gaff in the King's Road. He was calling himself Alfred Sidney all this time; only when he reached the haven of Vestris's 1839 Covent Garden company, fell ill, was nursed by and then married Leonora, did he become the grown-up Mr Wigan. He became a respected and intellectual performer, but remained off-centre, a player in 'a narrow groove' of roles, chiefly French or other broken-English characterisations. It was Leonora who had the 'stage knowledge and *flair*'[52] to drive them to eminence as a supporting couple to the leading managements, and eventually to take on successfully the management of the Olympic, 1853–7, and the St James's, 1860–3. Plays were written to suit them, with an eccentric Frenchman for him and a bustling, often lower-class comic woman part for her – such pieces as Lady Dufferin's *Finesse*, which came to them at the St James's too late in their management, so that they carried it with them and offered it to Buckstone when they were engaged at the Haymarket the next year. Leonora's role in this piece, as a ladies' maid with a funny-melodramatic line in disaster stories about her family that are called to her mind by everything that happens in the play, is a substantial vehicle for a certain kind of female comic.[53]

THE KEELEYS

The Keans have been given too much prominence in the received account of the mid-century creation of the West End, and the Wigans have been too completely sidelined. The Keeleys – Mary Ann Goward (1805–99) and Robert Keeley (1793–1869) – are generally understood to have been a mainstay of the commercial theatre for most of the century; but there is a great deal more to be said about them than that. In their careers, and especially in that of Mary Ann, the main characteristics of West End theatre came together and found their first full expression. I have already discussed her appearances in boy roles in the 1820s and 1830s. These need to be seen in the context of her stringent training and apprenticeship, and her subsequent pre-eminence. She was seven years under the musical tuition of Mrs Henry Smart before her début as a soprano, brought out in York in 1823 by Mrs Smart's brother-in-law Sir George, and a transition

---

[52] *DNB.*
[53] Sarah Lane, managing and arranging her repertoire to suit herself out at the Britannia in Hoxton, has left a similar body of work.

to acting roles and a London début under the wing of Fanny Kelly.[54] After her boyish days, she moved on to a long career as a star and intermittently as a leading manager. She met Bob Keeley in her début season in 1825 at the English Opera House, and by 1827 they had developed their comic double act as a contrasting pair of servants in *The Sergeant's Wife*, a performance described by the *Examiner* critic on 29 July 1827 as an example of how much acting improves upon a text. They were married in June 1829 and had their first daughter Louisa by March 1830. Both of them were working hard on the theatrical front line throughout the 1830s, making a good income by touring the provinces and also America together, and individually as well as sometimes in tandem supporting the last seasons of patent performance at Covent Garden, and at Drury Lane under Macready. In between they were exploring possibilities for the new West End theatres, becoming the main drawing cards of seasons at the Marylebone, the Strand and the Adelphi. After the act in 1843, therefore, they were ready to take on their own management, and at Easter in 1844 the Lyceum announced an opening under the management of Mrs Keeley. The company included the Wigans, and the house dramatists soon included Albert Smith acting as dramaturg to bring Dickens's novels and stories to the stage. The little theatre took off with enormous verve. They printed a publicity leaflet headed 'Theatre Royal Lyceum / Under the management of Mrs Keeley. / Gazette Extraordinary!! Gratis!!!', which included Mrs Keeley's opening address – full of political allusions about her heading up a new style of government, and claiming that the legitimacy of the drama they staged would be defined not by tedious length, but by the talent it brought to the stage. The reprints from their opening reviews repeat the personae they had established in their acting partnership, now expressed not only on stage but also in her leadership in management, and his support:

It is impossible to imagine this clever, versatile, and lively actress as otherwise than successful in whatever part she assumes . . . She has an original way of doing everything, and is always charming and always natural. Her husband is clever in another style; it is a happy contrast to see them. Her intelligence is so sparkling that it beams from her eye and speaks from her features. Her face and her action are more eloquent than words. The audience perceive a deeper meaning than the dramatist ever expresses, more wit than ever he intended; she makes a character out of anything, and will serve up dull dialogue with such a *sauce piquante* as to

---

[54] See Bush-Bailey, *Performing Herself*, p. 35: one of Kelly's most important melodramatic roles was in *The Sergeant's Wife*, which was also a major piece in the Keeley's repertoire, discussed below.

throw the house into raptures with what would tire it from other lips. The great merit of her husband, on the contrary, is the extraordinary mass of stupidity and dullness he can throw into his face ... his air of offended dignity is always irresistible.[55]

They were successful, but not, apparently, successful enough to make them willing to meet the demands of the escalating lease they had signed with the theatre owner Sam Arnold Jnr, which committed them to pay £700 more for the theatre in the 1847/8 season. After an acrimonious debate in the public press about the issue,[56] the Keeleys retreated from management to starring at the Haymarket. Eventually Arnold and the 'renters' – shareholders – of the Lyceum were wise enough to let the theatre to Madame Vestris, now trading as Mr and Mrs Charles Matthews, and so resume the movement towards a new West End style: see below, Chapter 6, for a discussion of the artistic achievements of the 1840s and 1850s at the Lyceum.

The Keeleys successfully undertook management once more in 1850, opening the Princess's in collaboration with the Keans, where they did the comedy and Ellen and Charles looked after the serious drama, but the Keeleys dropped out after the first season and returned to starring, now including their daughter Louisa in their family success. They continued to work with all the other managements discussed here, and lived amongst the acting elite in Brompton, but did not return to management. Perhaps there were difficulties they did not relish about recruiting and holding a company: all was not necessarily always sweetness and light amongst the West End group, as Scott had fondly imagined. In the Victoria and Albert Theatre Collection there is an intriguing letter from Alfred Wigan to Bob Keeley, dated 15 June 1847:

Your note of yesterday admits of but one interpretation – while the evil reports and insults to my wife were the work of Mrs Keeley, I remained comparatively passive, under the idea that Mrs Keeley's long standing reputation as a breeder of dissension and ill blood was of itself a protection – now however that you whose character for justice has always stood so high in the esteem of myself and my wife have been brought to believe these things it is just possible that other persons whose good opinion I value may be similarly acted upon – the matter therefore becomes serious ... I trust your sense of justice and gentlemanly feeling for the future to do your part as I shall mine to prevent the probability of our ever again coming into collision on this most disgusting subject.

---

[55] From '*The Britannia*', reprinted in the nonce publication described; copy available in the Victoria and Albert Theatre Collection, Lyceum file.

[56] See, e.g., *The Sun*, 24 March 1847; *Era*, 28 March 1847.

Wigan was notoriously a touchy and easily insulted man; but one may imagine the imperious (but pretty) little Mary Ann, and the large and commanding (but less attractive) Leonora falling out spectacularly. Neither couple stayed in management for very long at a time. The Keeleys retired in 1859, and Bob died ten years later, but Mary Ann survived into a celebrated old age; in 1895 Queen Victoria came out as her leading admirer, inviting her ahead of any other member of the theatrical profession to make a private visit to the Palace, and then, eventually, sending carriages and attendants to take her out during her last illness. In 1893 she was still young and mischievous enough, in her 89th year, to amaze a visiting journalist by kicking a large, heavy hassock across the room 'with evident glee and all the energy of a schoolboy at football' (see Figure 8).[57] According to Joseph Knight,

She left the substantial sum of £17,812 17s. 2d. Her funeral was at Brompton cemetery on 16 March and was almost a public ceremonial. She was a small, neatly made person, not beautiful, but an actress of wonderful variety, with a 'laughing devil in her eye'. She was also a promising amateur painter: one of her landscapes was owned by the Savage Club.[58]

CONCLUSION: THE BANCROFTS AND THE NEXT GENERATION

I opened this chapter by referring to Tracy Davis's discussion of 'wo-managers', with its case studies of Eliza Vestris and Marie Wilton. More has been written about Marie Wilton, Mrs Bancroft, than about any of the other women whose lives I have outlined here. The story Davis has told of her graduation from boy roles at the Strand to management on her own account at the up-and-coming Prince of Wales's, her recruitment and grooming of the hack Tom Robertson to produce the plays she needed, through to her marriage three years after she took the theatre to a stable, respectable man who could front the enterprise and converse with the gentleman capitalists, is a central example of my argument about marriage and management. I do not need to rehearse the well-known story once more: their enterprise sailed henceforth under the name of 'the Bancrofts', and is thoroughly inscribed into theatre history; I shall consider its contribution to the

---

[57] F. G. Edwards, 'Mrs Keeley and "Oberon"', *Musical Times* 40, 1 April 1899, 240–1, 240.
[58] *DNB.*

Figure 8   Mary Ann Keeley at her desk

shaping of West End style in the next chapter. I have, however, come across one reference to her which suggests that her story could have been written quite differently: that, if the necessary evidence had been available, her career as part of an eminently respectable married couple might have been neglected in favour of a reversion to an earlier construction of the successful actress as a kept woman.

The Harvard Theatre Collection has a file of letters from Marie Bancroft. At the back of it there is a cut-out printed engraving of a portrait of her, with a piece of paper stuck to it on which is written in pencil 'Miss Marie Wilton / now / Mrs Bancroft. / formerly kept / by Alfred Shoolbred / who left her / £30,000'. The first 's' in 'Miss' is long, suggesting a contemporary inscription. I have attempted in vain to find any corroboration of this assertion. In her own memoirs she does not of course mention any such liaison, although she does describe two of her admirers, and makes quite a dramatic scene of a moment when she almost lost her head and ran away with one of them, but was restrained by thoughts of her family. There was a Shoolbred family among the merchant classes in London at this date, beginning with a Scottish tailor whose initial is A, and who traded from a smart Jermyn Street address from around 1830, specialising in formal menswear and inventing elastic corsets. He was fifty years her senior, and disappears from the record in the 1840s, when she was still a small child, so is hardly a candidate. He may or may not have been the father of the founder of a large drapery shop that operated in the Tottenham Court Road; a son of this house was called Alfred, and he was more or less Marie Wilton's contemporary. He died unmarried in 1872, which would have enabled him to leave her money, even as much as £30,000, since he was a wealthy bachelor. Except that he did not do so. His will makes no mention of any such bequest. She had undertaken management in 1865, so the Prince of Wales's venture could never be said to have been funded by any such bequest, and she and Bancroft, whom she married in 1867, did not move to take on the Haymarket until 1880, by which time his entrepreneurial skills would have ensured there was no shortage of capital for the larger venture. There is a remark in her autobiography, however, which is interesting in this connection, and otherwise not entirely explicable: speaking of her success at the Prince of Wales's, and its precarious but successful financing by £1,000 borrowed from her brother-in-law, she says: 'I have tried to tell *why* I became a manager, and *how*. Let me add that not one shilling further was ever borrowed by me from, or given to me by, anyone living or dead in connection with this enterprise.'[59] The denial is vehement, but unexplained in her text. It might appear that she was trying to dismiss the rumour about Shoolbred without actually repeating it.

A dispassionate assessment would suggest that the story, however circumstantial and apparently factual, does indeed owe more to the actress/ whore trope than to reality. It is therefore an attempt to besmirch and explain away her power and prestige. Marie Bancroft was the inheritor, not of a fortune from a keeper, but of skill and judgement in her own business which enabled her to make her way independently and to secure a professionally advantageous and eminently Victorian marriage. Fortunately history has, in her case, recognised her success; but many less well documented women managers stood behind and around her, and are written out of the account, or their achievements belittled by the way their stories are told.

CORRECTING THE RECORD

Mrs Bancroft was born in 1839. Two or even three generations of professional women went to the making of the modern West End: Vestris, Fanny Kelly and Jane Scott, all born in the previous century, were joined by a whole generation from the time of the Napoleonic Wars, born in the 1800s; and Marie Wilton had contemporaries in the likes of Henrietta Hodson, Patty Oliver, Louisa Herbert and Mathilda Wood. Where they have left accounts of themselves, the high Victorian generation of actresses often recall their training with the professional women of the previous generation. Such stories have tended to pass into the mainstream of theatre history, where they are noted at all, in terms of the demonisation of these tutors as ferocious *grandes dames*, intimidating children in the exercise of their authority; Ellen Terry's account of her training by Ellen Kean, for example, gives an excellent example of a directorial method which has still not dropped out of use, when she describes her storming at and slapping the little girl into sobbing mortification, to get her to find and then capture the pleading terror of the little Prince Arthur in *King John*. Later at the Royalty, Madame de Rhona trained her to scream effectively by flying at her 'like a wild-cat' and then getting her to reproduce and enlarge her terrified response.[60] Ellen Kean also taught

[59] *Mr and Mrs Bancroft On and Off the Stage*, 2 vols. (London: Richard Bentley 1888, vol. i, p. 189. But see also the family history website oldwhitelodge.com (visited 18.06.11) which demonstrates one birth of a son Charles to Marie Wilton in 1863, and speculates whether the father was the actor William Kendal, or Edward VII. Perhaps he was Alfred Shoolbred.

[60] Terry, *Story*, pp. 26, 38.

her technical essentials – how to simulate laughter, to clarify vowel sounds, to walk with a long train – just as, later, Leonora Wigan taught her the value of standing still on the stage.[61] This was not the normal training of the mid-Victorian girl child; and it is scarcely surprising that talented young people so trained were not content with a normal middle-class girlhood and a subsequent career of self-effacement. What the likes of Vestris and Louisa Swanborough and Ellen Kean passed on to the girls in their companies was a professional competence that wielded for their own purposes a deliberate consciousness of their own physical and emotional powers.

Before Nina Auerbach picked up Terry's story[62] and pointed out this legacy of female empowerment, it was usual to repeat as historical characterisations the contemporary amusement at Ellen Kean's clinging to her crinoline, Mary Swanborough's malapropisms and plebeian speech, Fanny Stirling's insistence that her pupils project themselves 'Bigger, my dear, bigger!', Mary Keeley's unflagging physical exuberance – all tending to downgrade female power into mere eccentricity. The habit continued: Liz Schafer has pointed out the determined tendency to cut Lil Bayliss, a woman manager of great power in the twentieth century, down to size by relentless insistence upon her wispy bun, her round glasses, her untheatrical expressions and general dottiness.[63] Even Ellen Terry cannot resist telling us an anecdote of 'Dear old Mrs Wigan!' who looked like a toad: that she prided herself on her gentility and mixed socially with the aristocracy, until the day her drunken cab-driving father turned up at the stage door. This sits very uneasily with the letter that Terry has just quoted, in which Mrs Wigan praised and described Terry's own acting, a letter full of insight and perfectly correctly expressed, from a woman whose father, as far as objective accounts go, had died when she was a child.[64] But perhaps Terry may be forgiven for assuming that the power and importance of that generation of female theatre managers could be taken for granted, and would not be diminished by her putting on record her own youthful rebellions against them as well as the debt she owed them. She should not have been so confident that they had already defeated the occlusions of history. The next chapter will seek to put their work back into the story, and to give a positive account of what they gave to the theatre.

[61] ibid., p. 70.   [62] Auerbach, *Ellen Terry*, esp. pp. 30–69.
[63] Elizabeth Schafer, *Lilian Baylis: A Biography* (Hatfield: University of Hertfordshire Press, 2006).
[64] Terry, *Story* pp. 70–2.

CHAPTER 6

Showtime

The final question, then, to which the previous chapter and indeed the whole book, leads, is: what part did these theatre managements, in which women were leaders or equal partners, play in the formation of the stage as it is in London today? How might the history of the drama, between the select committees of 1832 and 1866, be reconceived in the context of the development of the West End that I have suggested here?

To ask the question in this form is to refocus attention on the abjected commercial performance culture that has been almost universally despised. The mid-nineteenth-century drama has been generally understood, not only in the wake of Modernism but also by the literary leaders of taste in its own time, to have been in deep darkness, waiting for a new dawn that did not appear until Ibsen was translated. But I am telling a different story, one that takes more account of the vigour and indeed the experimentation and innovation of that mid-century performance culture. Its leading edge was not Shakespeare, despite the committee men's obsessions, nor the beginnings of a minor kind of realism, the 'cup and saucer' drama that has been retrospectively discovered as a precursor to Naturalism. The stage was not a pale equivalent of the dominant realist novel that was developing in the 1840–60s. It was rather, I would argue, the beginning of contemporary theatre, expressed in music, excitement, visual delight and comedy. It offers an opposite and equal response to the pressures of the Real – not by mirroring it with a constrictive 'realism', but by defying those limits, while still taking hold of the moment; by theatricality, exuberance and excess, in fantasy and burlesque.

The difference made by the contribution of women to this anti-naturalistic development can be seen even within the realm of serious drama and the valorisation of Shakespeare: Madame Vestris brought a sumptuous understanding of Shakespearean fable to her production of *A Midsummer Night's Dream* in November 1840, a play which dominant Victorian culture found hard to deal with precisely because it refuses a literal interpretation, and insists upon the physical presence on stage of six-foot-high fairies. Again, Mary Warner was as important as Samuel Phelps in founding the Sadler's Wells venture in 1844, and it was she who attempted to bring the serious drama back into town at the Marylebone Theatre, though neither of them ultimately succeeded in making a profit. Her power was in the intensity and energy of emotional evocation, exemplified by what Dickens called the 'defiant splendid Sin' of her performance as Evadne in *The Bridal*.[1] Similarly, Ellen Kean contributed an other than realistic dimension to the celebrated but unprofitable Shakespeare seasons at the Princess's in the 1850s. Charles focussed his offering to modern sensibility on antiquarian authenticity in support of patriotism, while she worked on the company's acting, and on her own performances, which she made thrilling and affective without the benefit of any such realistic trappings. She played Hermione in *A Winter's Tale*, for example, in utter disregard for her husband's attempt to make it an historical rather than a mythological play, acting with searing emotional truth and a huge crinoline.[2] Meanwhile, Fanny Kemble made an excellent living for twenty years by solo performances of seventeen Shakespearean texts – more than any theatre had attempted to stage for a century – playing, rather than merely reading, all the roles herself, from Bottom to Othello. Henry James thought the 'human thunder-roll' she produced in Lear's lamentation for Cordelia – 'Howl, howl, howl!' – incomparably great.[3]

A less puckish, more foundational female artistic agency can be argued in relation to female management and performance in the art that most people preferred to Shakespeare: the musical theatre. At the high end, grand opera emerged, in the mid century, as the performance art most valued by intelligent and cultivated London society. The Queen, the fashionable world, and also now the intelligentsia, were finding their most exciting theatre in the new Royal Opera House eventually established post-1843 at Covent Garden; these audiences were eagerly seeking transcendence, rather than realism, from divas such as Giulia Grisi and Jenny Lind in the works of Balfe, Meyerbeer, Donizetti, Verdi and Berlioz. Opera's management – though not of course its performance – remained in the hands of men. Indeed, masculine power was reinforced as the opera house practices of the early part of the century, which had made the social event, directed by the aristocratic and often female holders of the boxes, more important than the artistic offering on stage, gave way to the middle-class

---

[1] Quoted in *DNB*. [2] See Terry, *Life*, p. 14.
[3] Henry James, 'Frances Anne Kemble', *Temple Bar*, April 1893, 503–25, 508.

practice of asserting status through aesthetic superiority and a focus on the appreciation of high art.[4] Music, however, was central to performance at many other levels, and comic opera, operetta and the emergence of the new forms which have dominated the West End ever since – musical comedy, revue, the spectacular musical – were much more the work of women. Chapter 2 has suggested the importance of the German Reeds in this development, their contribution to popular song culture, the introduction of Offenbach's music to London and the development of the *opera da camera*, all of which fed into the high Victorian development of Gilbert and Sullivan operetta, and eventually the modern musical. This chapter will pick up other strands of stage musical theatre, especially extravaganza/burlesque, as it was begun by Vestris at the Olympic and then developed at the Strand theatre under the Swanboroughs.

The starting point is the work of the Keeleys, the Wigans and Webster with Madame Celeste, at the Lyceum, the Olympic and the Adelphi, all in or around the Strand. Their managements interlaced: at the Adelphi Elizabeth Yates briefly continued her widow's tenure until 1843, then Ben Webster became lessee and Celeste what we would call artistic director from 1844 to 1858; the Keeleys also took the Lyceum from 1844, until 1847; and then the Mathews's had a critical but less of a financial triumph there in 1847–56. The Wigans managed at the Olympic from 1853 to 1857, before reverting to the less risky practice of working together under other managements. Celeste took the Lyceum lease from 1859 to 1862, and in 1859 the lengthy reign of the Swanboroughs began at the Strand Theatre, where many managements, both male- and female-directed, had come and gone during the earlier decades. These new West End theatres[5] did musicals and spectacular shows, farces, one-, two- and three-act plays, burlettas and burlesques, and unlabelled events, songs, dances and *jeux d'esprit*, in a brilliant, no doubt tinsel kaleidoscope. After forty years of plunging from moments of heady, illegal success to sudden failure and persecution, the Theatres Act in 1843 finally freed them to find their feet, and experiment with a new kind of dramatic programming. This was not a matter of growing realism, though it drew upon the Real and offered a response to it. As the Romantic melodrama ceased to convince, audiences did not lose

[4] See Hall-Witt, *Fashionable Acts*, pp. 160–84 and passim for discussion of this shift with the transition from the Haymarket Opera House to Covent Garden.
[5] The term in its nineteenth-century form. 'West-end theatre' came into use at this time: the *Theatrical Times*, already showing the West End propensity to venerate long runs, claimed on 22 January 1848 that the Adelphi had been open for 1,000 consecutive nights, 'a circumstance without parallel in the history of the West-end theatre'.

their taste for emotion extroverted, and relationships vividly dramatised; and, in the face of the lurid and often frightening life of the metropolis in the 1840s, they particularly liked to laugh.

The ideological grip of the new middle-class imperatives, of domesticity and the separate spheres, expressed in the dominant form of the mid-century novel, was felt on stage, but modified in significant ways. Theatre, I will argue, engaged with the modern world, and the challenge of a negotiation between the Real and the Ideal, to offer new models of identity and relationship not available in the novel; deploying spectacle, transformation and affective performance. These were (and are) the strengths of the stage and, especially, of women on stage. The female managements were at the heart of that process, and offer evidence for this characterisation of the West End show.

THE KEELEYS AND 'SALIQUE MANAGEMENT' AT THE LYCEUM

The theatres along the Strand had already found new models for the good night out, beginning with Vestris's success at the Olympic in 1831. A decade later her influence can be seen to have developed into the style of thing on offer at the little Strand Theatre, where Mrs Keeley was a 'tower of strength' in the company of a Mr Hall, previously an Adelphi manager. *The Era* described the ambience they created:

the management appear determined to go-ahead. New pieces are produced at a railroad pace, fresh recruits fill up the ranks, and crowded audiences, and sides aching with laughter, cram the 'small circle'. Here are no lugubrious looks, and deep-drawn sighs – no melo-dramatic starts, no domestic dismals, no tragic situations, no woeful sympathies awakened – but in their stead – and a capital exchange it is – we have mirth, humour, wit, and fun! There is no stinting in quantity, and the quality is unexceptionable. And then there is such a comfortable, cozy, English air about the little place – such an agreeable tea-table shake-hands sort of familiarity with the company and the actors – that we feel more like calling in upon a party of genial friends, than making a set voyage to a theatre. The pieces, too, are short, and this is of exceeding advantage; for, supposing the particular piece does not suit the particular taste, there is still plenty to select from: so all are sure to be suited. You have but to go early, get a decent seat, and enjoy yourself *ad lib*. You do not require a double achromatic telescope of a forty-eye power to catch the varying shades of expression of the actors' features; nor need you strain the tympanum of the ear to listen to the modulation of the actor's voice: nature has fair play, and you have the real worth of your money.[6]

---

[6] *Era*, 26 September 1841.

So Vestris's novel formula, of several light, enjoyable pieces begun promptly and over by eleven, with high production values, wit and elegance, and in the auditorium comfort, good order and an unthreatening, informal but exciting atmosphere, had become embedded, and at the Strand Theatre embraced a much larger section of the potential middle-class audience. It is the foundation of one of the most important of the 'feminised', that is the familial and familiar, aspects of West End management: a femininity that gives more weight to the pleasure of the audience than to its edification or elevation, recognises and caters for, and possibly leads, modern taste rather than seeking to reprimand it; its values are those consigned to the domestic rather than the heroic sphere in mid-Victorian thought.

That is not to say, however, that such an artistic agenda was inevitably conventional, conservative or unadventurous. The programmes of the little theatres in the Strand became the matrix, after 1843, for the introduction of elements that were more satirically or formally experimental, were intellectually interesting and could be deeply emotionally charged; that explored the affect and the anxieties of the modern world somewhat indirectly. Such a practice allowed the audience to remain within a safe context, but still offered them challenges, new things, and looked hard both for, and at, novelty and change. Plays and other performances that were of the stage, stagey, displaced from the world outside, but therefore had large-than-life impact while still carrying cultural significance that reflected upon the mundane from an imaginative distance, were accommodated within the pattern.

Mary Ann Keeley learnt from Hall's policy at the Strand, and her own management across the road at the Lyceum from Easter 1844 to June 1847 was the result. *The Era* pontificated at its close that

under the Salique management of Mrs Keeley, the Lyceum has attained a dramatic status, and a coherency which it had failed to achieve under any preceding management ... in every instance female rule in theatricals has ever been triumphant. Madame Vestris and Mrs Keeley may be (with reverence be it spoken) considered as the Elizabeth and the Victoria of the dramatic kingdom.[7]

She and her husband recruited a strong team of performers, including Louisa Fairbrother, Julia Fortescue, Frank Matthews (who was a Vining) Sarah Woolgar and the Wigans. They maintained a relationship with a

---

[7] *Era*, 2 May 1847.

band of writers including Albert Smith, Gilbert Abbott A'Beckett and Mark Lemon, while also drawing on the work of major established dramatists such as Edward Stirling, J. R. Planché and Douglas Jerrold, and giving a first opening to newcomer Tom Taylor. They were an immediate success, and their audiences listed week after week in the *Morning Post* were high-ranking and fashionable, overlapping with those listed as visiting the Opera or the French plays at the St James's. The plays were mostly new, and, as Mary Ann pointed out in her opening address, their claim to be 'legitimate' was based on their quality – what she calls their 'talent' – not their length. The bill regularly included either three or four pieces. Some were short farces, others one-, two- or three-act comedies, the night normally climaxing in a burlesque spectacular in comic rhyming couplets with much scene-changing, music and dancing, the forerunner of the high Victorian pantomime, but with more bite.

Within such an apparently light-weight, miscellaneous pattern a great deal could be achieved. Nothing was fixed, so nothing was a disaster. Successful pieces could come back or extend their run while new things were readied and brought out, a play that failed on its first night could be cut and amended, giving it a further chance while established favourites kept the house full. Half-price admittance meant that a piece could be run while it was drawing at full price and then be brought out as a new attraction later in the bill for the half-price audience, or a late-night success could be shunted forward for the early comers to appreciate. Experiments could be tried without emptying the box-office, and fashionable successes like a children's dance troupe they had created, or the favourite polka sequence from a play they had done the previous season could be used to boost the programme at a thin moment.

The arts that developed best under such circumstances was, perhaps inevitably, comic – including the art of the farce. Michael Booth argued that 'the golden age of nineteenth-century farce was the forties, fifties and sixties' when the stage was swept by a tide of 'materiality and domesticity'. [8] This influence which, he felt, rather engulfed and sentimentalised comedy and prevented the development of the serious drama, was nevertheless creative, in the farce and 'petite comedy', of a new, current and expressive art form. Within such an unpretentious, practical programme as the Keeleys and their peers in the new West End offered, we therefore may find unexpected things, including not only a sharp

[8] Michael R. Booth, *English Plays of the Nineteenth Century*, vol. IV, *Farces* (Oxford: Clarendon Press, 1873), Introduction, p. 22.

irreverence about the more pretentious arts but even a concern with wider political issues: a lightly carried acuteness that upsets the conventional reading of the long mixed bill as mere mass entertainment. Both performers and writers were responsible for this radical edge; and it was not confined to the farces. The spectaculars and many of the one-act pieces were also written by the semi-attached stable of dramatists, Albert Smith, A'Beckett and Lemon. These men were the leading Bohemian writers but, more than that, they were at that moment the highly successful team responsible for the sensational success of the satirical journal *Punch*, from 1842 taking the journalistic world by storm with insistent deflationary laughter and a Radical political bias. By 1846 the weekly had become 'a national institution, the official comic organ of the English middle classes'[9] and not only its editor Lemon and its leading writers, including Douglas Jerrold, but also its lesser lights like Mildenhall and its newcomers such as Tom Taylor, wrote also for the Lyceum. Their stage work, in farce or fantasy forms, can be as radical as the early *Punch*. The plays are, for example, peppered with sideswipes at the New Poor Law, one of the journal's chief targets.

Important aspects of their agenda were indeed better served by the stage than by the press. Dramatic form ensures that all its characters may speak for themselves, and in the Lyceum pieces the working-class figures, present in *Punch* chiefly as caricatures or as objects of pity, were presented by stars like the Keeleys as substantial flesh and blood, and might therefore become worthy of consideration and indeed admiration as people. Booth points out the importance of lower-class characters and the comic techniques that go with them in the farces;[10] Bob Keeley made such figures as Jacob Earwig, the strategically deaf and eternally self-satisfied inn servant in Selby's *The Boots at the Swan* (Strand 1842), endearingly funny as well as obstreperously intractable.

More significantly to my argument for the agency of Mrs Keeley and her female peers is the way in which the extravaganzas and burlesques, depending as they do on the work of leading actresses, could become rather less misogynistic than the magazine jokes. In the *Arabian Nights'* romp *Open Sesame* at the beginning of the season, for example, Lemon and A'Beckett gave Mary Ann Keeley the role of a low servant girl called Morgiana who does comic imitations of Carlotta Grisi's ballet-dancing but also represents herself as an independent woman. Faced with a friend in distress over her husband's

[9] Sutherland, *Victorian Fiction*, p. 94.   [10] Booth, *English Plays*, p. 22.

debts, she offers help from her own savings – which are in the Savings Bank,[11] where she has put by her tea and beer allowance:

> Though bred a servant may I not pretend
> Once and away a five pun' note to lend?[12]

Later she even has an heroic couplet apparently straight out of melodrama:

> A nation with *one slave* can ne'er be great
> May all the world slave bonds repudiate!

To which her lover replies

> 'amen to that sweet prayer' – but you shall be
> No slave, dear Morgy – I'm for making free[13]

and she has to slap his hands away, supplying a claptrap sentiment and its comic undercutting in a single quatrain.

The patrons of the Lyceum were expected to appreciate not only these characters and a stream of topical allusions but also lightning impersonations of Macready and Jenny Lind and elaborate burlesques of Shakespearean verse, to recognise the wit of a score woven from a pastiche of current operatic and popular hits, identified in the manuscripts of the plays as for example 'the air from Esmeralda', *l'elixir d'amore*', 'the Druid march in *Norma*', or 'Who'd be a governess?' and to be able to distinguish the polka as danced by Henry and Payne from that of Fairbrother and James, or indeed Perrot and Grisi. They would apparently recognise glancing allusions to the current shows like the Ojibbway Indians and the Wizard of the North, and also, more overtly politically, respond to characters on stage repudiating the wage-slavery of seamstresses and celebrating the triumphs of the Rebecca rioters against turnpike tolls. The impression of empty-headed fun that the exclamatory bills give us is, to this extent, deceptive; even knock-about burlesque at the Lyceum, generated by the *Punch* men and delivered by the Keeleys, was politically committed and aware, if only of quite easily supported Radical causes.

Similarly, the endless translations from the French, so complained of by the critics (who were often the same men who wrote them, or those

---

[11] Savings banks explicitly catering to labouring customers, with a minimum deposit as low as 6d, were set up in Britain from Henry Duncan's pioneering start in 1810; there was apparently by 1844 some sense that they were not as flexible as their customers might reasonably expect, since Morgiana goes on to complain that she can't get her money out in under three weeks.
[12] Add. MSS 42974, fos. 325–85, fo. 335r.   [13] ibid., fo. 371r.

whose native English work was being eclipsed), can, on closer examination, seem less unrewarding. The Lyceum writers were well aware of the imputation that all London got its plays from Paris – there is a pun in the Christmas burlesque of 1844, *Valentine and Orson* by Albert Smith and Charles Kenney, which has Oberon the fairy king doubt that anyone is inventing plots against him:

Invent a plot! You're wrong in what you've stated.
Plots ain't invented now: they're all translated.[14]

This was particularly comic from the multilingual Kenney, all of whose stage work was in various kinds of translation. His greatest success was the translation of the libretto for the first full-length Offenbach opera seen in London, *La Grande-duchesse* (Covent Garden 1864).[15] Other things besides opera, burlesques and cleaned-up farces came from the French, however, and one of the less successful pieces on which the Keeleys took a punt, on 20 October 1844, was *The Seven Castles of the Passions*, an experimentally constructed piece from a French fable by the established dramatist Edward Stirling. He had the Keeleys appearing in a series of set pieces, with elaborate staging and satirical dialogue, illustrative of the deadly sins, to each of which they enthusiastically succumbed. The *Morning Chronicle* thought it 'good wholesome satire' and the performances very funny, but the *Examiner*, and the public, found it flimsy, and by 28 October they had rapidly mounted a new Planché piece instead.[16] They nevertheless in June 1846 accepted a more successful experimental piece of Stirling's from a French original, called *Above and Below*, in which they physically divided the stage and played two stories – of rich and poor – at once, to the puzzlement of some critics and the professional admiration of *The Era*, which was deeply impressed by the clever writing and the ensemble playing required.[17]

New dramatists as well as old were encouraged by the Lyceum, and sometimes their work, however French its origins, struck the critics as fresh and original and went down well with audiences. Tom Taylor, who by 1860 was felt to have become England's leading living dramatist,[18] arrived in London from a fellowship at Trinity Cambridge in 1844, pursuing careers as an academic and barrister, but also immediately joining *Punch* and beginning to write for the Lyceum. Over two years

[14] Add. MSS 42980, fos. 526–82, fo. 529r.   [15] *DNB*.
[16] *Morning Chronicle*, 22 October 1844; *Examiner*, 26 October 1844.
[17] *Era*, 19 July 1846.   [18] *DNB*.

he had a hand in at least seven plays there, his first single-authored piece being the accomplished, successful and apparently entirely original farce *A Trip to Kissingen*, which they put on in November 1844 just after the failure of Stirling's *Seven Passions*. It is a four-hander, with the Wigans as aristocratic German bank fraudsters and the Keeleys as a big-mouthed, lecherous British journalist called Crisis and his angry wife. The most interesting thing about the copy of the play that survives in the Lord Chamberlain's collection[19] is that it bears the marks of extensive correction and revision, mostly in the form of cuts – not the work of the censor, but of someone who had gone over the script before or during rehearsal. A few cuts are of material that would possibly have given offence – as when Bob Keeley's character was called upon to name the contents of his suitcase, and included his underwear in the list – but mostly the cuts are dramaturgical, tightening, speeding on, removing elaborations or repetitions unnecessary to a point already made. One cannot tell whether this was the work of one of the Keeleys, leading the new dramatist by the hand, or of one of his friends on *Punch* who went over it before it went to the theatre; but he was clearly being inducted into a successful playmaking team as a contributor with whom trouble should be taken.

THE NEW INSPIRATION: CHARLES DICKENS AND THE WEST END DRAMA

The most important new source of dramatic material in 1844 was, however, not a newcomer. Charles Dickens was already the most famous writer of his day, and his work had hit London's stages, as well as its bookstalls, a decade before: Mary Ann Keeley had appeared in *A Bloomsbury Christening* at the St James's in 1834, though she may not even, at that date, have known that it was adapted from one of the *Sketches by Boz*. But in the feeding frenzy that followed the appearance of an apparently heaven-sent new creative force on the English scene, Dickens came to expect and anticipate that everything he wrote was, in effect, written for the stage as well as the page.[20] He came to terms with the eager players and rapacious adapters, through the Keeleys in particular, actively making common cause with them. His relationship with the Keeleys had developed into a trusting friendship – it was to Bob Keeley that he had

[19] Add. MSS 24979.
[20] 'Every writer of fiction, though he may not adopt the dramatic form, writes in effect for the stage.' Dickens's speech at the Royal Theatrical Fund Dinner, 1858.

applied for acting lessons when he thought of taking to the stage himself; but it was much more. The Keeleys' managerial and acting work, the dramaturgy of their house writers, and the creative power of the greatest original of the day, meshed into a fruitful whole that made Dickens the nearest thing there is to a Victorian Shakespeare. His work is seen today on more stages and screens, especially in the West End, than that of any other 'classic' writer, Shakespeare included.[21]

Dickens's work is, I want to argue, one of the major foundations of the modern West End. Unwilling to confine himself to the impecunious Bohemian subworld of the career dramatist, but utterly unable to leave the theatre alone, the greatest Victorian author wrote for the stage only indirectly; but his work is nevertheless radically part of it. In literary terms, Dickens is the lost leader, the major modern dramatist sought for in vain by Macready and his supporters. Macready's literary snobbery, his narrow conception of the dignity of the Drama, blinded him when at last the opportunity he had sought for years, the chance to enlist a major writer for the stage, presented itself in the form of the eager young Charles Dickens, offering to adapt his latest novel for Macready's season at Covent Garden. The patent house manager told the author that *Oliver Twist* was utterly impracticable for the stage.[22] But the new West End managements knew a good thing when they saw it. There were multiple, competing stagings of each of Dickens's early writings, successful plays that happened all across London before his part-novels were even completely published; the theatre recognised the modernity, the instant and indispensable signifying power of the characters he created.[23] Here was the writer whom the public wanted to shape and embody their everyday lives and aspirations in ideal and fantastic forms. The Lyceum and the Adelphi were more than willing to collaborate with him, whether or not they were invited to do so.

As discussed above, in Chapter 4, Smike in a dramatisation of *Nicholas Nickleby* was one of Mary Ann Keeley's most admired impersonations at the Adelphi in 1839, where she alternated the role with her famous Jack Sheppard. Dickens not only tolerated this representation but went to rehearsals to give advice, the only part of which that has survived being his damning of Stirling's saccharin addition of little robins to one of

---

[21] In a single week in December 2007, for example, there were seventeen works inspired by Dickens listed in the guides to Christmas entertainment in London and on British television.

[22] See J. C. Trewin, ed., *The Journal of William Charles Macready* (London: Longmans, 1967), p. 126.

[23] See H. Philip Bolton, *Dickens Dramatized* (Boston, MA: G. K. Hall & Co., 1987) for extensive listings of the plays derived from each story and novel.

Smike's speeches.[24] Mrs Keeley he thought was otherwise excellent. Martin Meisel suggests that 'it is arguable that Dickens was influenced by her Smike' in creating a character so suited to her line as the title role in his next novel – Barnaby Rudge.[25] She gave a rumbustious realisation of the boy in 1841 during her engagement at the Strand, but the adaptation sailed too close to the political wind for the press, who thought its gutsy staging of the riots dangerous, and found her 'art and experience' in representing Barnaby alarming – the operatic version with the leggy Miss Fortescue was to be preferred.[26] When she opened at the Lyceum, therefore, Mrs Keeley had substantial experience in Dickensian drama, and put on first *Martin Chuzzlewit* in an adaptation by Stirling done with Dickens's permission. The author himself – having written to Bob Keeley saying it was all against his principles[27] – spent time and energy at its rehearsals, and his friend Albert Smith wrote a prologue which Mary Ann spoke on the first night. It begins with the already familiar repudiation of old-fashioned drama: this will be

No ghostly legend from some mouldering page,
And 'carefully adapted to the stage'.
No grand romantic drama, deep and dire,
Full of 'terrific combat' and red fire
Boast we tonight. No flimsy plot shall trench
Upon our scene 'translated from the French';

But rather, the play is 'one in deep emotion far more rife – The powerful romance of common life'. Dickens, he claims, is the master of this genre, this new theatrical form:

We owe this story of the present hour
To that great master-hand – whose graphic power
Can call up laughter – bid the tear to start,
And find an echoing chord in every heart,
Whom we have learn'd to deem an household friend.[28]

Dickens wrote to personal friends congratulating himself on having at last managed to keep hold of his own work and put it on the stage. But he was

---

[24] Mentioned by him in a letter to John Forster, 23 November 1838; and see Goodman, *Keeleys*, p. 79.
[25] Martin Meisel, *Realizations: Narrative, Pictorial, and Theatrical Arts in Nineteenth-century England* (Princeton University Press, 1983), p. 260.
[26] See Chapter 4 above, p. 128.
[27] Dickens to Robert Keeley, 24 June 1844; *The Letters of Charles Dickens*, ed. Mamie Dickens and Georgina Hogarth, 2 vols. (London: Chapman & Hall, 1880), vol. 1, p. 57.
[28] Reported in *Age and Argus*, 13 July 1844.

startled by one thing, in the production: Mary Ann's own chosen role was
not, as he expected, Ruth Pinch – which would have made him feel safe,
he said[29] – but another of her boy roles, Bailey the boots at Todger's
lodging-house. She played it alongside her husband as Mrs Gamp, to
universal satisfaction:

> Mrs Keeley's Bailey was the delight of the house. Shrewd, sly, intelligent little
> cockney – witty, and fully aware of the fact – knowing and assuming the
> innocence of a babe – the *beau ideal* of the 'tiger' – the essence of premature
> assurance, slang, and precocious boyhood.[30]

In this way she avoided the pitfalls of pathos she had found in Smike, and
brought salt and scepticism – a kind of realism, within the obvious fantasy
distancing of cross-dressed performance – as her particular contribution
to the Dickensian picture of modern life. Her comic ability to capture
characters from the bottom rungs of the social scale and make them
appear as living reflections of the new world, actual human beings not
yet made over into art, was perhaps something she had been developing as
she assimilated the *Punch* Radicalism of her writers; a slightly acerbic,
unsentimental but delightfully moving common touch remained her
contribution as an actress in the ensuing collaboration with Dickens.

The Adelphi is often regarded as the leading Dickensian house, and the
plays tended to appear simultaneously there and at the Lyceum, with
Dickens himself holding out a hand to each. The Keeley management had
begun too late to be able to undertake what is probably the most popular
of all the Dickens plays: *A Christmas Carol* appeared, as a book and a stage
phenomenon, over Christmas 1843/4. Dickens gave Stirling permission to
dramatise it at the Adelphi, but the *Carol*'s runaway success, which is still
not over in the twenty-first century, brought him little personal profit. He
did, however, realise that he had almost accidentally stumbled on a perfect
form for his dramatic creativity. For each of the next four Christmases he
produced a book that was deliberately designed to come out simultaneously in print and on the West End stage. At Christmas 1844/5 *The
Chimes*, probably Dickens's most Radical fiction, was dramatised for the
Adelphi by Lemon and A'Beckett and for the Lyceum by Stirling. So
mindfully was Dickens writing for the stage that his friends from *Punch*
were able to reproduce the dialogue 'nearly word for word from the book,
the four quarters of whose Chimes form the four acts'.[31] Stirling could do

---

[29] Dickens to Robert Keeley, 24 June 1844, *Letters*, vol. 1, p. 57.   [30] *Age and Argus*, 13 July 1844.
[31] Bolton, *Dickens*, p. 269, quoting an unattributed review.

the same for the Lyceum, and by all accounts gave a more interesting, effectively fantastic shape to the 'goblin' elements, including two 'dream' acts; both theatres used Dickens's name on the bill, with Celeste at the Adelphi able to boast his 'especial permission'. They used remarkably similar bill designs of imps on bells to emphasise the subtitle: *a Goblin Story* (see Figure 9). At both houses the anti-Political Economy speeches and, especially, the character of the oppressed labourer Will Fern were received with unusual attention, for a serious Christmas piece, and with great applause. On 28 December the Chartist newspaper *Northern Star*, which was only just at this point venturing into theatrical reviewing, noted:

Keeley's fun formed the support of the piece. Probably the character of Trotty could not be made to yield a greater number of hits than he brought into play. His dress and appearance were admirably in character. But no one could look or dress any character better than Mr Emery as Will Fern. He was a haggard, three-quarters starved labourer, with a fierce desperation in his looks at one time, yet, at another, sinking, cowed, and heartbroken under the pressure of want, with a reality that was almost startling. Mrs Keeley as Margaret, or Meg Veck, drew great applause in the passionate scene where Lillian dies at her feet.

The Keeleys were a little out of their comfort zone here, perhaps; but they kept the play going as the traditional serious prologue to their Christmas burlesque, *Valentine and Orson*, into February, and their audiences apparently enjoyed the whole bill, which is not so disparate in feeling as it might appear. *The Chimes* makes its serious points through the use of transformation scenes and supernaturalism; Albert Smith's burlesque begins with a sequence in which a fairy orphanage committee meet and lament the great increase of foundlings upon their hands since the passing of the New Poor Law.[32]

Valentine and Orson, based on a favourite 'serious pantomime' or proto-melodrama of the early years of the century, which in its turn took the story of a nursery tale, was familiar to everyone. It has a central scene, done in mime, in which twin brothers, parted at birth (whom we might read as the two sides of the self) confront each other. One is the courtly hero, fresh from triumph in love and war, who carries a mirrored shield as he sallies forth to rid the countryside of a wild man, brought up by a bear, who is of course his lost brother. Nurture conquers nature, as nature,

---

[32] See Add. MSS 42980 fos. 526–82, fo. 527r.

(a)
(b)

Figures 9a and 9b   Adelphi and Lyceum bills for *The Chimes*

seeing itself in a mirror for the first time, recognises itself as human. The naked symbolism of the melodrama remains, in the Lyceum version; but the audience is invited to laugh about the complexities of being human, and being male. The antics of the Keeleys – she was the courtly Valentine, he the wild man Orson – and of Emery, as the bear foster-mother who dies of drink, carried off in apparent light-hearted playfulness an evening otherwise tending towards the savagely satirical, especially on the part of Emery, since he had also played Will Fern. When *The Chimes* came off in February, *Valentine and Orson* continued alongside a revival of Jerrold's comedy *The Prisoner of War*, which had been made a success at Drury

Lane by the Keeley's performances.[33] This carried the programme through to Easter, when *Martin Chuzzlewit* was brought back compressed into two acts to entertain the visitors, who no doubt by this date expected there to be something by Dickens for them to see.

The next year, 1846/7, saw the Christmas book/play phenomenon at its height, in the shape of *The Cricket on the Hearth*. Dickens sent proof sheets to Albert Smith, and the Lyceum company launched the piece simultaneously with the presses; Thackeray, reviewing not the play but the book, in the *Morning Chronicle* on Christmas Day, made it quite clear where the inspiration and the form for Dickens in his role as 'master of ceremonies for Christmas' was now coming from – he has amalgamated the serious, 'feeling' play with the following Boxing Night pantomime. With his customary sly amiability, Thackeray begins: ' "The cricket on the hearth" has the effect of a beautiful theatrical piece: it interests you as such – charms you with its grace, picturesqueness, and variety – tickles you with its admirable grotesque.' He quotes the opening at length – 'The kettle began it', etc., and asks: 'is this like nature, or like the brilliant ballet-pantomime to which I have compared it? All the properties on the little stage waken into ludicrous life as they will in the pantomime tomorrow night'. Smith had had very little to do, as Thackeray implies: the book is written in three sections (called 'chirps') that neatly transpose to three acts; the dialogue lifts intact, and the effects – the overseeing of the conversation between Dot and the stranger, the fireside visions of Caleb, and so forth – are conceived in perfect stage terms, and are then simply realised on stage.[34] *The Times* – in an editorial fury because Dickens was about to launch a rival daily paper – decided to scupper the enterprise with a slashing review, and announced that 'whatever may be its defects, criticism is disarmed by the somewhat startling announce-ment that it was concocted chiefly with a view to its production at the Lyceum theatre' and that is sufficient explanation for its unnatural dia-logue and generally repulsive staginess. The Lyceum produced their effects, as forecast, and less biased critics loved it, with Mrs Keeley as Dot, Emery as John, and Robert making a personal success as Caleb while introducing their 15-year-old daughter Mary to the stage in her début role, as Caleb's blind daughter Bertha.

---

[33] See Michael Slater, *Douglas Jerrold 1803–1857* (London: Duckworth, 2002), pp. 127–8.
[34] For discussion of the techniques of pictorial realisation in Dickensian plays, see Meisel, *Realizations*, pp. 250–65.

Thus one could say that the Keeleys and Dickens were involved in a series of collaborative creations. Next year the novelist was actually at the Lyceum with them, directing their rehearsals of *The Battle of Life*, 'working harder than I ever did at the amateur plays' despite a streaming cold.[35] His suitability to the role of director is explicit in a later letter about the collaborative act of stage creation: 'As to the play itself, when it is made as good as my care can make it, I derive a strange feeling out of it, like writing a book in company'.[36] He was directly professionally involved in 1846 at the Lyceum, having again conceived the piece in three parts, like a play's three acts, with not only a company but the scenic effects he wanted already in mind; he charged Keeley £100 for the rights to the piece.[37]

The reviews, moreover, began to rebalance the honours in favour of the theatrical end of the show. *The Illustrated London News* for 26 December 1846 says the sisters Grace and Marion were dull, and almost caused disapprobation, but the whole was rescued by the Keeleys. The reporter assumes the readers all know the plot already – a day elapsed between publication and first night, which he seems to assume was long enough for this. It was followed closely, only altered as was necessary 'for the exigencies of the stage; and the result was a most unqualified success. For this, however, be it understood, the author and dramatist were mainly endebted to the unequalled acting of Mrs Keeley as *Clemency Newcombe* . . . otherwise the piece was somewhat wearisome'. She rescued it by her 'exquisite pathos' in the third act. *The Spectator* was even more convinced that the whole evening was Mrs Keeley's, and told its readers that she had a 'private arrangement' to obtain the proof-sheets of the book from the author, but having found it made only a 'dreary' drama had 'perceived that she must carry through the play single-handed' and had rescued the evening by making it 'succeed as a monologue'.[38] At the end, the principals were called, and Dickens, who was not in the house, and then Albert Smith, who was, and whom Mary Ann led on to take his bows.

Dickens always left the country both for the day of publication of his books and for the first nights of his professional productions; but he was by this stage, I would argue, equally responsible for both – even when, as

---

[35] Dickens to Kate Dickens, 21 December 1846, *Letters*, vol. 1, p. 85.
[36] Letter to Sir James Tennent, 9 January 1857; see T. Edgar Pemberton, *Charles Dickens and the Stage* (London: George Redway, 1888), p. 220.
[37] Dickens to Robert Keeley, 31 August 1846, *The Pilgrim Edition of the Letters of Charles Dickens*, ed. Madeline House, Graham Storey and Kathleen Tillotson, 12 vols. (Oxford: Clarendon Press, 1969–2002), vol. IV, p. 616.
[38] *Spectator*, 26 December 1846.

in *The Battle of Life*, the greater share of the creativity involved actually belonged to Mary Ann Keeley. Her observed, unmawkish sentiment, her creation of lower-class characters with minds of their own, was served by Dickens's writing, and in turn served his creations well. George Henry Lewes summed it up, saying she was 'intense and pointed', like a kitten 'eager to make a mouse of any moving thing'. Speaking of her 'picture of a London "slavey", a stupid, weary, slatternly good-natured drab' in a little play called *Furnished Apartments*, he says: 'It was so grotesque, yet so real, that laughter ended in a sigh.' He summed up the Keeleys' career with less ambiguity: it was 'one uninterrupted triumph, and they live in the memory of playgoers with a halo of personal affection round their heads'. [39] The season at the Lyceum was generally seen as a triumphant success, but the advocates of the revival of the national drama resented it: in for example the column written by 'The Trunkmaker' in *The Fine Arts Journal*, 1 May 1847, the writer complains about actor-managers failing to uphold the legitimate.[40] He makes an exception for Madame Vestris, whom he hopes is about to take Drury Lane, but the Keeleys are reprimanded for losing 'a glorious opportunity' to 'resuscitate' the Drama. This refusal to see the value of what Mary Ann Keeley did in creating a new national stage is not unconnected with the long occlusion of Charles Dickens as its primary writing force to emerge from the Victorian period. The West End continued, and continues, to rely heavily upon him as its classic dramatist; a revival of Lionel Bart's jolly musical *Oliver!* was the highest grossing box-office hit in the whole of the history of Drury Lane soon after it opened at Christmas 2008/9, and two years on was advertising itself with a line adapted from one of its songs – 'Never before has a show given more!' The theatrical materials of the 1840s remained Dickens's most successful stage work, and they have had a long life; but some of his later novels, as well as his own stories cut into the dramatic readings he gave during his last eight years, have also proved hugely successful West End fare. *A Tale of Two Cities* (1859), for example, was convertible into stage property well worth fighting about, and was at the centre of acrimonious authorial disputes. It has been a stage success many times over,[41] but was at first a very sore point

---

[39] George Henry Lewes, *On Actors and the Art of Acting* (London: Smith, Elder & Co., 1875), pp. 81, 84, 87.

[40] 'The Trunkmaker', 'The Manager-Actor', *Fine Arts Journal*, 1 May 1847, 403–5, 404.

[41] See Joss Marsh, 'Mimi and the Matinée Idol: Martin-Harvey, Sydney Carton, and the Staging of *A Tale of Two Cities*, 1860–1939', in *Charles Dickens, A Tale of Two Cities and the French Revolution*, ed. Colin Jones, Josephine McDonagh and Jon Mee (London: Palgrave Macmillan), 2009.

between Ben Webster and Celeste, and also between Dickens and the dramatist Watts Phillips, who was convinced Dickens and Webster had taken its plot from his play *The Dead Heart*, a manuscript Webster had had in hand since 1858. Whether or not the play actually caused their personal estrangement, Celeste left Webster and the Adelphi, and her Madame Defarge was the first success of her independent management at the Lyceum in 1860.[42] An emotional and female-centred melodrama, full of sexual tension and physical extremes, *A Tale of Two Cities* was a classic 'Adelphi drama'. Under Celeste's sole direction from 1845 to 1853, the Adelphi regained and strove to maintain its particular niche in the market with such materials, and drew a particular audience whose tastes they met.

'A PECULIAR REPUTATION': CELESTE AND WEBSTER AT THE ADELPHI

If the Lyceum succeeded by carefully eschewing 'the dismals' and all too affecting incidents, laughing quite kindly at everything and conducting itself like a cosy tea party, the Adelphi was made of stronger stuff: according to John Cole in 1859,

[o]ne of the smallest and most incommodious of London theatres, it had long enjoyed a peculiar reputation. The Adelphi had its own audience, its own authors, actors, and pieces. In all these there was an uninterrupted family inheritance, never disputed, but duly descending from generation to generation. How many names of celebrity are conjured up to memory, when we glance hastily back on the fifty-three years' life of this celebrated histrionic temple, devoted to red-hot melodrama, burlesque, domestic tales of intense interest, and 'screaming farce'.[43]

A 'screaming farce' is physically extreme and frequently coarse; the main pieces were spectacular melodrama, non-naturalistic and 'terrific'. The audiences here were still treated as friends – but more likely to be masculine, hail-fellow-well-met friends, who liked a thrill as well as a belly laugh, to whom a nod was as good as a wink. The house was decorated regularly, but remained until a major rebuild in 1858 crammed,

---

[42] See Webster, *Same only Different*, p. 79.
[43] John William Cole, *The Life and Theatrical Times of Charles Kean, F.S.A. Including a Summary of the English Stage for the Last Fifty Years, and a Detailed Account of the Management of the Princess's Theatre, From 1850 to 1859*, 2 vols. (London: Richard Bentley 1859), vol. II, p. 260.

cramped and less than comfortable; it seems to have been the last West End theatre openly to admit sex workers, ignoring a steady barrage of press outrage; and its front-of-house staff were notoriously surly and demanding, making it an ordeal, and often a considerable expense, to get hold of a good seat. But it enjoyed a loyal following, who wanted no change.

There had been some concern when Fred Yates, the long-serving manager who, with his wife Elizabeth, actor/author John Baldwin Buckstone and leading comedian John Reeve, had been the driving force of the Adelphi's particular culture, died prematurely in the summer of 1842. Ben Webster took over the Adelphi lease in 1845 while still spending most of his personal time on his 'legitimate' enterprise at the Haymarket. He therefore installed and relied upon Celeste as 'directress', trusting her to restore the particular ambience of the place. Reeve had died in 1838, and Buckstone had gone to America and returned to act at the Haymarket, where his contract forbade him to write for other theatres – though Webster could now, of course, lift that embargo.

Before that could happen, however, Celeste made a beginning with her own style of strong drama: a development of her early highly physical, cross-gendered multiple performances (see above, Chapter 4) in *The Mysterious Stranger*, a play so called to get it past the Lord Chamberlain's office, since the French original named Satan in the title. According to *The Examiner* on 2 November 1844 'the old Adelphi audiences seem rallying again' to this piece, in which the *Era* reported:

The drama is of peculiar interest and novel idea; the mind is kept in a state of mystery throughout, but the dénouement clears all up satisfactorily. It is written with great literary talent, and is of an infinitely higher order of excellence than the original. The principal character *Satan* is excellently fitted for the peculiar talent of Mme Celeste; and indeed, with the exception of Mrs Keeley, whose forte is in characters of this description, we know no other actress on the English stage, who could so ably have embodied the creation; a character combining so much of the ideal with the real, and in which the various phases of character and of expression are continually shifting, would have been a task worthy of Mrs Keeley's dramatic powers, the development of which would have added largely to her legitimate and well-earned fame. We hear that the character was originally intended for her, but some matters interfering, it was refitted for Mme Celeste. The circumstance has proved fortunate for that talented lady, as well as the theatre to which it is attracting crowded audiences . . . Mme Celeste, as the mysterious stranger, played with great talent, and received most flattering applause. In the course of the piece she personates a variety of characters; first, a well-whiskered Parisian dandy, then a street *gamin*, anon a Russian princess, and a military officer, the brother of the

Princess, and lastly, the intended bride of the count, all of which were represented with considerable tact.[44]

'Tact' would appear to have been an important part of Celeste's French
heritage: she could do outrageous things with a kind of almost insolent
cool. A German critic, attempting to characterise the contradictions of
British vulgarity and prudery in 1853, wrote a little dialogue about the
audiences in the Strand:

'their taste is unrefined, but they are inclined to respect grace and dignity. Look
at Madame Celeste. She carries everything before her by the grace of her
untraditional movements.'
    'But then she is a pretty French woman,' said Mr Baxter, laughing, 'and pretty
women, you know, will carry every thing before them'.[45]

All her sangfroid was, one imagines, called upon when she took to the
stage in February 1845 in Buckstone's new play, *The Green Bushes*. It was
written for her performance strengths but, apparently, without regard for
any embarrassment there might be for her in the plot, which mirrors her
own socially unacceptable position as partner to the still-married Webster.
In the play the hero has left his wife behind in Ireland and formed a new
liaison with Miami – Celeste's character – in America. She apparently did
not mind: it was a perfect role for her.[46] Buckstone's strength as the
dramatist on the Adelphi team had always included not only a sense of
what its audience wanted, but also his actorly sensitivity to the capacities
of, and possibilities presented by, the players he worked with and for
whom he wrote. The team under Yates had been, according to one of its
leading members O. Smith, a tight-knit ensemble all of whom knew their
own business and built and improved upon roles written for them.[47]
Presented with a new challenge, '[t]o bring the great and opposite talents
of Mrs Yates, Mrs Fitzwilliam, and Madame Celeste, before the public in
one production' Buckstone took his time, and then claimed a triumphant
result in which he was 'proud to acknowledge how much he owes to the

[44] *Era*, 3 November 1844.
[45] Max Schlesinger, *Saunterings In and About London* (London: Nathaniel Cooke, 1853), p. 272.
[46] There is a study waiting to be made of the resonances between the roles chosen by actresses in
      nineteenth-century plays and their personal circumstances: see Bush-Bailey, *Performing Herself*,
      p. 39 on Fanny Kelly in *The Sister of Charity*, and Virginia Surtees, *The Actress and the Brewer's Wife*
      (Norwich: Michael Russell, 1997), pp. 44 and 48, on Louisa Herbert in *Going to the Bad* and
      Ticklish Times.
[47] *Recollections of O. Smith, Comedian*, ed. William Appleton, Performing Arts Resources 5
      (New York: Theatre Library Association, 1979), p. 68.

exertions of those ladies – exertions of the highest order of dramatic excellence, unrivalled now, as they have ever been'.⁴⁸

It took until the end of January 1845 to produce *The Green Bushes*, but when it came it was all it promised to be. When the theatre closed in 1858 for its rebuilding, *The Times* singled out the play's arrival as marking the success of the last phase of the old theatre, asserting it could

fairly be pronounced a perfect monster of success; inasmuch as fourteen years of scarcely interrupted wear and tear have proved insufficient to destroy its popularity. Many pieces have been brought out with various degrees of success since first Miami crossed the bridge, with her rifle on her shoulder, and Muster Greenidge and Jack Gong convulsed London with their eccentricities; but nevertheless, Mr Buckstone's 'Green Bushes' will always remain in the memory of the present generation of playgoers as the type of the old Adelphi.⁴⁹

Perhaps those patrons who saw the situation of the play as distortedly reflecting the real life of the directress simply enjoyed it the more; no one mentioned the circumstance in the press. The most interesting critical characterisation of the play was that '*The Green Bushes* is a novel divested of its minor particulars, but retaining all the outline of an exciting tale.' This writer (in the *Age and Argus*)⁵⁰ is clearly not prepared to admit that he personally is impressed by Buckstone's 'celebrated melodramatic apt-ness' and adds that this is a skeleton 'so ingeniously dressed as to beguile the observer into notions of its vitality. Prepared to fascinate – to produce an effect – it fully realises the author's expectations, and gratifies the lovers of such compositions'. The idea that a successful drama – one acknow-ledged to be original, derived from no French or narrative source, but created whole from a study of its prospective players and audience – could be a displaced, unnatural type of the novel, the hegemonic form of the day, is highly suggestive.

The play is historical, like many of the novels of the day – *Barnaby Rudge* and *Jack Sheppard* were completed in 1841 and 1840, Lytton's *The Last of the Barons* in 1843, and Thackeray's *Barry Lyndon* would appear in 1846. Its setting is Ireland and America 'one hundred years ago', with a plot involving an Irish rebel leader who flees to America and contracts a bigamous marriage to Miami, Celeste's character, who is half Native American and half French aristocracy. When his wife – Mrs Yates,

⁴⁸ John Baldwin Buckstone, *The Green Bushes, or a Hundred Years Ago* (London: Webster & Co., [1845]), advertisement, p. iii.
⁴⁹ Quoted in Cole, *Life of Charles Kean*, p. 261.   ⁵⁰ 1 February 1845.

lachrymose and persecuted – arrives and Miami sees them together, she shoots him dead, and throws herself into the raging river. In the final act in Dublin, Fanny Fitzwilliam, playing a devoted peasant step-sister, seeks the missing daughter of the family by singing the folk song of the play's title, and Celeste, not drowned but now embodying her character's French inheritance as Madame St Aubert, rescues both ladies and the daughter too before dying of a broken heart. The resemblances of such a plot to Celeste's earlier triumphs are obvious, but this wild and haughty woman does not pretend to be a boy, and her intense interactions with the other women are at the heart of the melodrama, as was the Adelphi pattern. O. Smith played a repulsive traitorous old peasant, and the new low comics of the establishment, Paul Bedford and Edward Wright, had classic scenes of melodramatic comedy in which they too went to America and brought back a woman, as wife and fairground exhibit. Some critics found this strand of the piece coarse and resented its interference with the pathos and high emotion of Celeste and Elizabeth Yates, but that was what the Adelphi offered: melodrama in all its extroverted contrasts, its dreamlike alternation of bizarre extremes.

Buckstone's next piece for them was not ready until March 1847, but when it came was another great success, and *The Flowers of the Forest* also took a lasting place in the Adelphi repertoire. It is another melodrama focussed on extremes of emotion acted out by contrasting female figures in a pastoral, archaic/exotic setting. Celeste played Cynthia, an Italian 'zingara' or Romany, and Fanny Fitzwilliam was Bess, another slightly simple-minded girl, a British gypsy who talks too much, and is very fond of money and of her beloved childhood sweetheart Lemuel – a gypsy boy played by Sarah Woolgar. Celeste was by now in her thirties, and while she always kept her athletic figure and continued for many years more to perform with energy, she was apparently willing, as a manager, to make use of a younger talent in boy roles, perhaps especially since Lemuel is weak and cowed: he impulsively commits murder because a gentleman has beaten him for poaching but then hides behind his girlfriend's skirts and allows another to take the blame. The scene in which Celeste and Fanny Fitzwilliam fought over the boy, Celeste's character determined to take him to court to vindicate Alfred, the man she loves but will not marry because he is, as the play has it, 'a Gentile', was second only in its sensational success to the finale. In that climactic scene of action her father demanded that she should kill Alfred to regain her place in the tribe, and

LIGHTNING. – A movement amongst the Gipsies is observed; they separate; Pharos removes the tent cloth hanging from the fir branch, and Alfred is seen, sleeping; music; Cynthia grasps her knife and waves them back; Bess utters a sharp cry, but is seized by Pharos, who places his hand over her mouth; they all retreat in silence; Cynthia stands, regarding Alfred; she looks around, and perceives the eyes of the tribe watching her from every part of the scene; she raises the knife; Alfred stirs in his sleep; she pauses; The Gipsies make a simultaneous movement, but in silence; the lightning flashes strongly upon the group; Cynthia bends over Alfred, and looks intently at his features; she sobs bitterly; then, with a sudden effort, again raises the knife and plunges it into her own heart; the loud screams of the women, who rush forward and surround Cynthia, wakes Alfred; he looks around in astonishment; Leybourne, Mayfield, Linton, and Lady Agnes appear down the descent, with others, R.H.U.E.; They approach Alfred, who points in horror to Cynthia, while Bess raises up her head as she crawls on her knees; plaintive music; kisses Alfred's hand, then springs up, and with a shriek, falls dead; the Wolf, with a glance of hatred towards Alfred, and a cry of despair, stands over the form of Cynthia; the Gipsies group round them; thunder heard and the lightning plays vividly.[51]

The Adelphi had, then, its own particular stamp, a tradition of strong melodrama which carried some of the charge of the Romantic theatre forward into a more cynical age, by enacting its extremes as a demonstration of female power, represented as fatally dangerous and ultimately self-destructive. It is striking that this play takes up a central, highly charged motif of Romantic melodrama, the dumb innocent wrongly accused or helplessly carrying the knowledge that will free another from wrongful accusation, and presents it through little Sarah Woolgar, whipped on stage in the first scene, dragged out of hiding between two strong women at the climax and delivered up to justice in the final act off stage. The charged symbol of the courtroom is not shown, but substituted by a kind of anti-masque or antithesis, in an ante-room to the court where the low comedians dress up as cartoon lawyers and rob the real (but very loquacious) innocent, Bess, of her savings, with which she is trying to rescue the boy from (rightful) conviction for the murder. Meanwhile the most deeply felt emotion of the piece is manifested by Celeste, a tragic outsider, a dutiful daughter of the wild whose passion for an Englishman is self-censored, self-suppressed to the point of violent suicide.

---

[51] John Baldwin Buckstone, *The Flowers of the Forest, a Gypsy Story* (New York: Samuel French, n.d.) pp. 52–3.

At Christmas 1852 Lemon and Taylor created the most successful
British dramatisation of Harriet Beecher Stowe's sensationally successful
novel *Uncle Tom's Cabin* for the Adelphi. Celeste had just returned
from a year-long American tour and she reopened there with an
enhanced company, adding leading players from the old Lyceum company. Called *Slave Life*, the Adelphi's contribution to the *Uncle Tom*
fever featured Emery as Simon Legree, Sarah Woolgar as Eliza, Alfred
Wigan as George Harris and Mary Ann Keeley as Topsey.[52] At Easter
1853 Webster, now aged 55, gave up his unrewarding task of upholding
the legitimate drama at the Haymarket and passed the tenure there to
Buckstone. He arrived at the Adelphi, and they staged a little show,
tellingly called *Webster At Home*, dramatising their own situation, in
which he, the Wigans and the Keeleys invade the Adelphi green-room
and 'Mme Celeste proposes to abdicate the managerial throne in favour
of Mr Webster – who, however, insists on her retaining the sceptre'.[53]
Webster sought to continue her successful policy. She was still a draw,
and an inspiration for dramatists able to supply her: in 1853 Dion
Boucicault wrote for her *Geneviève, or, The Reign of Terror;* in 1854
there was Tom Taylor's and Charles Reade's *Two Loves and a Life* and
the role of Mademoiselle Marco in Selby's *The Marble Heart*. In 1855
Boucicault, now a rising dramatist, wrote the pair a 'modern melodrama of the best kind',[54] *Janet Pride*, suited to both their talents: Ben
played a drunken husband and father and Celeste his wife who dies in
the first act and his daughter in the third, fourth and fifth, the pair of
them staggering and agonising though a series of 'striking situations'[55]
for four hours. The successes of that season were, however, a new
Lemon extravaganza called *Domestic Economy* and assorted revivals,
not only *Green Bushes* but also, given the Keeleys' presence, *Open
Sesame* and *Valentine and Orson*. The Queen decided to come to the
Adelphi, enjoying the Christmas pantomime *Jack and the Beanstalk*, in
combination with a 'drama of serious interest' called *Like and Unlike* in
which Celeste played an innocent girl and a 'reckless Countess', with
presumably rather predictable contrasting effects. Victoria was pleased;
she took a royal box, and came again. Ben began upon plans to rebuild

[52] See Sarah Meer's interesting discussion of the play in *Uncle Tom Mania*, pp. 137–60.
[53] *Athenaeum*, 2 April 1853 quoted in the Adelphi Calendar consulted at www.emich.edu/public/
english/adelphi_calendar/ (visited 27.04.2011).
[54] *Morning Post*, 13 February 1855.   [55] *Examiner*, 10 February 1855.

the theatre, but he was to say ' "When my theatre was dirty and old and uncomfortable it was always crowded. The public made me rich and I tore down the old hovel and built them an elegant theatre to show my gratitude. Confound them! They won't come to it!" '[56]

But by 1859, when the 'elegant theatre' opened, the old Adelphi company was gone: Wright, unreconstructed low comedian to the end, succumbed to some unspecified and probably discreditable illness immediately after the reopening, fled to Bologne to escape either debts or domestic trouble, and died by Christmas. Celeste and Webster fell out, and she opened a rival enterprise at the Lyceum. In 1860 they were both surprised by the reappearance in London of Dion Boucicault, who had been making a great success for himself and his wife Agnes in New York, under Laura Keene's management. He returned to London and applied to Celeste for an engagement, but her programme at the Lyceum had no gap for him. He went instead to the Adelphi with the first of his newly named 'sensation dramas', *The Colleen Bawn*. It was an immense success, the first long, uninterrupted run of a play in West End history, and became the first West End touring production.[57] Webster had, however, a tiger by the tail, and before the next year was out Boucicault had forced him to sign away artistic control of his theatre to the dramatist, and before long they were in the courts. Boucicault decamped with his plays to take a lease on Drury Lane.[58] Perhaps Celeste was canny to turn him down; but she might have handled the turn of events somewhat better.

Madame Celeste never returned to the new Adelphi, preferring her own management at the Lyceum (see above); after the notable success of her Defarge she played there another pair of characters – two brothers, a French nobleman and his wild gypsy avatar, in a Parisian melodrama originally by de Kock and Barrière called *The House on the Bridge of Notre Dame*. Her shape-shifting was marvelled at as she exited as the nobleman and entered as the gamin in and out of the many 'practicable' rooms, corridors and staircases of the titular house on the bridge, constructed on stage against a city landscape of Old Paris painted by Mr Calcott. But by 1863 she had had enough of West End management, and departed on a five-year American tour.

---

[56] Webster, *Same only Different*, p. 86.
[57] See Richard Fawkes, *Dion Boucicault* (London: Quartet Books, 1979), pp. 120–4.
[58] ibid., pp. 126–32.

SETTLING OUT? GENTILITY AND THE BURLESQUE

One might see the 1850s and 1860s in the West End as a time of settling and fixing, a clarification of the elements that had grown and expanded since 1844 to create an interlocking web of performance. This partly involved organising audiences differently inside the theatres, as more establishments adapted or rebuilt their auditoria to provide booked and price-segregated seating. Some theatres had a long-term, well-known character that would guide the patrons to the level and type of entertainment they sought. The Adelphi, holding on to its uproarious and interactive character acquired even before the act, might be regarded as the flipside of a programme of planned gentrification undertaken by the Bancrofts. Marie and Squire Bancroft have been both praised and vilified in subsequent commentary for making this deliberate management choice when, in the later 1860s, they abolished the pit, cut off communication across the footlights and even eventually picture-framed the stage in gold, to appeal to an upper-middle-class taste. But to suggest that the audiences for these two styles were distinct and separate, not influenced or informed by each other, would be to oversimplify a densely hatched, intricate picture, in which all the elements of the West End experience remained, I would argue, in play, accessed in some sense by all the people who went there.

The overlapping and interweaving in which I am interested shows up under one roof in the Mathews management at the Lyceum 1847–54. Vestris, who was older than Celeste, 50 when her final management began, had perhaps had enough of performing her kind of glamorous spectacle by this point. The Lyceum was always said on the bills to be under her direction, but Clifford John Williams argues that this was for her publicity value only:[59] she was no longer its artistic driving force, and this was the period of Charles James Mathews's maturation as a performer and director. This may indeed in one sense be so: Mrs Mathews was certainly often unable to appear through illness during these years, and did nothing one might regard as a new departure in her own performances. But she did appear, and this was the period of the most spectacular of her extravaganzas, written by Planché, and of the clever, rather near the knuckle burlesque performances in which Charles Mathews and Priscilla Horton played off each other to the accompaniment of a comical cascade of classical allusion – see above, Chapter 4, for examples. Williams argues

[59] Williams, *Madame Vestris*, pp. 204–8.

that at this point Mathews came into his own as a 'fine comedian' of a new, more naturalistic and gentlemanly kind than had previously been seen.[60] It is at least worth asking whether the preference of posterity for his contribution, noticing and valuing chiefly his modern French-style comedy, might owe more to critical than public opinion. Maybe people in general, as distinct from the writers for the press, went to see the extravaganzas, and put up with the genteel comedy. Or possibly they liked them both equally well. Certainly the critical opinion that emphasises the French-style comedies is hardly unbiased, since it is led by George Henry Lewes, who, under the name of Slingsby Lawrence, was writing the new material in question: he was so much the house dramatist of the Lyceum under the Mathewses that he had a writing room in the theatre.[61]

The writerly lobby was becoming more self-assertive, as the 1850s progressed, in its assessment of the new West End managements and their offerings. The critics now had not only the decade of French-language plays at the St James's under Mitchell, but also the French-based works of the Mathewses at the Lyceum, to use as contrast with the homely emotionalisms of Mary Ann Keeley and the passionate Adelphi offerings. New managements like the Wigans at the Olympic were therefore congratulated on practices and plays the commentators regarded as being, by these measures, an improvement, partaking of a new and more polished, restrained, genteel style. In 1856, for example, *The Era* congratulated Mr Wigan on the occasion of his annual benefit for having 'given to this theatre such a high-class reputation for the production of the best pieces in the best manner' with his 'quiet, finished style', and claimed he had been rewarded by the attendance of the highest classes of society for his efforts 'to escape from the effete traditions of the stage, and make the tone and development of the incidents depicted on these boards approximate nearer to reality'. These genteel patrons were also delighted, apparently, by 'the extreme refinement that pervades every department of the theatre, and the studious manner in which he has regarded the comfort, as well as the amusement of his visitors'. One notes again the feminised virtues of domestic comfort for the 'visitors'; but reinforced now by textual and actorly refinement, the damping down of the somatic and the affective on stage. In 1856 an *Era* writer claims that such pieces and performances as '*Delicate Ground*, which was one of the favourite Lyceum pieces during the Matthews dynasty' and 'the marked evidence of the careful study with

---

[60] ibid., pp. 210–14 and see Lewes: *On Actors*, pp. 59–72.
[61] Williams, *Madame Vestris*, p. 211.

which every phase of emotion is delineated' by Wigan will refute the critics of the theatre by drawing in 'the most fashionable audiences'.[62] His tone strikes the note, combining intellectual and social snobbery, that characterises the construction of the West End that has been passed down to us.

But a different aspect of the Wigan Olympic programme at this moment shows how partial such an assessment is. In 1853 the couple took on, at that theatre, not only the lease but also, on Leonora Wigan's insistence, the previously leading comic performer Frederick Robson, whom she thought a genius.[63] Robson has been treated in memoir and subsequent history as an extraordinary phenomenon, *sui generis*, a unique creature of humour and pathos over whose memory heads are shaken and glasses raised. In fact he was, from the descriptions of his work, quite like many other comics of the time, but he is hailed as unique in theatre history because of the uneven formation of the entertainment world of the mid century. Most of his comparable contemporaries – men such as W. G. Ross, Mackney, J. H. Stead – worked not in theatre, but in the new form, the music hall. They are legends too, but in the history of 'popular culture'. The distinction was not quite so set at the time, perhaps: in 1861 a critic in *The Player, a Dramatic, Musical and Literary Journal* declared '[i]n his diversity of genius Mr Mackney is as remarkable as Mr Robson' and called him 'the Robson of the Singing Hall and the Concert Room'.[64] One might with equal justice say Robson was the music hall comic of the West End theatre. Having begun in the private Minor Theatre in Catherine Street and been taken up by Thomas Rouse at the Grecian Saloon in Hoxton, he came to the West End, appeared before 'the most fashionable audiences', and was greeted as a wonder. Before the Wigans arrived he was playing at the Olympic in burlesque Shakespeare, and at his benefit in September 1853 had apparently involved 'Baron' Renton Nicholson, of the extremely dubious 'Judge and Jury' entertainments, normally seen in a night-house off the Strand, as the judge in the case of Shylock *v.* Antonio – in a burlesque written by the real, and highly respectable, lawyer Thomas Noon Talfourd.[65]

This alarming prodigy became part of the Wigans' refined enterprise, and men like Albert Smith and Tom Taylor wrote for him; his comic

---

[62] *Era*, 13 July 1856.
[63] Erroll Sherston, *London's Lost Theatres of the Nineteenth Century* (London: John Lane and the Bodley Head, 1925), p. 91.
[64] 3:60, 16 February 1861.
[65] *Reynolds's Newspaper*, 11 September 1853 – but the report might be a jest, one feels.

talent, a capacity for excessive, grotesque caricature, rude hilarity and pathos with lightening transitions to intense, demanding emotional moments that were rapidly swept away again into laughter now super-charged by shock, was thus opened to a middle-class audience's appreci-ation and susceptibilities. The new management opened with Taylor's *Plot and Passion*, and the press enthused about both Wigan and Robson, the latter 'taken out of the burlesque' to act 'a vigorous masterpiece' with only a few touches of vulgar caricature, alongside Wigan, who has laboured long 'towards elevating acting into an art'.[66]

On the first night bill *Plot and Passion* played after an *à propos* Planché extravaganza, *The Camp at the Olympic*, greeted by the press as comfort-ably familiar, all the better because it was reassuringly old hat, created off the back of several preceding pieces by the same, now aging, writer. In its first moment the two Wigans walked on to a bare stage in street dress, arm in arm, congratulating each other that

MR W. Well, come what may, at least behold us here!
  I hope you're satisfied? (*to Mrs Wigan*)
MRS W.   So far, my dear,
   The house is ours. We've nothing now to do
   But –
MR W.   Fill it. Do you call that nothing, too?[67]

And they plunge into a domestic squabble, resolved by the appearance of 'Fancy' – played by the newly-wed Mrs German Reed. The continuity from theatre to the world of the drawing-room entertainments, where the Reeds would always squabble like this at the outset of a piece (see Chapter 4), is as clear as that between the theatre and the halls is in the presence of Fred Robson, who soon enters to play 'Burlesque'.

AND SO TO THE STRAND

Burlesque has figured on most bills discussed in this chapter; it is a dramatic form we might think has passed away, that starts with the likes of Fielding, *Tom Thumb* and the anti-heroics of the early eighteenth century and finally trickles off into a leg-show, its content lost, its name appropriated by an American popular art that died out in the twentieth century. But the kind of burlesque that abounded in the early years of the

[66] *Lloyd's Weekly Newspaper*, 23 October 1853.
[67] J. R. Planché, *The Camp at the Olympic*, in *Plays*, ed. Donald Roy (Cambridge University Press, 1986), p. 174.

London West End was neither (and both) of these things; and the essence of what it more completely was is still alive in British entertainment today, in, most clearly, the TV sketch show. Dawn French and Jennifer Saunders, for example, producing their personal three-minute versions of films – heroic, huge, romantic films from *Gone with the Wind* to *Braveheart* and *Titanic* – are doing exactly the kind of thing that went on at the Strand under the Swanboroughs. Both work in the classic manner by reduction to absurdity, making game of the conventions of the heroic – its huge settings, its operatic acting styles, its intense but often bathetic dialogue are reproduced very unnaturally on a very very small scale. To this they add visual inversions, the great heart-throb of the day impersonated by a flouncing fat woman; and physical comedy. The stock of iconic images drawn upon is in both cases both classic and topical: the 1850s equivalents of *Gone with the Wind*, the classic romance in everybody's memory bank, were *The Miller and his Men*, *The Maid and the Magpie* and *Black-ey'd Susan*; and the Strand also took up the very latest hits – their *Titanic* was *Uncle Tom's Cabin*. So burlesque in this sense is not yet an outdated mode; but there are some grounds for arguing that it was a new, or relatively new, one in the 1840s. William Davenport Adams, putting together *A Book of Burlesque* in 1891, spoke of 1831 as 'the starting-point of a new theatrical era' and of the Strand under the Swanboroughs as 'the palmy days' of the genre.[68] Before that point melodrama had contained extreme heroics and their undercutting, and the audience had been able to accept both inflated claptrap, expressive of romantic idealism or of British heroism, and almost simultaneously the skilled deployment of deflationary humour, immediately beside it, within the play – a process still alive in the Adelphi melodramas discussed above. This made for long plays and large casts, and a pace that, while it included rapid alternation, took a long time to get to its end. Attack this at a 'railroad pace' in short pieces and on a small stage and the heroics stand up less well; better to keep them in the mind of the viewer, conjured up there by visual and verbal puns. Sherston observes that

The playgoers of the day, especially the pit and gallery, knew 'The Miller and His Men' and 'The Red Rover' by heart ... The public in general had devoured eagerly all the novels of Walter Scott ... the stalls and boxes knew all about the plots of the Italian operas, many of them supremely ridiculous. Byron – H. J. of that ilk – recognized the possibilities of the situation and for years concocted

---

[68] William Davenport Adams, *A Book of Burlesque: Sketches of English Stage Travestie and Parody* (London: Henry & Co., 1891), pp. 34–43.

parodies bristling with puns, crowded with bright songs and gay dances, and the fortune of the hitherto unlucky little house was changed as by magic from the year 1858.[69]

Add to that system of intertextual reference the complex, delightful intertheatricality of the familiarity of the performers themselves, the patrons' memories of the other roles they had seen the company members do – as every British twentieth-century TV viewer had a rich palimpsest of Morecombe and Wise Christmas Shows, or Victoria Wood *As Seen on TV*, to inform and stimulate their expectations of the next one – and you have a pattern for West End success.

   This was the heart of the Strand's offerings. From the moment Louisa Swanborough took on the management in 1857 a steady, as far as possible unvarying management policy delivered a comedy, a farce and a burlesque every night, changing individual pieces only when they were exhausted, boasting in the advertising of the length of the runs each successful item of the show achieved. Harley Granville-Barker recalled that this meant it became 'the manly habit of the day' to book a seat there – the reserved seat kept free for you all evening was part of the new West End arrangements – 'dine comfortably' and turn up in time for the burlesque, which was 'a romp, a riot of absurdity, and pretended to be nothing else'.[70] Much quoted in any attempt to understand the appeal of the Strand is Henry Barton Baker's observation that

There certainly was a 'go', an excitement about burlesque at the Strand in those days that was never approached by any other house. The enjoyment of the performers was really, or seemingly, so intense that the wild ecstatic breakdown into which they broke at the end of almost every scene seemed perfectly spontaneous; it was a frantic outburst of irrepressible animal spirits, and they seemed to have no more control over their legs than the audience did over their applause. You might call it rubbish, buffoonery, vulgarity, anything you liked, but your temperament must have been abnormally phlegmatic if you could resist the influence of that riotous mirth.[71]

The 'breakdown' is part of the minstrel show format, and blackface songs like Zip Coon and Jim Crow were also indispensably part of the burlesque of opera and classic plays. Lightning, layered reference to other immediate amusements was also required, as well as Byron's often tortuous way with words. Perhaps most important of all was the relationship with the deeply

[69] Sherston, *Lost Theatres*, p. 218.
[70] Quoted in Jim Davis, ed., *Plays by H. J. Byron* (Cambridge University Press, 1984), p. 3.
[71] H. Barton Baker, *The London Stage*, 2 vols. (London: W. H. Allen & Co., 1889), vol. II, p. 135.

remembered but not longer directly accessible, melodramatic simplicities
of feeling. The only way a modern audience can allow itself to go back to
Brief Encounter, one might say, is in a TV sketch that sends it up, but the
archetypal romantic film is still being enjoyed for itself, somewhere within
that experience. Similarly, then, perhaps the old plays were being enjoyed
at the Strand, as they were simultaneously burlesqued by the very titles of
the shows, by which a version of Victor Hugo's *The Hunchback of Nôtre
Dame* becomes in 1861 *Esmeralda, or, the Sensation Goat*, and Fanny
Kelly's burletta success *The Maid and the Magpie* (Drury Lane and the
English Opera House, 1815) becomes *The Maid and the Magpie, or, The
Fatal Spoon* in 1858.

   Charles Dickens was impressed by Marie Wilton as Pippo in this once
famous piece, exclaiming about the miraculously inoffensive freedom of
her performance, 'so stupendously like a boy'.[72] For my analysis the
important point about Pippo is that he is stagestruck. Wilton began her
performance with a long solo in which she complained

> To think that I – one born to tread the boards
> And wield the heaviest of combat swords,
> Whose mission is to wear a spangled dress
> And succour lovely women in distress,
> To single handed fight against a crowd,
> To gasp and fall, then rise with accents loud
> Shout 'Recreant robbers come! Come one, come all!'
> And with a guggle and a stiff back fall
> Conquered by treachery, and fearful odds
> Bring down the curtain, and the Gods,
> One born to ride, what in the bills we read
> Described as 'The fiery untamed steed'
> That wild and most obedient of coursers,
> That *I* should have to wash up cups and saucers –[73]

Working the audience's memory of the original play, of *Timour the
Tartar*, and of the conventions of all such plays, with this kind of clever,
affectionate material was not a matter of pouring scorn upon the theatrical
past. Byron, who had written this for her and pleaded that only she could
carry it off,[74] gave Wilton a way of invoking and sharing her admirers'
deep affection for, and memories of, a simpler time, and an easier access

---

[72] Quoted in *DNB* entry on the Bancrofts.   [73] Add. MSS 52976H, fo. 8r.
[74] *Mr and Mrs Bancroft On and Off the Stage*, vol. 1, p. 78.

to emotion, as they laughed with the woman behind the boy, and shared her aspirations to freedom from the everyday.

As Baker identified, while there were stars in the Strand company it was, essentially, a performing team, and their relationship with each other was shared with the audience. Outstanding members of the early companies, particularly Marie Wilton and Pattie Oliver, were to carry the creative package away and develop it further. Marie Wilton involved Byron himself in the setting up of the Prince of Wales's, though she soon outgrew him, as she had anticipated: she asserted that her venture on her own there was chiefly an attempt to get away from being always cast as a burlesque boy.[75] Martha 'Pattie' Oliver, who has not enjoyed the same historicisation as Wilton, was just as much one of the Strand stars, and her subsequent career followed a surprisingly similar trajectory, though one which has not been noticed. She was, according to Sherston, 'one of the most refined and accomplished actress [*sic*] of her day in many lines. She was equally good in emotional drama as in burlesque. She could make you cry one minute and laugh the next'[76] – like Fred Robson, one might say. Like Wilton, Oliver moved on to management on her own account, taking another versatile Strand actor, H. T. Craven, with her as a dramatist – as Wilton took Byron. She managed the Royalty from 1866 to 1870, rescuing Fanny Kelly's tiny theatre from degradation – as Wilton had rejuvenated the Prince of Wales's. She staged successful burlesques and other pieces by her own Bohemian protégé, Andrew Halliday – as Wilton had taken up and made Tom Robertson. Having achieved her own substantial managerial success without a front-man, Oliver then married a much younger man from outside the theatre and left the stage, as Jane Scott had done two generations before, and Louisa Swanborough in the previous decade.

At the same point (in 1868) John Hollingshead, Bohemian writer, Radical journalist for *Punch* and *Household Words*, drama critic on the *Daily News* and manager and effectively creator of the Alhambra in Leicester Square, took the next step in the development of West End burlesque. He gathered a company including Alfred Wigan, Robert Soutar and his wife Nellie Farren the ultimate actress of boys, who had met at the Olympic, and a young Madge Robertson, who was to become Madge Kendal, and took the newly built Gaiety Theatre, opposite the Strand, on the old site of the Lyceum. There he carried on the Strand Theatre model, opening with an operetta, a comedy from the French

[75] ibid., pp. 171–5.   [76] Sherston, *Lost Theatres*, p. 222.

translated and led by Alfred Wigan, and a burlesque of the opera *Robert the Devil*, starring Nellie as Robert and written by W. S. Gilbert. For eighteen years, as he said, he kept 'the sacred lamp of the burlesque'[77] burning there.

CONCLUSION

I hope I have demonstrated that the West End theatre of the subsequent 130-odd years can be claimed, in large part, as the creation of women, the legacy of Vestris and Celeste, the Swanboroughs and Wigans and Keeleys; and that there is much more to it than cup-and-saucer comedy and class segregation of the auditorium. The burlesque view of the world, its emotional excess and its hilarious physical extremity, is, I have argued, the true descendant of the exhilaration, the somatic and emotional release, of the Romantic melodrama; the relationship between the two is a passionate intertheatrical game, in which players and audience could consciously take part. In an age which craved such theatrical release but was increasingly too inhibited and also too sophisticated to surrender to it, women like Celeste and Marie Wilton gave opportunities for extremes of emotional response within a frame that marked them as clearly of the theatre, unreal, and therefore not threatening to the painstakingly con-structed Victorian self. Unlike the dominant form of the day, the novel, the stage did not offer to fit people into their demanded social slots, and so to naturalise relationships of power. Instead it released them, gave them a space within which they could still laugh and cry and feel, all together. This was the promise held out by the glittering portal – the space of fairyland that is the West End.

---

[77] *DNB* quoting him.

Conclusion

Beginning with Clement Scott, it has been a given of theatre history that when in 1865 Marie Wilton created the Prince of Wales's Theatre in the Tottenham Court Road a new era began. Her management – or rather, that of 'The Bancrofts' – has been hailed as, first, the dawn of naturalism on British stage, and, later, as the central betrayal perpetrated by the West End, leading to 'mismanagement and snobbery' that stifled the drama for a century. 'The Bancrofts' are credited with picture-framing the stage and so cutting off the dynamic flow between audience and players; with segregating and curtailing the demographic of the audience by higher prices and reorganised, segregated seating; with shortening the long mixed bill to a single piece, even sometimes without a 'curtain-raiser', to accommodate the changes in the fashionable hour of dining; and with inventing the long run, the box set and the society play, and so subordinating text to upholstery, and everything to profit.[1] In fact, as I hope I have shown, most of these things had been begun, changed, adopted or discarded by the earlier managements I have been discussing. Vestris, one of the most visionary and innovative London managers of the century, had done everything from shortening the times of performance and modifying the auditorium to hiring co-ordinated set designers and costumiers at the Olympic in the 1830s. There had been experiments with evening-long single plays at most of the theatres, but the audiences had found them boring. Every new management of these jerry-built little theatres tried to clean them up and make them warmer, or cooler, and more comfortable. Marie Wilton learnt from her predecessors, and moved onwards through her own career with great good sense. For a time, these were the developments that worked; the second half of the nineteenth century saw many of these things become normal, because they were commercially successful.

[1] Pick, *West End*.

The London theatre has always been a commercial theatre; since Davenant and Killigrew, all that happened on its stages was intended to be what would bring in a paying audience. The nineteenth-century managers, especially the women, were alert to the desires of their nineteenth-century customers, and the developments in programming that I have been discussing were their best estimate of what would work. Rather than wishing them away, wishing that theatre had been delivered more quickly into the hands of visionaries rather than stage professionals, that its centre was the dramatist rather than the event, I have tried in the foregoing chapters to think about what it was they offered and why their audiences liked it; why they succeeded. I have been attempting to look at those performances for themselves, in the context of all the other offerings of entertainment in the West End at mid-century, without accepting the prejudices and prescriptions of later generations; and the picture is lively, indeed bizarre; often funny, sometimes emotionally supercharged, both vivid and coarse. Not dull. By no means mundane or socially exclusive. Dickensian affect – the emotional overload of Smike and Pickwick, Barnaby and Dot – is accompanied by alienation effects like a female criminal hero wielding a carpenter's plane and burlesque fairies discussing the Poor Law in punning couplets. Fantastically clad women fighting or weeping, shooting their husbands or stabbing themselves in pantomime are intercut with beloved comics acting drunk and winking at the audience. Spectacular moving scenery and ghostly apparitions surround women in crinolines who shake audiences with Shakespeare's lines, and the never-never land of the stage gives back colour and feeling to anxious lives.

AND THEN?

The legacy of the West End left by these feminised managements can be seen most clearly, perhaps, in a very masculine successor: Sir Henry Irving at the Lyceum. Irving has come to epitomise all that is implied, whether we like it or not, by the magic of the stage. Robertson Davies characterises Irving's theatre by saying that for him

the sub-text, provided by himself, and to which the total production offered an objective correlative, was supreme. It was this imaginative element that created the atmosphere of phantasmagoria and dream grotto that was the mark of every Lyceum production, even when the author was Shakespeare.[2]

---

[2] *DNB.*

At the Lyceum from 1879 to 1899 Irving built an enduring archetype of the stage, and grossed more than a million pounds in the currency of the time, amidst 'an extraordinary aura of priestly opulence'.[3] Resting briefly, as a final stage in this journey, on this last pillar of the theatre history bridge across the nineteenth century may suggest how much the West End theatre as we understand it owed to the mid-century work of the men and women I have been describing.

Ellen Terry, Irving's co-star, resembled the theatre-managing women who taught her and whom she described in her memoirs (see Chapter 4) in many ways as a performer and as an independent woman, but she was not the Lyceum's co-manager. She was hired by Irving to play opposite him when he took over the management – from Mrs Bateman. Irving's absolute power at the Lyceum from 1879 and in the popular imagination of the time came about at least in part, I would suggest, because he built upon a management practice created by women, but in doing so took back to himself the attributes that two previous generations of actors had eschewed as feminised. Irving came from a 'serious' background – his mother was a strict Methodist who never got over her hatred of the theatre – and he aspired to be a member of the elite, even though he left his wife because she was a short-sighted snob. He succeeded – he was the first knight of the British theatre; but he was not merely what his wife and mother wanted, an ordinary gentleman in black. His achievement was to gather up all that had been done by the West End managements to make theatre part of the imaginary of the British public once more, and take it back into the image he created, of the Great Actor. His black clothing famously included a huge, theatrical hat and a swirling cloak, and he spoke and walked and looked like an actor, as much as Robert Elliston had done in the days before Victoria was crowned. On stage, he was the centre of a throng of supers and all the many limelights, and his partner Ellen Terry's costumes had to blend into the background of the colours Irving wore; as Mephistopheles, in skin-tight red from head to foot, he fenced with an electrically wired sword that flashed sparks as he struck. He deployed all the theatrical forces there were, and invented more; he topped the century's tradition of elaborate Shakespearean staging, spending sums of money on it that read like budgets for a Hollywood movie, and were occasioned by the same desire to deploy absolute realism to create surpassing fantasy. Dancing oddly across the stage as a supernatural being of attractive evil and amusing allure, he was following in the

---

[3] Pick, *West End*, pp. 88–9.

footsteps of Celeste; arranging masses of supers to dress the stage in a ravishing realisation of Shakespeare-land, he was following Vestris's 1841 initiative in *Midsummer Night's Dream*, applying to the Drama the traditions of the diorama and the musical theatre. In his own acting, he brought out with a flourish the queer melodramatic power that had been carried through the mid-century under the wing of burlesque: if there is anything that the twenty-first-century man in the street knows about Irving's performances, it is the combined laugh and shudder evoked by his staring eyes and clutching hands as he exclaimed 'The Bells! The Bells!' It is assumed now that Irving was entirely serious about this trademark melodrama, but it is interesting that from its very first night in 1871, *The Bells* was frequently preceded in the evening, and therefore of course on the playbill, by *Jingle*, a Dickensian farce which gave the actor his best comic character.[4] The delightful interaction of shock and laughter, the sly self-burlesque, could hardly be more knowingly signalled.

Irving's work has recently been argued to be worth revisiting as 'one of the harbingers of modernist theatre' for his precise, studied, artificial theatricality, which Jim Davis compares to the acting theoretics of Stanislavski and Meyerhold; simultaneously, Davis also suggests, we should regard him as the last of the great Victorians, one of those who 'aspired beyond the mundane and everyday in realising their vision of the world around them'.[5] In both these things – in his physical, technical perfection, deployed to create affective and somatic engagement with the deep desires of his audiences – I would argue that Irving acted like the professional women whose work was the foundation of the Victorian theatre. Out of their work grew the art of theatre as London understood it for a century; but, as Irving pointed out, they knew and passed on to him the understanding that 'the theatre must be carried on as a business, or it will fail as an art'.[6] In this book it has been my intention to insert these powerful businesswomen and artists, Irving's foremothers Mary Ann Keeley and Leonora Wigan, Madame Vestris, Mrs Charles Kean and Madame Celeste and the rest of the all but forgotten female theatre-makers of the century, into a new history of creative energy, the theatrical magic that is the West End.

---

[4] Thanks to Professor James Davis for this information.
[5] Jim Davis, '"He danced, he did not merely walk – he sang, he by no means merely spoke": Irving, Theatricality and the Modernist Theatre', in Richard Foulkes, ed., *Henry Irving: A Re-evaluation of the Pre-eminent Victorian Actor-Manager* (Aldershot: Ashgate, 2008), pp. 27–36, pp. 27, 35
[6] Quoted in Jeffrey Richards, *Sir Henry Irving: A Victorian Actor and his World* (London: Hambledon & London and Continuum, 2005), p. 7.

Bibliography

MANUSCRIPTS

British Library Add. MSS, Lord Chamberlain's Plays
British Library Add. MSS 59888, plays by J. T. Haines
Harvard Theatre Collection, letter from Robert Keeley to W. C. *Macready* 12 *April* 1841
London Metropolitan Archives, diaries of Henrietta Thornhill, catalogue ref. IV/81

ONLINE REFERENCE WORKS

New Dictionary of National Biography, www.oxforddnb.com, abbreviated in notes to *DNB*
Survey of London, www.british-history.ac.uk/surveyoflondon, especially volumes 18, 20, 36, 41

NINETEENTH-CENTURY NEWSPAPERS AND PERIODICALS

The following have been consulted online at www.galegroup.com
  Age and Argus
  Bell's Life in London
  Caledonian Mercury
  Daily News
  Era
  Examiner
  Liverpool Mercury
  Lloyd's Weekly Newspaper
  London Review
  Morning Post
  Odd Fellow
  Reynolds's Newspaper
  Saturday Review
  Theatrical Times
  York Herald

WORKS CONSULTED

Accounts of the Total Population, 1841, *British Parliamentary Papers*, 1841, ii (Sess. 2, 52), 277

Adams, James Eli, *Dandies and Desert Saints: Styles of Victorian Masculinity*, Ithaca, NY: Cornell University Press, 1995

Adams, William Davenport, *A Book of Burlesque: Sketches of English Stage Travestie and Parody*, London: Henry & Co., 1891

Allen, Percy, *The Stage Life of Mrs Stirling: With some Sketches of the Nineteenth-century Theatre*, London: T. Fisher Unwin, 1922

Altick, Richard, *The Shows of London*, Cambridge, MA: Harvard University Press, 1978

Andrews, Malcolm, *Charles Dickens and his Performing Selves: Dickens and the Public Readings*, Oxford University Press, 2006

Anon., 'Lucid Intervals of a Lunatic No. 8', *Bell's Life in London, 30 Jan* 1842

Armstrong, Isobel, *Victorian Glassworlds: Glass Culture and the Imagination 1830–1880*, Oxford University Press, 2008

Arnold, Matthew, 'Equality', *Fortnightly Review* 23:135, 1878

Ashton, Rosemary, *G. H. Lewes, a life*, Oxford: Clarendon Press, 1991

Auerbach, Nina, *Ellen Terry, Player in her Time*, London: J. M. Dent, 1987

Bailey, Peter, *Leisure and Class in Victorian England: Rational Recreation and the Contest for Control, 1830–1885*, London: Routledge & Kegan Paul, 1978

'The Victorian Middle Class and the Problem of Leisure', *Victorian Studies* 21, autumn 1977, reprinted in *Popular Culture and Performance in the Victorian City*, Cambridge University Press, 1998, 13–29

Baker, H. Barton, *The London Stage, 2 vols.*, London: W. H. Allen & Co., 1880

Bancroft, Squire and Marie, *Mr and Mrs Bancroft On and Off the Stage, 2 vols.*, London: Richard Bentley, 1888

Barringer, Tim, 'Equipoise and the Object: The South Kensington Museum', in Martin Hewitt, ed., *An Age of Equipoise? Reassessing Mid-Victorian Britain*, Aldershot: Ashgate, 2000, 68–83

Blackmer, Corrine E., *En Travesti: Women, Gender and Subversion*, New York: Columbia University Press, 1995

Blanchard, E. L., 'Licensed Victuallers, their Manners, and their Parlours', *The Town*, 20 April, 1839

The Life and Reminiscences of E. L. Blanchard, with Notes from the Diary of Wm. Blanchard, ed. Clement Scott and Cecil Howard, 2 vols., London: Hutchinson & Co., 1891

Bolton, H. Philip, *Dickens Dramatized*, Boston, MA: G. K. Hall & Co., 1987

Booth, Michael R., *English Plays of the Nineteenth Century*, vol. iv, *Farces*, Oxford: Clarendon Press, 1873

Brannan, Robert Louis, *Under the Management of Mr Charles Dickens: His Production of 'The Frozen Deep'*, Ithaca, NY: Cornell University Press, 1966

Bratton, Jacky, *New Readings in Theatre History*, Cambridge University Press, 2003

'Mirroring Men: The Actress in Drag', in Maggie Gale and John Stokes, eds., *The Cambridge Companion to the Actress*, Cambridge University Press, 2007, 253–71

'Fanny Kemble, Shakespearean', in Gail Marshall, ed., *Great Shakespeareans*, vol. VII, *Jameson, Cowden Clarke, Kemble and Cushman*, London: Continuum, 2011, 92–132

Brecht, Bertolt, 'The Modern Theatre is the Epic Theatre: Notes to the opera Aufstieg und Fall der Stadt Mahagonny'. 1950, in *Brecht on Theatre: The Development of an Aesthetic*, ed. and trans. John Willett, London: Methuen, 1964

Brook, Peter, *The Empty Space: A Book about the Theatre: Deadly, Holy, Rough, Immediate*, London: MacGibbon & Kee, 1968

Brooks, Peter, *The Melodramatic Imagination: Balzac, Henry James, Melodrama, and the Mode of Excess*, New York: Columbia University Press, 1985

Brough, Robert, *Marston Lynch: His Life and Times, his Friends and Enemies, his Victories and Defeats, his Kicks and Halfpence, with a Memoir by G. A. Sala*, London: Ward & Lock, 1860

Buck-Morss, Susan, 'Walter Benjamin – Revolutionary Writer (1)', *New Left Review* 1:/128, July–August 1981, 50–75

Buckstone, John Baldwin, *The Green Bushes, or a Hundred Years Ago*, London: Webster & Co. [1845]
The Flowers of the Forest, a Gypsy Story, New York: Samuel French, n.d.

Bunn, Alfred, *The Stage: Both Before and Behind the Curtain*, 3 vols., London: Richard Bentley, 1840

Bush-Bailey, Gilli, *Treading the Bawds*, Manchester University Press, 2006
Performing Herself: Autobiography and Fanny Kelly's Dramatic Recollections, Manchester University Press, 2011

Butter, Frances Anne, *Records of Later Life*, 3 vols., London: Richard Bentley, 1882

Cannadine, David, *Class in Britain*, Harmondsworth: Penguin, 1998

Carlisle, Thomas, *On Heroes, Hero-Worship and the Heroic in History*, 1840, London: Chapman & Hall, 1872

Castle, Terry, *Masquerade and Civilization: The Carnivalesque in Eighteenth-century English Culture and Fiction*, London: Methuen, 1986

Certeau, Michel De, *The Practice of Everyday Life*, trans. Steven Randall, Berkeley: University of California Press, 1984

Clark, Maribeth, 'The Quadrille as Embodied Musical Experience in 19th-century Paris', *Journal of Musicology* 19:3, summer 2002

Cole, John William, *The Life and Theatrical Times of Charles Kean, F.S.A. Including a Summary of the English Stage for the Last Fifty Years, and a Detailed Account of the Management of the Princess's Theatre, From 1850 to 1859*, 2 vols., London: Richard Bentley, 1859

Coleman, John, *Players and Playwrights I have Known*, 2 vols., London: Chatto & Windus, 1888

Davidoff, Leonore and Hall, Catherine, *Family Fortunes: Men and Women of the English Middle Class 1780–1850*, London: Hutchinson, 1987

Davies, Robertson, *The Mirror of Nature: The Alexandra Lectures 1982*, University of Toronto Press, 1983

Davis, Jim, ed., *Plays by H. J. Byron*, Cambridge University Press, 1984

Davis, Jim,"'He danced, he did not merely walk – he sang, he by no means merely spoke": Irving, Theatricality and the Modernist Theatre', in Richard Foulkes, ed., *Henry Irving: A Re-evaluation of the Pre-eminent Victorian Actor-Manager*, Aldershot: Ashgate, 2008, 27–36

Davis, Jim and Emeljanow, Victor, *Reflecting the Audience*, University of Iowa Press, 2001

Davis, Tracy C., *The Economics of the British Stage 1800–1914*, Cambridge University Press, 2000

  'Female Managers, Lessees and Proprietors of the British Stage (to 1914)', *Nineteenth-century Theatre* 28:2, winter 2000, 115–44

  '"I long for my home in Kentuck": *Christy's Minstrels in Britain (1857–64)*', conference paper in progress, delivered first at TaPRA, 2010

  The Broadview Anthology of Nineteenth-century British Performance, Peterborough, Ont.: Broadview Press, 2011

Dickens, Charles, *The Letters of Charles Dickens*, ed. Mamie Dickens and Georgina Hogarth, 2 vols., London: Chapman & Hall, 1880. Vol. I, Project Gutenberg e-book no. 25852

  The Pilgrim Edition of the Letters of Charles Dickens, ed. Madeline House, Graham Storey and Kathleen Tillotson, 12 vols., Oxford: Clarendon Press, 1969–2002

Duncan, Barry, *The St James's Theatre, its Strange and Complete History 1835–1957*, London: Barrie & Rockliff, 1964

Dyos, H. J. and Wolff, Michael, *The Victorian City, Images and Realities*, 2 vols., London: Routledge & Kegan Paul, 1973

Ebers, John, *Seven Years of the King's Theatre*, London: Ainsworth, 1828

Edwards, F. G., 'Mrs Keeley and "Oberon"', *Musical Times* 40, 1 April 1899, 240–1

Edwards, P. D., *Dickens's 'Young Men': George Augustus Sala, Edmund Yates and the World of Victorian Journalism*, Aldershot: Ashgate, 1997

Eliot, George, *The George Eliot Letters*, ed. Gordon S. Haight, Oxford University Press, 1954

Ehrenreich, Barbara, *Dancing in the Streets: A History of Collective Joy*, New York: Metropolitan Books, 2007

Fawcett, F., *Dubrez, Dickens the Dramatist on Stage, Screen and Radio*, London: W. H. Allen, 1952

Fawkes, Richard, *Dion Boucicault: A Biography*, London: Quartet Books, 1979

Fasick, Laura, *Professional Men and Domesticity in the Mid-Victorian Novel*, Lampeter: Edwin Mellen Press, 2003

Fielding, K. J., 'Thackeray and the "Dignity of Literature"'parts I and II, *TLS*, 19 September 1958, 536; and 26 September 1958, 552

Fitzsimons, Raymund, *The Baron of Piccadilly: The Travels and Entertainments of Albert Smith 1816–1860*, London: Geoffrey Bles, 1967

Flanders, Judith, *Consuming Passions: Leisure and Pleasure in Victorian Britain*, London: HarperPerennial, 2007

Fraser, Hilary, Green, Stephanie and Johnson, Judith, *Gender and the Victorian Periodical*, Cambridge University Press, 2003

Garber, Marjorie, *Vested Interests: Cross-Dressing and Cultural Anxiety*, London and New York: Routledge, 1992

Gernsheim, Alison, *Victorian and Edwardian Fashion, a Photographic Survey*, New York: Dover Publications, 1963, 1981

Gilbert, W. S., 'From St Pauls to Piccadilly', *Belgravia* 2, March 1867, 69–74

Glavin, John, *After Dickens: Reading, Adaptation and Performance*, Cambridge University Press, 1999

Goodall, Jane, *Performance and Evolution in the Age of Darwin*, London and New York: Routledge, 2002

Goodman, Walter, *The Keeleys, on the Stage and at Home*, London: Richard Bentley, 1895

Grazia, Victoria de and Furlough, Ellen, eds., *The Sex of Things: Gender and Consumption in Historical Perspective*, Berkeley: University of California Press, 1996

Haines, John Thomas, *The French Spy; or, The Siege of Constantina*, Dicks plays no. 680, n.d.

Hall, Jennifer Lee, 'The Re-fashioning of Fashionable Society – Opera-going and Sociability in Britain 1821–1861', unpublished Ph.D., Yale University, 1996

Hall-Witt, Jennifer, *Fashionable Acts: Opera and Elite Culture in London, 1780–1880*, Durham: University of New Hampshire Press, 2007

Halliday, Andrew, ed., *The Savage Club Papers*, London: Tinsley Brothers, 1867

Hardwick, J. M. D, ed., *Emigrant in Motley: Unpublished Letters of Charles and Ellen Kean*, London: Rockliff, 1954

Harvey, John, *Men in Black*, London: Reaktion Books, 1995

Hewitt, Martin, ed., *An Age of Equipoise? Reassessing Mid-Victorian Britain*, London: Ashgate, 2000

House, Madeline and Storey, Graham, eds., *The Letters of Charles Dickens*, vol. II, *1840–1841*, and vol. IV, *1844–1846*, Oxford University Press, 1969

Howard, Diana, *London Theatres and Music Halls 1850–1900*, London: Library Association, 1970

Hudson, Derek, *Munby: Man of Two Worlds. The Life and Diaries of Arthur J. Munby 1828–1910*, London: Abacus, 1974, 1st published 1972

Hyman, Alan, *The Gaiety Years*, London: Cassell, 1975

James, Henry, 'Frances Anne Kemble', *Temple Bar*, April 1893, 503–25

John, Juliet, *Dickens's Villains: Melodrama, Character, Popular Culture*, Oxford University Press, 2001

Kemble, Frances Anne, *Records of Later Life*, 3 vols., London: Richard Bentley, 1882
    Records of a Girlhood, New York: Henry Holt, 1883

Kent, Christopher, 'The Whittington Club: A Bohemian Experiment in Middle-Class Social Reform', *Victorian Studies*, 18:1 September 1974, 31–55

'The Idea of Bohemia in Mid-Victorian England', *Queen's Quarterly* 80, 1973, 360–9

'British Bohemia and the Victorian Journalist', *Australasian Victorian Studies Journal* 6, 2000, 25–35

King, W. D., *Henry Irving's Waterloo: Theatrical Engagements with Late-Victorian Culture and History*, Berkeley: University of California Press, 1993

Koven, Seth, *Slumming: Sexual and Social Politics in Victorian London*, Princeton University Press, 2004

Leach, Joseph, *Bright Particular Star*, New Haven, CT: Yale University Press, 1970

Lewes, George Henry, *On Actors and the Art of Acting*, London: Smith, Elder & Co., 1875

Linton, Eliza Lynn, *The Autobiography of Christopher Kirkland*, 1885, transcribed, encoded and proofed by W. Charles Morrow, ed. Perry Willett, for the Victorian Women Writers Project Library, Library Electronic Text Resource Service (LETRS), Indiana University

Loehlin, James, ed., *Romeo and Juliet*, Shakespeare in Production series, Cambridge University Press, 2002

Marsh, Joss, 'Mimi and the Matinée Idol: Martin-Harvey, Sydney Carton, and the Staging of *A Tale of Two Cities*, 1860–1939', *Charles Dickens, A Tale of Two Cities and the French Revolution*, ed. Colin Jones, Josephine McDonagh and Jon Mee, London: Palgrave Macmillan, 2009

Marshall, Gail, ed., *Great Shakespeareans*, vol. VII, *Jameson, Cowden Clarke, Kemble and Cushman*, London: Continuum, 2011

Mathews, Anne, *The Life and Correspondence of Charles Mathews, the Elder, Comedian, by Mrs Mathews, a new edition, abridged and condensed by Edmund Yates*, London: Routledge, 1860

Meer, Sarah, *Uncle Tom Mania: Slavery, Minstrelsy and Transatlantic Culture in the 1850s*, Athens: University of Georgia Press, 2005

Meisel, Martin, *Realizations: Narrative, Pictorial, and Theatrical Arts in Nineteenth-century England*, Princeton University Press, 1983

Morley, Henry, *The Journal of a London Playgoer from 1851 to 1866*, London: Routledge, 1866; Leicester University Press, 1974

Morley, Malcolm, *The Old Marylebone Theatre*, London: St Marylebone Society, 1960

Nead, Lynda, *Myths of Sexuality: Representations of Women in Victorian Britain*, Oxford: Blackwell, 1988

Victorian Babylon: People, Streets and Images in Nineteenth-century London, New Haven, CT: Yale University Press, 2000

Newey, Katherine, *Women's Theatre Writing in Victorian Britain*, London: Palgrave Macmillan, 2005

Nicoll, Allardyce, *A History of Early Nineteenth Century Drama 1800–1850, 2 vols.*, Cambridge University Press, 1930

A History of the English Drama, vol. VI, *A Short-Title Alphabetical Catalogue of Plays . . .* Cambridge University Press, 1959

Orr, Lyndon, *Famous Affinities of History*, New York: Harper, n.d. [1912], no. IV, Charles Reade and Laura Seymour; www.authorama.com/famous-affinities-of-history-iv-1.html (visited 30.12.2010)

Pemberton, T., *Edgar, Charles Dickens and the Stage: A Record of his Connection with the Drama as Playwright, Actor and Critic*, London: George Redway, 1888

Perugini, Mark Edward, *The Omnibus Box*, London: Jarrolds, 1946

Pick, John, *The West End: Mismanagement and Snobbery*, Eastbourne: John Offord, 1983

Pilbeam, Pamela, *Madame Tussaud and the History of Waxworks*, London: Hambledon & London, 2003

Pierce, Charles E., *Madame Vestris and her Times*, London: Stanley Paul & Co., n.d.

Planché, James Robinson, *Plays*, ed. Donald Roy, Cambridge University Press, 1986

Porter, Roy, *London, a Social History*, London: Hamish Hamilton, 1994; Harmondsworth: Penguin, 1996

Pulling, Christopher, *They Were Singing, and what they sang about*, London: George Harrap & Co., 1952

Poovey, Mary, *Uneven Developments: The Ideological Work of Gender in Mid-Victorian* England, London: Virago, 1989
   Making a Social Body: British Cultural Formation, 1830–1864, University of Chicago Press, 1995

Powell, Kerry, *Women and Victorian Theatre*, Cambridge University Press, 1997
   'Gendering Victorian Theatre', *The Cambridge History of British Theatre*, vol. II, *1660–1895*, ed. Joseph Donohue, Cambridge University Press, 2004, 352–68

Prowse, Jeffrey, *Nicholas's Notes and Sporting Prophesies, with some miscellaneous poems, serious and humorous*, ed. Tom Hood, London: Routledge, [1870]

Purbrick, Louise, 'The Bourgeois Body: Civic Portraiture, Public Men and the Appearance of Class Power in Manchester, 1838–50', *Gender, Civic Culture and Consumerism: Middle Class Identity in Britain 1800–1940*, ed. Alan Kidd and David Nicholls, Manchester University Press, 1999, 81–98

Rappaport, Erika Diana, *Shopping for Pleasure: Women in the Making of London's West End*, Princeton University Press, 2000

Rendell, Jane, *The Pursuit of Pleasure: Gender, Space and Architecture in Regency London*, London: Athlone Press, 2002

Richards, Jeffrey, *Sir Henry Irving: A Victorian Actor and his World*, London: Hambledon & London and Continuum, 2005

Rowell, George, *Queen Victoria goes to the Theatre*, London: Elek, 1978

Sala, George Augustus, *Twice Round the Clock; or The Hours of the Day and Night in London*, 1st published 1858; introduction by Philip Collins, Leicester University Press, 1971
   Gaslight and Daylight, London: Chapman & Hall, 1859
   Life and Adventures of George Augustus Sala, written by himself, 2 vols., 2nd edn, London: Cassell & Co., 1895

Schafer, Elizabeth, *Ms-Directing Shakespeare*, London: Women's Press, 1998
    Lilian Baylis: A Biography, Hatfield: University of Hertfordshire press, 2006
Schlesinger, Max, *Saunterings in and about London*, London: Nathaniel Cooke,
    1853
Schoch, Richard, *Shakespeare's Victorian Stage: Performing History in the Theatre
    of Charles Kean*, Cambridge University Press, 1998
    Wot Shakespheare: Bardolatry and Burlesque in the Nineteenth Century,
    Cambridge University Press, 2002
    'Performing Bohemia', *Nineteenth-Century Theatre and Film* 30:2, Winter
    2003, 1–13
    'Theatre and Mid-Victorian Society, 1851–1870', *The Cambridge History of British
    Theatre*, vol. II, *1660–1895*, ed. Joseph Donohue, Cambridge University Press,
    2004, 331–51
Scott, Clement, *The Drama of Yesterday and Today*, 2 vols., London: Macmillan,
    1899
Scott, Mrs Clement, *Old Days in Bohemian London*, London: Hutchinson &
    Co., n.d.
Sedgwick, Eve Kosofsky, *The Epistemology of the Closet*, Harmondsworth:
    Penguin, 1994; 1st published Berkeley: University of California Press, 1990
Seigel, Jerrold, *Bohemian Paris: Culture, Politics and the Boundaries of Bourgeois
    Life, 1830–1930*, Baltimore, MD: Johns Hopkins University Press, 1986
*Select Committee on Theatres and Places of Entertainment with Proceedings,
    Minutes of Evidence, Appendix and Index*, British Parliamentary Papers
    Report, 1892
Sennett, Richard, *The Fall of Public Man*, Cambridge University Press, 1976
Shattuck, Charles H., ed., *Bulwer and Macready: A Chronicle of the Early
    Victorian Theatre*, Urbana: University of Illinois Press, 1958
Sheppard-Skaerved, Peter, Palmer, Frances and Snowman, Janet, *John Orlando
    Parry and the Theatre of London*, London: Janet Snowman, 2010
Sherston, Erroll, *London's Lost Theatres of the Nineteenth Century*, London: John
    Lane and the Bodley Head, 1925
Slater, Michael, *Douglas Jerrold 1803–1857*, London: Duckworth, 2002
Smith, Albert, *The Natural History of the Gent*, London: D. Bogue, 1847
    The Natural History of the Ballet Girl, London: D. Bogue, 1847
Smith, Richard John, *Recollections of O. Smith, Comedian*, ed. William Appleton,
    Performing Arts Resources 5, New York: Theatre Library Association, 1979
Smith, John Harrington, *The Gay Couple in Restoration Comedy*, Cambridge,
    MA: Harvard University Press, 1948
Spielmann, M. H., *The History of 'Punch'*, London: Cassell & Co., 1895
Stephens, John Russell, *The Profession of the Playwright: British Theatre 1800–
    1900*, Cambridge University Press, 1992
Stobart, Jon, Hann, Andrew and Morgan, Victoria, *Spaces of Consumption: Leisure
    and Shopping in the English Town c. 1680–1830*, London: Routledge, 2007
Straub, Kristina, *Sexual Suspects: Eighteenth-century Players and Sexual Ideology*,
    Princeton University Press, 1992

Sustees, Virginia, *The Actress and the Brewer's wife*, Norwich: Michael Russell, 1997

Sussman, Herbert, *Victorian Masculinities: Manhood and Masculine Poetics in Early Victorian Literature and Art*, Cambridge University Press, 1995

Sutherland, John, *Victorian Novelists and Publishers*, London: Althone Press, 1976
Victorian Fiction: Writers, Publishers, Readers, London: Macmillan, 1995

Terry, Ellen, *The Story of my Life*, London: Hutchinson, 1908

Thackerary, W. M., 'Men's Wives: The Ravenswing', *Ballads and Tales*, London: Smith, Elder, 1869

Tomalin, Claire, *The Invisible Woman: The Story of Nelly Ternan and Charles Dickens*, Harmondsworth: Penguin, 1991

Trewin, J. C., ed, *The Journal of William Charles Macready*, London: Longmans, 1967

Tyldesley, William, *Michael William Balfe*, Aldershot: Ashgate, 2003

Vandenhoff, George, *Dramatic Reminiscences; or, Actors and Actresses in England and America*, ed. Henry Seymour Carlton, London: Thomas Cooper & Co., 1860

Wahrmann, Dror, *Imagining the Middle Class: The Political Representation of Class in Britain, c. 1780–1840*, Cambridge University Press, 1995

Wallace, James D., 'Race and Captivity in Cooper's *The Wept of Wish-ton-wish*', *American Literary History* 7, 1995, 189–209

Webster, Margaret, *The Same only Different: Five Generations of a Theatre Family*, London: Victor Gollancz, 1969

White, Jerry, *London in the Nineteenth Century*, London: Jonathan Cape, 2007

Williams, Clifford John, *Madame Vestris – A Theatrical Biography*, London: Sidgwick & Jackson, 1973

Williams, Raymond, *The Long Revolution*, Harmondsworth: Penguin Books, 1965, first published. London: Chatto & Windus, 1961
Marxism and Literature, Oxford University Press, 1977

Wilson, Elizabeth, *Adorned in Dreams: Fashion and Modernity*, London: Virago, 1985
Bohemians: The Glamorous Outcasts, London: J. B. Tauris & Co., 2000

Wood, Gillen D'Arcy, *The Shock of the Real: Romanticism and Visual Culture, 1760–1860*, London: Palgrave, 2001

Yates, Edmund, *My Haunts and their Frequenters*, London: D. Bogue, 1854
Edmund Yates: His Recollections and Experiences, 2 vols., London: Richard Bentley, 1884
'Bygone Shows', *Fortnightly Review*, May 1886, 633–47

Index

Printed in Great Britain